Fannie Lou Hamer

THE LIBRARY OF AFRICAN AMERICAN BIOGRAPHY

General Editor, John David Smith
Charles H. Stone Distinguished Professor of American History
University of North Carolina at Charlotte

The Library of African American Biography aims to provide concise, readable, and up-to-date lives of leading black figures in American history, in widely varying fields of accomplishment. The books are written by accomplished scholars and writers, and reflect the most recent historical research and critical interpretation. Illustrated with photographs, they are designed for general informed readers as well as for students.

Fannie Lou Hamer: America's Freedom Fighting Woman, Maegan Parker Brooks (2020)
Jackie Robinson: An Integrated Life, J. Christopher Schutz (2016)
W. E. B. Du Bois: An American Intellectual and Activist, Shawn Leigh Alexander (2015)
Paul Robeson: A Life of Activism and Art, Lindsey R. Swindall (2013)
Ella Baker: Community Organizer of the Civil Rights Movement, J. Todd Moye (2013)
Booker T. Washington: Black Leadership in the Age of Jim Crow, Raymond W. Smock (2010)
Walter White: The Dilemma of Black Identity in America, Thomas Dyja (2010)
Richard Wright: From Black Boy to World Citizen, Jennifer Jensen Wallach (2010)
Louis Armstrong: The Soundtrack of the American Experience, David Stricklin (2010)

Fannie Lou Hamer

America's Freedom Fighting Woman

Maegan Parker Brooks

ROWMAN & LITTLEFIELD
Lanham • Boulder • New York • London

Published by Rowman & Littlefield
An imprint of The Rowman & Littlefield Publishing Group, Inc.
4501 Forbes Boulevard, Suite 200, Lanham, Maryland 20706
www.rowman.com

6 Tinworth Street, London SE11 5AL, United Kingdom

British Library Cataloguing in Publication Information Available

Library of Congress Cataloging-in-Publication Data

978-1-5381-1594-7 (cloth)
978-1-5381-1595-4 (electronic)

♾ ™ The paper used in this publication meets the minimum requirements of American National Standard for Information Sciences—Permanence of Paper for Printed Library Materials, ANSI/NISO Z39.48–1992.

For Evie, Sawyer, and the next generation of freedom fighters

Contents

Introduction

"To Tell It Like It Is"

In a smoke-filled Atlantic City hotel ballroom, Fannie Lou Hamer limped toward the dais. White purse clutched in her right hand and a Mississippi Freedom Democratic Party (MFDP) badge affixed to the chest of her flowery dress, she took her seat. Hamer shifted nervously as a microphone was fastened to her lapel. One hundred and eight credentials committee members sat in rows across from her. The credentials committee was tasked with determining which delegation sent from Mississippi would be seated at the 1964 Democratic National Convention (DNC). Would it be the party known as the "Regulars," an all-white delegation, representative of the state's white supremacist election machinery? Or would the credentials committee members risk a southern "Dixiecrat" walk-out and vote to replace the segregationist delegation with the racially integrated MFDP?

Camera crews from all three major networks lined the back of the ballroom. The sixty-eight members of the segregationist Mississippi delegation sat, arms crossed, glowering at Hamer as she spoke. "Mr. Chairman, and to the Credentials Committee, my name is Mrs. Fannie Lou Hamer and I live at 626 East Lafayette Street, Ruleville, Mississippi, Sunflower County, the home of Senator James O. Eastland and Senator Stennis." With this seemingly straightforward introduction, Hamer defied the white supremacist norm of refusing black women the courtesy title "Mrs." She boldly shared her address with terrorists, including those who had recently flooded her home with threatening phone calls, as well as those who had fired shots into a home where she had taken refuge. And with this seemingly simple introduction, Hamer set the stage for a core claim that would animate her activist career: "Nobody's free until everybody's free."

Over the next thirteen years, Hamer unpacked this aphorism for audiences across the nation. Hamer told audiences from Harlem to Seattle that because the white supremacist election machinery in her state sent representatives to the US Senate and to the House of Representatives and because these legislators sat on powerful committees and voted for laws and policies that gov-

1

erned us all, voter discrimination in Mississippi was not just a problem for black people in her home state. Voter discrimination posed a death threat to our democracy.

On that late August afternoon in the Atlantic City hotel ballroom, Hamer provided evidence of her oppression to expose the limits of America's foundational ideals. She told the 1964 DNC credentials committee about being fired and evicted from the Delta plantation where she had labored for eighteen years because she tried to register to vote. She testified that white supremacist nightriders had shot sixteen bullets into the home where she fled after her eviction. And Hamer stunned the nation when she described how she was arrested, beaten, and sexually assaulted in a Mississippi jail cell on her return trip from a civic education workshop. "All of this," Hamer declared, her strong voice wavering slightly as tears rolled down her cheeks,

> is on account of we want to register, to become first-class citizens. And if the Freedom Democratic Party is not seated, *now*, I question America. Is this America? The land of the free and the home of the brave, where we have to sleep with our telephones off of the hook because our lives be threatened daily, because we want to live as decent human beings, in America?

Hamer's credentials committee testimony sent sitting President Lyndon B. Johnson into a state of outright panic. Just moments into her eight-minute-long address, Johnson called a press conference to divert the media's attention away from Hamer's scathing indictment of the nation he led. Even as the nation's gaze temporarily shifted from Hamer to Johnson, whom media outlets assumed had called the press conference to announce his running mate, Hamer's testimony shocked her immediate audience. In response to her words, a hush fell over the previously bustling ballroom as many credentials committee members fought back tears. Once the television networks realized they had been duped by Johnson—who did not announce his running mate, but rather used the dubious press conference to mark the nine-month anniversary of the assassination of President John F. Kennedy—stations across the country replayed Hamer's testimony during their evening programs. In this way, Johnson's attempt at diversion backfired. Hamer's mid-afternoon credentials committee testimony became a prime time news feature, reaching millions more Americans. Viewers responded to her heart-wrenching address by flooding their Democratic Party representatives with telegrams in support of the MFDP. The widespread popular support that Hamer's testimony garnered forced Johnson to negotiate with the MFDP and compelled the Democratic Party to vow they would never again seat a racially segregated delegation. Commentators have suggested that Hamer's speech both "turned the tide" of this particular convention and literally "changed the face of American politics," as white southern Democrats flocked to the Republican Party in retaliation for the Democratic Party's commitment to racial integration.

While Hamer's testimony at the 1964 Democratic National Convention is undoubtedly her most famous speech, it was neither the first nor the last time she foregrounded her personal experiences to expose America's white supremacist underpinnings. Catapulted into the national limelight by this speech, and supported by national civil rights organizations like the Student Nonviolent Coordinating Committee (SNCC), Fannie Lou Hamer traveled across the country—and even to the west coast of Africa—testifying about her experiences growing up poor and black in one of America's most viciously-segregated states. Hamer was the granddaughter of enslaved persons and she spent the first forty-four years (1917–1962) of her life on the Delta's sharecropping plantations. Hamer spoke out about exploitative labor practices and the lack of economic and educational opportunities for rural black people. As the most outspoken representative of SNCC's campaign to empower masses of southern black people, Hamer testified about how white supremacists withheld basic human necessities like food, water, shelter, and health care to punish black activism in Mississippi.

Over the course of her fifteen years as a human rights activist (1962–1977), Hamer shared platforms with the likes of Martin Luther King, Jr., Stokely Carmichael, Ella Baker, Pete Seeger, Gloria Steinem, Betty Friedan, and Malcolm X. It was Malcom X, in fact, who introduced Hamer to an audience in Harlem as "the country's number one freedom fighting woman," inspiring the title of this book. Hamer also marched with Ambassador Andrew Young and demonstrated alongside Congressional Representatives John Lewis and Eleanor Holmes Norton. Hamer spoke at the 1964, 1968, and 1972 Democratic National Conventions. She was a founding member of the National Women's Political Caucus, and she was one of the very first civil rights activists to publicly speak out against the war in Vietnam—months before SNCC issued a formal statement and nearly two years before King delivered his famous "A Time to Break Silence" speech. Hamer regularly spoke on college campuses, including the University of Wisconsin-Madison, Harvard, Duke, Florida State, and Seattle University. And when she challenged the legitimacy of the US congressmen sent from her state during a MFDP demonstration in Washington, D.C., Hamer was among the first three black women *in history* to be seated on the floor of the US House of Representatives. Hamer parlayed her national notoriety into material support for her economically destitute Mississippi Delta community. She helped hundreds of Mississippi residents acquire decent housing, she encouraged thousands of black people to register and vote, and she secured millions of dollars' worth of food, clothing, farm equipment, and monetary donations from northern supporters of poverty programs in the South.

In short, Hamer was a dynamic activist in her time, and she stands as a powerful activist exemplar for ours. *Fannie Lou Hamer: America's Freedom Fighting Woman* seeks to enrich public understanding of Hamer by offering a concise, accessible, and up-to-date portrait of this lesser-known, yet no less important, human rights activist. *America's Freedom Fighting Woman* unfolds chronologically, beginning with the first forty-two years Hamer spent struggling to survive on exploitative Delta plantations, all the while learning lessons from her family and her Black Baptist church about black empowerment, resistance, and liberation. I center W. E. B. DuBois's concept of "double-consciousness" to demonstrate how Hamer's complex self-conception formed from competing visions of who she was and who she had the potential to become. I then reconstruct Hamer's initial foray into political activism and the life-threatening repercussions she endured as a result. I chronicle the bold local, state, and national challenges that Fannie Lou Hamer waged against what bell hooks has more recently labeled the "imperialist white supremacist capitalist patriarchy." Throughout the book, I detail Hamer's political victories as well as her many defeats. *America's Freedom Fighting Woman* shines a light on Hamer's personal hardships too, detailing the challenges of caregiving while living in poverty, of caring for one's self in the midst of all-consuming movement work, of living with health conditions common to those raised without access to adequate medical care or sufficient food staples, and of surviving trauma wrought by sexual assault and police brutality.

Hamer's life story is vivid, inspirational, and harrowing—a tale that has captivated audiences for decades through its universal thematic tensions of struggle and victory, defeat and perseverance, human connection and devastating loss. Hamer's life story endures, in part, because of these universal themes, which reach audiences across time and across the particular boundaries of social location. *America's Freedom Fighting Woman* engages these universal themes while also emphasizing that Hamer's life story is particularly relevant in our contemporary context. The struggles that Hamer fought during her lifetime—against white supremacy, police brutality, sexual assault, voter disenfranchisement, segregated education, food insecurity, health care access, and governmental control over reproductive health—are strikingly similar to the challenges facing many Americans today. Hamer's life story offers solidarity and strength in this difficult time, demonstrating that these battles have been waged for decades and reminding contemporary activists that there are wells of wisdom upon which to draw.

What's more, learning from Fannie Lou Hamer's life story encourages contemporary readers of *America's Freedom Fighting Woman* to value the broad range of knowledge that ought to inform movements for social, political, and economic change. Hamer championed intersectionality long before it became a central feature of academic, political, and social analyses. Throughout her life, Hamer reasoned from her diverse range of life experiences and she chided those who spoke on her behalf without valuing her experiential wisdom. Through Hamer's example, readers of *America's Freedom Fighting Woman* will develop a healthy disrespect for respectability politics. The principled stances Hamer took, her propensity to "speak truth to power," and her embodied disruptions of systemic exclusion prove Hamer to be a powerful forerunner to and an activist exemplar for contemporary movements like Black Lives Matter, the Fight for $15, the "Me Too Movement", and the Immigrant Justice Network.

Further still, the story of Hamer's life as recounted in the pages of *America's Freedom Fighting Woman* is significant because it troubles what Jeanne Theoharis refers to as the "national fable of the civil rights movement." In her book, *A More Beautiful and Terrible History: The Uses and Misuses of Civil Rights History*, Theoharis contends that this fable functions as a "a veil to obscure enduring racial inequality, a tool to chastise contemporary protest, and a shield to charges of indifference and inaction." The fable accomplishes these repressive ends by reducing the complexity of the most powerful movement for social, political, and economic change in American history to a triumphalist tale featuring white-washed versions of a few larger-than-life leaders. In the ubiquitous fable's retelling of the movement, larger-than-life leaders are transformed into what Hasan Kwame Jeffries has dubbed "convenient heroes"; their words and actions plucked from radical contexts to diminish the persistence of white supremacy, to avoid inflicting defensive feelings of "white fragility," and, most ironically, to support the fiction of a post-racial society. The well-known fable of the civil rights movement foregrounds national victories like the 1954 *Brown v. Board of Education* decision and the 1965 Voting Rights Act, while papering over the hard-fought local struggles that led to these national victories and omitting the violent white supremacist retaliation to these civil rights gains—retaliation so severe that it often impeded the implementation of national legislation at the local level. The triumphalist overtones of this ubiquitous narrative suggest that our country has moved past struggles for racial equality; the inequality that remains, therefore, becomes the fault of individual failings rather than institutionalized racism. The national fable's promotion of white-washed versions of leaders and protests, moreover, conceals the range of advocates who effected change and belies the radical nature of the demonstrations that brought about the social, political, and economic victories of the mid-twentieth century civil rights movement.

As a corrective to the national fable of the civil rights movement, Theoharis suggests that "we need fuller histories—uncomfortable, sobering histories—that hold a mirror to the nation's past and offer far-reaching lessons for seeing the injustices of our current moment and the task for justice today." Hamer's life story provides one such history. The life story of a disabled, impoverished, middle-aged black woman from the rural Mississippi Delta challenges widespread perceptions of who participated in—as well as how they influenced—mid-twentieth century movements for social, political, and economic change. Hamer's life story, for instance, demonstrates that women were not only organizing and fulfilling vital supporting roles, but they were also on the front lines of significant movement challenges. Further, many activists like Hamer promoted complex ideologies, simultaneously supporting the causes of civil rights, Black Power, and Women's Liberation, even as they acknowledged the flaws of separationist ideologies, critiqued aspects of the push for integration, and warned feminists about the danger of building coalitions before acknowledging important differences in women's lived experiences. Perhaps most significantly, engaging the complexity of Fannie Lou Hamer's life story brings us face to face with persistent exclusions in American society. As Hamer told an audience gathered at Harvard University in 1968, "The wrongs and the sickness of this country have been swept under the rug, but I've come out from under the rug, and I'm going to tell it like it is."

To write this book, I drew upon the historiographical shift in black freedom movement studies ushered in by landmark works like Charles M. Payne's *I've Got the Light of Freedom: The Organizing Tradition and the Mississippi Freedom Struggle* and John Dittmer's *Local People: The Struggle for Civil Rights in Mississippi*. Influential works like Payne's and Ditmer's challenge the national fable of the civil rights movement with more complex community studies that foreground the myriad contributions of grassroots activists and organizations. *America's Freedom Fighting Woman* also benefited from foundational biographical studies, including Kay Mills' *This Little Light of Mine: The Life of Fannie Lou Hamer* (1993), Chana Kai Lee's *For Freedom's Sake: The Life of Fannie Lou Hamer* (1999), and my previous book, *A Voice that Could Stir an Army: Fannie Lou Hamer and the Rhetoric of the Black Freedom Movement* (2014). Even as I drew upon these authors' insights, I sought to distinguish *America's Freedom Fighting Woman* from previous biographical works by telling Hamer's story through the mode of creative or narrative nonfiction. I favor the narrative nonfiction form because it more closely approximates the vividness of Hamer's life than past renderings by ascribing to the fundamental principle of great storytelling— "show, don't tell." To foreground Hamer's voice and the voices of those who knew her well, and to recreate the complexity of the historical scenes in which she acted, I engaged in a multilayered process of historical reconstruction. My narrative nonfiction account of Hamer's life story draws upon details gleaned from primary sources I've gathered over fifteen years of Hamer-related research. These include personal letters, public speeches, photographs, television and radio interviews, film footage, newspaper clippings, and campaign platforms culled from over twenty archival and private collections across seven states. I combined the details gleaned from primary sources with over thirty oral history interviews I conducted and hundreds of informal conversations I had with Hamer's friends, family members, and fellow activists. I then set this primary source material against a backdrop of illuminating secondary sources including documentaries, biographies, and historical accounts relevant to Hamer's compelling life story. To bring all of this material to life, I employed creative techniques such as omniscient narration, scene-setting, and the recreation of dialogic encounters, all the while remaining firmly rooted in the historical facts of Hamer's life and times. The result of this creative historical reconstruction is an intimate and accessible portrait of a multifaceted freedom fighter—a complex story of Hamer's life set against the backdrop of the enduring struggle for black freedom in America.

As a white woman from the North, I'm often asked: Who am *I* to write such a narrative? I clearly lack experiential insight regarding Hamer's identity as a disabled black woman from the rural South. I have been inspired to write Hamer's story, however, by the perspectives we share in common. As a daughter raised at times on public assistance in the rural North, as a mother, a wife, and a survivor of sexual assault, I relate to particular facets of Hamer's identity as I narrate how she variously reasons from, grapples with, overcomes, and is overwhelmed by who she is and where she's from.

As an anti-racist teacher and scholar, moreover, I am also inspired to tell Hamer's life story because I believe in its transformative power. I recognize how her experiences and her activism fundamentally challenge the white supremacist ideologies propagated by the national fable of the civil rights movement. And I understand the dismantling of white supremacy to be everybody's work—perhaps *especially* the work of white people, who have benefited from this pernicious ideology and therefore hold privileges and resources to deconstruct it.

The very antiracist activist and scholarly commitments that compel me to share Hamer's story as a counterpoint to the national fable of the civil rights movement, however, also caution me against joining a historical legacy of interpretive exploitation marked by what Jacqueline Jones Royster describes as the "free touching of the powerless by the power-full." In her landmark keynote address, "When the First Voice You Hear Is Not Your Own," delivered in her role as chair of the Conference on College Composition and Communication, Royster shares both her visceral and intellectual responses as a black woman listening to people from outside her community make sense of her life experiences. She admits that "when the subject matter is me and the voice is not mine, my sense of order and rightness is disrupted." This disruption, Roys-ter acknowledges, has brought her to the "very edge of a principle" she values "deeply as a teacher and as a scholar," namely: "the principle of the right to inquiry and discovery." Although she recognizes it might be far less problem-atic to do so, Royster does not advocate restricting scholars' rights to inquiry and discovery to those specific communities to which they belong or to those life experiences they have personally endured. Instead, Royster uses her influ-ential address-turned-widely-circulated essay to emphasize the need for accountability, for the acknowledgment of interpretive limitations, and for the development of "codes of better conduct in the interest of keeping our bound-aries fluid [and] our discourse invigorated with multiple perspectives."

Inspired by Royster's call for codes of better cross-boundary interpretive conduct, informed by the metaphor of hospitality that is woven throughout her essay, and based upon the many interviews I conducted at kitchen tables across the Mississippi Delta, I have come to approach research and writing about Hamer as if I were a dinner guest in her home place. As a dinner guest in the Mississippi Delta, I am ever-mindful that I should not arrive empty-handed. In practice, this has meant sharing primary sources with K-12 public school teachers in Mississippi and beyond. As a dinner guest in the Delta, I also recognize that I should never expect to be invited into one's home, but rather that I should show gratitude when I am granted interviews and provided access to rare research material. This display of gratitude, not unlike helping your host set the table or clean up after a meal, ought to provide tangible support to the community. In practice, this has meant serving in supportive roles on projects like the Fannie Lou Hamer Statue Fund initiated by activists in Hamer's home-town. As a dinner guest in Hamer's home place, moreover, I am careful to never "eat and run." I strive to nurture longstanding relationships with mem-bers and organizations in her home community, such as the decade-long docu-mentary film partnership I forged with Hamer's great grandniece, Ms. Monica Land. Mindful of the egregious pattern of white scholars who have come into the Mississippi Delta, taken what they needed for their projects, and left the community with little to show for their vital involvement in the scholars' research, my dinner-guest ethic of cross-boundary conduct has also made me cautious about overextending my welcome. While I believe my intentions to be ethical, I am careful to recognize that black Deltans have good reasons to be wary of my presence.

Beyond simply being the right thing to do, the ongoing and reciprocal nature of my research relationship with Hamer's home community has filled many of the gaps in my outsider's understanding of who Hamer was, how her life circumstances shaped her existence, and what motivated her to act. Never-theless, there is simply no substitute for experiential wisdom. *Fannie Lou*

Hamer: America's Freedom Fighting Woman, therefore, is best read through what Royster describes as the "lens of subjectivity"—it is unavoidably partial and necessarily limited to the expanse of my socially located perspectives. This book is the culmination of fifteen years of archival, oral history, and community-based research, and it is also, at its core, an interpretation of Fannie Lou Hamer's life written by a guest who frequently visits, but is not from, Hamer's home place.

I am profoundly grateful that Hamer's friends, family members, and fellow activists have shared insights and precious primary sources with me. I am also grateful that they continue to hold me accountable for how I represent their community. Through my representation of Hamer's life story, I hope readers will recognize both the complexity and the continuity of freedom struggles; I hope Hamer's example will compel readers to appreciate the diverse sources of knowledge that ought to inform our contemporary movements for political, social, and economic change; and I hope that we might all draw strength from a powerful, yet relatable, freedom fighting woman.

· 1 ·

Visions that Transform

It is a peculiar sensation, this double-consciousness, this sense of always looking at one's self through the eyes of others, of measuring one's soul by the tape of a world that looks on in amused contempt and pity. One ever feels his two-ness, an American, a Negro; two souls, two thoughts, two unreconciled strivings; two warring ideas in one dark body, whose dogged strength alone keeps it from being torn asunder.

—W. E. B. DuBois, *The Souls of Black Folk*, 1903

*T*hrough heavy eyelids young Fannie Lou watched as the water turned pink, blood dripping from her mother's cracked knuckles. Lou Ella Townsend scrubbed and scrubbed. Laying on a heap of the plantation owner's dirty laundry, young Fannie Lou listened as her mother crooned:

> *Sheep-pie, sheep-pie where your little lamb?*
> *Way down in the valley*
> *Birds and the butterflies picking at his eye*
> *And the poor little thing he cried, "Mama"*

Those last few lines always left Fannie Lou feeling empty inside, evoking her earliest memories of being swaddled and set against a tree, shaded from the harsh sun, but removed from her mother, father, and siblings. In those early days, she could barely make them out in the distance—blurred figures hunched over waist-high cotton stalks, picking and wrestling with the stubborn boll. Tonight, Fannie Lou tried to stay awake long enough to hear her favorite verses of that somber song, passed down from her enslaved grandmother, Liza Gober Bramlett, to her sharecropping mother, and now—in these twilight moments of closeness—to her:

> *Go to sleep, go to sleep*
> *Go to sleep little baby*
> *Go to sleep little Bayou-bay-o-bay*
> *Won't you go to sleep little baby*

Young Fannie Lou fought sleep to catch a few more glimpses of her mama bustling around the cabin—scrubbing the plantation owner's laundry, boiling sweet potatoes for her own large family to eat in the fields tomorrow, and humming a melancholy lullaby to her youngest child.

On October 6, 1917, Fannie Alma Louise DuBois Townsend was born to sharecropper parents, James Lee and Lou Ella. When Fannie Lou—as she became more commonly known—was just two-years-old, her parents packed wagons full of their six girls and fourteen boys and moved from her birthplace of Tomnolen, in Montgomery County, to the city of Ruleville in Sunflower County, Mississippi. The Townsends arrived in Sunflower County during a particularly tumultuous period. Black veterans who returned from fighting the Great War abroad joined with black people who were generations removed from slavery and began to grow more outwardly resentful of their miserable living conditions, exploited labor, and lack of opportunities. Some black people left Mississippi for industrial jobs in northern cities, as part of what would become the Great Migration. Many of those who remained in the state were also on the move.

Large plantations across Mississippi had been infested by the boll weevil. A small beetle that feeds on cotton, the boll weevil devastated cotton crops across the South in the early 1900s. Sunflower County was spared from the insect's infestation and, as a result, the county experienced a population explosion during the 1910s—growing by more than 60 percent to over 40,000 inhabitants, making it the state's fourth largest county.

The Townsend family found sharecropping work at E.W. Brandon's plantation a few miles east of Ruleville. The city was named after the Rule brothers who built the town's first cotton gin in 1886, some forty years after the Choctaw Natives had been forced from the land. Early white settlers in this area relied on a labor force of enslaved black people to clear the densely wooded land and begin planting cash crops. Cotton, soybeans, rice, and corn all grow well in the rich soil that stretches across Mississippi's northwest region known as the Delta. This triangular portion of the state sits between the Yazoo and Mississippi rivers, boasting flatlands and a long growing season.

In the Delta region, where the black population outnumbered the white population—constituting 75 percent of Sunflower County's population in 1920—the exploitative system of sharecropping replaced slavery as a means of securing cheap labor and ensuring white supremacist social control during young Fannie Lou's formative years. Spared from the boll weevil's destruction and with the influx of new labor from families driven off plantations in other regions of the state, Sunflower County quickly became "the most productive cotton-growing area in the most productive cotton-growing state in the most productive cotton-growing country in the world," explained historian Chris Myers Asch. This distinction connected Delta planters to a global economy that yielded considerable profits for landowners—these profits were not, however, passed down to the sharecroppers, who labored in the hot, humid, mosquito-ridden, and snake-infested fields. In fact, sharecroppers were often kept in the landowners' debt through an exploitative credit-based system, against which impoverished workers had no recourse.

Plantation owners encouraged black families to live on their land and loaned them small amounts of money for living expenses throughout the year, to be paid back at harvest. When that time came, the plantation owner ostensibly split the proceeds from the season's yield with the sharecroppers. The main catch, however, was that the seed and fertilizer for planting, in addition to the family's housing, food costs, cash advances, and whatever else the plantation owner reckoned to be fair, was paid out of the cropper's half.

Add to this injustice, the cruelness of the cotton crop itself, which required near-constant tending—from planting in April, to chopping back the tiny plants into rows as they began to sprout in May, to weeding the rows in the steamy summer months—all before the eventual back-breaking, finger-splitting work of the fall harvest. Once the stubborn bolls had been plucked, they went through a ginning process to remove their seeds, reducing the weight of the harvest by at least two-thirds. What was worse, some plantation owners used a weighted measuring system to surreptitiously cheat workers out of fair compensation for their harvest. So even on a good year when a large family like the Townsends could pick fifty or sixty bales of cotton, they might earn slightly more than three hundred dollars—less than four thousand dollars in today's currency. With the average sharecroppers' wages ranging from just $1.25 to $3.00 a day during the 1920s and 30s, it was nearly impossible for black laborers to turn a profit. Unable to establish financial independence, therefore, the workers remained beholden to the landowner for their very survival.

Dawn came and carried her mother, father, and most of her older siblings into the fields before Fannie Lou woke. When the chirping ibises and the rustling of the cornstalks that filled her flour sack bed became too noisy for her to bear, Fannie Lou went looking for her older sister. The siblings too young to work in the fields would stay back to care for Fannie Lou and tend to their home. The Townsend home wasn't much more than a shack—built from discarded wood planks, nailed to a rickety frame, the sole source of heat and light coming from an open fireplace in the center of the makeshift structure. The large Townsend family shared an outhouse with several other sharecropping families working the plantation's fields. The communal structure became a breeding ground for viruses like polio, against which there was no vaccine and for which sharecroppers were never formally diagnosed or treated. Many suffered fevers, muscle aches, and stiffness and some, like Fannie Lou, were left with paralytic limbs for life.

That particular morning, Fannie Lou found her brother first. He was returning from the nearby river with the bucket her mama had used to scrub the Brandon family's clothes last night. The clothes now hanging tautly on the line, Fannie Lou's brother had been given strict orders to bathe his youngest sister. Fannie Lou had other ideas. She figured that tub of water would slow him down so she took off toddling toward the cotton fields. He soon caught up to her, though, and dunked her in the bucket. She didn't mind the bath much when her mama bathed her, gentle as Lou Ella was with her youngest child, but Fannie Lou struggled and fussed when her brother tried to wash her. Frustrated by the wrangling, worn out from fetching the water, and inexperienced with handling slippery babies—he dropped young Fannie Lou, hard. Her left leg took the brunt of the blow, popping loudly as it bent in an unnatural direction. Fannie Lou cried out from the pain and her sister rushed to console her, offering her the bud of a clover plant to suckle while she attempted to set Fannie Lou's limb, wrapping it with a cloth from the line as best as the young girl knew how. Fannie Lou spent the rest of the day convalescing close by her sister's side—still getting into most everything and slowing the pace of the chores, even as she grimaced from the throbbing pain in her left leg.

Their father was the first to enter the Townsend's cabin well after sunset. Fannie Lou looked up from the pan of water she was playing with, rice—the family's precious food staple—was scattered across the floor. She could see the anger rise up in her father's eyes as he took in the wasteful scene. Fannie Lou took off once again in the direction of the field, this time hobbling and yelping from the shooting pain in her leg, the makeshift cloth cast unraveling as she ran.

Trailing after her, James Townsend bellowed: "I'm going to whip her behind!"

Lou Ella scooped her youngest child into her arms and shot her husband a look that made it clear he would do no such thing.

> *Mama's gone, papa's gone*
> *Ain't nobody but the baby*
> *They shall bring some horses*
> *White and black, speckled and gray—all them pretty little horses*
> *When you wake, you'll eat a pancake and ride the pretty little pony*

Several years later, Fannie Lou hummed her mother's lullaby softly to herself, stomach growling, as she kicked rocks down the gravel road separating the cotton fields from the commissary store. Her mouth watered at the thought of fluffy bites of warm pancakes and her heart leaped at the thought of galloping atop a speckled pony.

Her daydream was interrupted by the sound of an engine slowing to a halt, red dust swirling around the truck's tires. The plantation owner slowly rolled down the truck's window and sized up young Fannie Lou with a cursory glance.

"Can you pick that cotton?" Mr. Brandon hollered at the child.

Fannie Lou averted her eyes, the suddenly shy girl simply shrugged her small shoulders.

"Yes. You can," he encouraged her. "And if you do I will give you things that you want from the commissary store—sardines, Crackerjacks, and Daddy Wide-Legs," Brandon said, a broad grin spreading across his sunburned cheeks.

Fannie Lou had noticed those treats he mentioned—especially those silly gingerbread man-shaped cookies with the long limbs—in his store when she tagged along with her mama, but their meager sharecropper wages never allowed for such indulgences. Food was scarce around the Townsend's home. Last night her mama cut the tops of the greens in the garden, mixed those up with some leftover grease and flour to make gravy. Then Lou Ella boiled the little rice they had left in the bag and stretched these meager provisions to feed her large and hardworking family.

That evening, Fannie Lou pleaded with her parents to try her hand at cotton-picking in hopes that she could bring home treats for her whole family to enjoy. They reluctantly agreed. During her first week, Fannie Lou picked thirty pounds of cotton and Brandon appeared to make good on his word, rewarding her labor with merchandise from his store. But because Brandon set the prices in his commissary and also controlled the sharecroppers' compensation, he told young Fannie Lou that she would need to pick twice as much cotton the following week to pay for the treats she already enjoyed. As an adult, Hamer reflected upon this exploitative practice of child labor and explained that through the promise of goods from his commissary, Brandon "was trapping me into beginning the work I was to keep doing and I never did get out of his debt again."

> *I would not be a white man*
> *White as a drip in the snow*
> *They ain't got God in their heart*
> *To hell they sure must go*

Briskly folding each piece of the Brandon family's clothing as she tore article after article down from the line, Lou Ella's voice carried over the sounds of sharecropping families in their cramped living quarters. Tired bodies stiff and sore from the days' labor struggled to fix dinner for tonight and searched for food to eat in the field tomorrow. Lou Ella's songs always drew Fannie Lou near, imparting understanding, comforting her, and passing down rhythms, tones, and melodies that stretched back to her African ancestors.

"But why wasn't *we* white?" Fannie Lou asked, attuned to the words her mother sang as she followed closely behind her.

Fannie Lou looked up to see her mother's astonished face.

"We work all summer and we work until it get so cold that you have to tie rags around our feet and flour sacks to keep our feet warm," young Fannie Lou explained. After all this work, she insisted, "we don't have anything. We don't have anything to eat, sometimes we don't have anything but water and bread! But the white landowners have very good food and they don't do anything." To her child's mind, the solution seemed simple: to make it you had to be white, and she wanted to be white.

Lou Ella turned away from the clothes hanging on the line. Wincing from the aches of the day, she nevertheless bent down to Fannie Lou's level. "There is nothing in the world wrong with being black. Be grateful that you are black," Lou Ella Townsend instructed her daughter. "If God had wanted you to be white, you would have been white, so you accept yourself for what you are and respect yourself as a black child." Lou Ella looked directly into young Fannie Lou's bright brown eyes and advised further. "When you get grown you respect yourself as a black woman and other people will respect you too."

In that pivotal moment, Hamer would later recall, Lou Ella compelled her to see "that it wasn't because this cat was the best," that he could relax and profit from black peoples' labor, rather "it was because of the kind of crook that he was. The white man was such a crook," young Fannie Lou realized.

> *I would not be a sinner*
> *I'll tell you the reason why*
> *I'm afraid my Lord may call me*
> *And I wouldn't be ready to die*

Lou Ella continued her song and through her allusion to Divine justice, Fannie Lou began to see that the exploitative system of sharecropping was shortsighted—garnering immediate earthly gains for its white beneficiaries, all the while damning their eternal souls.

Lou Ella's voice, as strong as it was sweet, woke the children each morning as she gathered their boiled sweet potatoes, jugs of water, and a large cast-iron pot covered with a dingy towel. Fannie Lou wondered why her mama brought that heavy pot back and forth into the fields and home again each day. Now indebted to the landowner at the tender age of six, Fannie Lou joined the rest of the Townsend family wading through the dewy grass, guided by a sliver of sun peeking above the horizon, and returning home along the dusty path only after the blazing Delta sun had stretched across the sky's expanse. From "kin to kain't," Fannie Lou's father called their workday schedule. From "can see to can't see," Fannie Lou soon came to understand.

In the fields, Lou Ella tried to bring small joy to the children during the most grueling harvest months. Initiating cotton-picking races between the siblings, she would enact the motions while singing out:

> *Jump down, turn around, pick a bale of cotton*
> *Jump down, turn around pick a bale a day*
> *Oh Lord, pick a bale of cotton*
> *Oh Lord, pick a bale a day*

Swept up in her plantation performance one afternoon, Lou Ella didn't initially notice the overseer approaching. But the rest of the family froze as the white man ambled toward her youngest son. Their fearful reactions alerted Lou Ella and she began sprinting toward her boy. By the time she caught up to the pair, the landowner's arm was raised to strike her son. Fannie Lou gasped as she watched Lou Ella grab the overseer's arm and pin it swiftly to his back. The sharecropping families spread across the field were divided—some looked on in horror and others anxiously averted their eyes. Humiliated, the overseer softly pleaded for his release.

"No white man was going to beat her kids," Hamer remembered her mother declaring. The dumbfounded overseer could tell by the force of her mother's grip that this was no idle threat.

Before Lou Ella made it back to the row they were working, curiosity got the best of Fannie Lou. She crouched down, lifted the corner of that yellowed towel, and peered inside the cast-iron pot. Fannie Lou fell back onto her bottom upon taking in the pot's contents: her mama had a 9mm Luger stowed in there! Collecting herself as she heard Lou Ella approaching, Fannie Lou smoothed the towel over the top of the pot and looked into her mother's eyes. Where she expected to see fear, she saw only fury.

That fury had built up over generations. Lou Ella had watched as her own mother, an enslaved woman, was passed around from master to master—birthing twenty-three children, only three of whom were the progeny of a consensual relationship with a black man. The remaining twenty children whom Liza Gober Bramlett carried to term were the result of rape. "White folks sure done Grandma bad," Fannie Lou's sister Laura Ratliff recalled, "this man would keep her as long as he want to and then he would trade her off for a little heifer calf. Then the other man would get her and keep her as long as he want." The rage Fannie Lou saw in her mother that day, as she confronted the white overseer, was a widespread feeling across the region. And Lou Ella was certainly not the only black Deltan who heeded Ida B. Wells' sage advice that the "Winchester rifle deserves a place of honor in every black home."

Just seven miles from the Townsend's Ruleville plantation, a man named Joe Pullum also lived and worked as a sharecropper. Like the Townsends, Pullum was also tricked and exploited by the landowner, who commonly withheld wages for his labor. "People think that Negroes just take whatever the white man puts out and likes it," exclaimed Hamer later in life. "Well, I know different." She knew the myth of black complacency was untrue from an early age because she had learned that folks like her mother and Joe Pullum refused to be exploited.

Though rural and remote, Sunflower County was not immune to either the national trends in rising black consciousness that occurred following World War I or the epidemic of racially motivated killings aimed to curtail black empowerment following Reconstruction. Black servicemen returned from war embodying the spirit of the "New Negro," no longer deferent to Jim Crow and eager to advocate for the same rights they had fought to secure for Europeans. Strands of Black Nationalism also cropped up in Sunflower County. Marcus Garvey's United Negro Improvement Association (UNIA), which was formed in New York the year of Hamer's birth, established a local chapter in Sunflower County in 1921, just two years after the Townsends moved their family there.

To quell black resistance in Sunflower County, white beneficiaries of the sharecropping system would make lurid examples of those black people who threatened racism's stronghold on the region. Lynching was the most barbaric method that white supremacists deployed to maintain the region's racial hierarchy. Though extreme in nature, lynchings were not all that uncommon—in 1919 alone there were eighty-nine reported lynching victims across the South. Between 1882 and 1951, furthermore, there were nearly 5,000 reported lynchings in the United States. And almost every state in the union was home to at least one race-based lynching, with 90 percent occurring in the South and the largest percent taking place in Mississippi, Georgia, Alabama, Louisiana, and Texas. In the state of Mississippi, in particular, at least 600 lynchings of black people were recorded between 1880 and 1940.

In 1923, at the height of this campaign of terror, the story of Joe Pullum from the Delta bayou spread like wildfire. As young Fannie Lou heard it, the landowner on the plantation where Pullum worked asked him to go out into the hill country and bring additional black families to his plantation to work.

The landowner gave Pullum $150 to bring them back to the town of Drew. But "Mr. Pullum didn't go to the hills to get the people," recalled Hamer. "He just figured since that man had never paid him, he would use the money to fix up his house and do different things he needed to do." Before long, however, the white landowner noticed that Pullum never brought back more workers. So the landowner brought another white man along with him to confront Pullum. And, as Hamer later recounted, when they arrived "Mr. Pullum told him what he'd done with the money and that he considered it his money because the man had robbed him of more than that anyway." This assertive response angered the white landowner, who shot Pullum in the arm. Joe Pullum, in turn, grabbed his Winchester rifle and shot the white landowner—dead. Terrified, the landowner's companion headed off toward the city center to gather a lynch mob. "I ain't never heard of no one white man going to get a Negro," noted Hamer. White people "are the most cowardly people I ever heard of."

Pullum didn't wait for the lynch mob to return. He headed to the nearby bayou and hid in the hollow of a tree. The mob quickly descended upon the bayou and "every time a white man would peep out, he busted him. Before they finally got him"—by pouring gasoline on the bayou and setting the entire marsh on fire—"he'd killed thirteen and wounded twenty-six, and it was a while before the whites tried something like that again," Hamer recalled with pride.

Most records suggest that Pullum killed three white men and wounded several others. Regardless of the actual death toll, however, this story exhibited to young Fannie Lou the bravery of a black man, who shared many of the Townsend's circumstances and who boldly resisted the abuse. The story, replete with its exaggerated death toll, emerged as the preeminent folk tale among black families in the Delta, trumping the message of intimidation that white supremacists attempted to concoct after the bayou standoff.

Young Fannie Lou would come to learn that the lynch mob did eventually find Pullum, whose dead body fell out of the burned tree stump once the fire had run its course. "They dragged him by his heels on the back of the car and paraded about with that man for all the Negroes to see. They cut his ear off and for the longest time it was kept in a jar of alcohol in a showcase in a store window at Drew," Hamer sighed, remembering. "I was about eight years old when that happened."

The standoff occurred on the night of December 15, 1923—Hamer would have actually been just six. The Pullum story circulated for years following his death, however, and it has become part of the Delta's greater mythology, so it is likely that Fannie Lou learned of the story a bit later in her childhood. And it is certain that the tale of armed resistance—much more so than the white mob's gruesome attempts at intimidating black Deltans—left a lasting impact on Hamer's consciousness.

The lessons of black pride that Fannie Lou learned from her mother and from the larger folklore circulating amidst her plantation culture led her to question the messages of racial inferiority she received during her several years of public schooling. Aside from the Holy Bible, the first books Hamer encountered were early readers supplied by the state and reflective of Social Darwinist beliefs. The Social Darwinist ideology combined ostensible laws of nature with the historical advances made by white people to suggest there was such a thing as an Anglo-Saxon race and that this race was the most fit for survival. They argued that white peoples' social dominance over other groups of people, whom they separated into the social constructs of race, was therefore warranted. White supremacists ignored advances made by people belonging to the other racial categories and they overlooked systemic and historical factors like colonialist oppression, clinging instead to an argument for natural dominance and declaring that black people were biologically inferior to whites. Stretching back to the days of slavery, white slave owners-turned-landowners propagated similar beliefs to justify everything from seizing the land upon which Native Americans lived to their social, political, and economic exploitation of black people.

"When I was in public school," Hamer remembered, "I read about a little child and this little child was black and his name was Epaminondas. First place, it was stupid to put a word that big in a book for a kid. Second place, it was a disgrace the way they had this little child and the things that he was doing."

Epaminondas and His Auntie, originally published in 1911, was a nonsensical fable written in the genre of a "numskull story," featuring a foolish black boy, who unwittingly destroys everything he takes from his aunt's house on his way back to his mother. Stories like this, portraying black children and adults as simple-minded racial caricatures, were popular across the state's elementary schools well into the 1960s.

"All I learned about my race when I was growing up was Little Black Sambo, who was a simple, ignorant boy," Hamer reasoned later in life. "I guess that's all they ever wanted us to know about ourselves."

The messages of inferiority black children were taught through the curriculum were reinforced by the meager physical resources made available to them. The segregated school that the Townsend children attended from December through March, after the cotton had been harvested and before planting season began, was a dilapidated one-room sharecropper's dwelling converted into a plantation schoolhouse. Their supplies were handed down from white schools, discarded books with the names of the white plantation owners' children scribbled on the inside, some pages torn out, others marked over. Operating under the "separate but equal" doctrine, the state of Mississippi spent approximately six dollars a year per black student, which was less than 20 percent of what it spent on each white pupil. Black schoolhouses were often rundown, lacking basic amenities such as chalkboards, desks, and chairs. Students of all ability levels were commonly taught together by teachers who often lacked any formal certification.

Fortunately, Fannie Lou had an impassioned teacher named Professor Thornton Layne. Since teaching jobs, let alone professorships, were difficult for even the most qualified black candidates to acquire, Fannie Lou and the other black sharecroppers' children in the Ruleville area benefited from Layne's advanced education. In Professor Layne, Hamer saw someone both relatable and aspirational. Like her, Layne's meager wages made basic amenities such as shoes difficult to come by. "He would wear his shoes the right way, for a while," Hamer remembered. "Then the heels wore down. So he would switch them to the wrong feet, and walk around like that, 'to let the heels straighten out,'" Layne explained to the bemused children.

Unlike the other adults in Fannie Lou's life, though, Layne had read widely and could recite poems and stories written by black artists. Layne recognized Fannie Lou's aptitude right away, encouraging her to grow as a reader and a writer through competitions like the schoolhouse spelling bee and through the performance of poetry. Lou Ella and James Townsend also encouraged young Fannie Lou, often setting her on top of the small table in the center of their modest cabin to recite the poetry Layne taught her, to sing hymns, and to tell stories. They relished showing off their daughter's intelligence to their adult friends. Fannie Lou delighted in the display of her knowledge as well. What's more she enjoyed the self-satisfaction that literacy incited. "When I was a child, I loved to read. In fact, I learned to read real well when I was going to school," Hamer later told an interviewer.

Witnessing their youngest daughter excel in school helped sustain the Townsends, who sacrificed mightily to provide the limited education Fannie Lou and her siblings received. "My parents tried so hard to do what they could to keep us in school, but school didn't last but four months out of the year and most of the time we didn't have clothes to wear," Hamer explained. Devoted to her children's well-being, Lou Ella Townsend would wear threadbare clothes herself, heavy with patches so that her children could have decent clothes to wear to school. The decent clothes the Townsends could provide for their children, though, were not warm enough to withstand Mississippi's coldest months, when temperatures dip below freezing. Since school was only provided for sharecropping children on the plantation when there was little work to do in the fields, and since weather during those months could be too cold to walk to school without shoes or a coat, Fannie Lou was like most other black children in the region whose education was patched together from a few months over the course of a few years.

Meanwhile, Mr. and Mrs. Townsend worked on the Brandon plantation year-round, clearing ground for planting by hoeing, raking, and burning brush in the early spring; working the fields from sun up to sun down during the summer and fall months. When there were no crops left to harvest or plant, James Townsend found work repairing farm machinery and structures across the plantation while Lou Ella cooked the planation owners' food and laundered their clothes—both working as hard as they could to provide for their twenty children. This work rarely resulted in payment sufficient to meet their large family's needs, so Fannie Lou's father also ran a small juke joint, bootlegging liquor to supplement their income. Further, Lou Ella would ask neighboring plantation owners if she could "scrap" their cotton, which entailed gathering what was left after sharecroppers harvested the fields in the fall. "We would walk for miles and miles in the run of a week. We wouldn't have shoes," Hamer remembered her mother tying the children's feet "with rags because the ground would be froze real hard. We would walk from field to field until we had scrapped a bale of cotton." Lou Ella would then sell that bale to buy what food she could afford from the commissary. When there was no more cotton to scrap, Lou Ella would offer to slaughter hogs in return for milk, butter, or leftover pieces of meat like the hog's head, feet, and intestines. In spite of her parents' best efforts, however, Hamer remembered that the sharecropping system often left the Townsends hungry. "Sometimes there'd be nothing but bread and onions. I know what the pain of hunger is about," Hamer recalled.

For a fleeting moment, however, it appeared that the large and industrious Townsend family had managed to beat the exploitative sharecropping system. By the time Fannie Lou reached early adolescence, her parents somehow managed to save up some money. "It must have been quite a little bit," she gathered, because Fannie Lou's father rented a small lot with a run-down cabin on it that they began fixing up. He also acquired a used car, a wagon, tools, a cultivator, and even some livestock. "My father bought three precious mules," Hamer recalled fondly. "I'll never forget their names because we loved them because they was ours. Ella was a white mule and Bird was kind of tan and Henry was jet black, they were beautiful to us." Even more than those three mules, the Townsend children adored the cow their father purchased; they named her Della. Della brought them nourishment and warmth, providing milk for the Townsend children, who also remembered warming their cold toes on the patches of ground where her large body lay.

As the Townsend family began planning for what promised to be a profitable planting season, white people in the area noticed that they were "doing pretty well" for themselves. Their relative affluence tipped the carefully regulated balance of power between the races. "White people never like to see Negroes get a little success," Hamer remembered.

Her family was staying in their old sharecropper shack on the Brandon plantation at night while they fixed up their cabin on the new lot during the day. One morning, when the Townsend children went to the new lot to fill the livestock's trough, they found one mule dead and the other two mules' bellies severely distended. Della's stomach, too, was swollen, and she moaned despairingly from the engorgement. What food was left in the trough from the previous day now glowed bright green. As the Townsends would soon learn, a white man had snuck onto their lot the previous night and mixed a gallon of "Paris Green," a brightly colored insecticide, into the trough, poisoning their precious livestock. "That white man did it just because we were getting somewhere," remembered Hamer. "That poisoning knocked us right back down flat. We never did get back up again."

Late in the evening, Fannie Lou would listen to the rhythmic sighs and snores of her brothers, sisters, and father while squinting to make out the shape of her mother bustling around their small shack in the dark. Lou Ella would finish the day's chores and then fall to her knees, nightly praying, asking God to watch over her children. The poisoning of their family's livestock was especially devastating for the Townsends because James and Lou Ella's bodies were giving out. Already up in their years when their twentieth child was born, a decade more of hard labor had worn them down by the time Fannie Lou reached adolescence. Add to this, Lou Ella's eyesight was fading fast.

In 1930, when Fannie Lou would have been twelve and her mother about sixty-years-old, the two were working along with a team of black men "deadening" a field—hard labor that consisted of clearing trees to cultivate new ground for planting. Lou Ella kept up with the male workers, steadily chopping the large trunks and removing their tangled roots. Fannie Lou followed close behind, gathering the brush and burning it in a large fire. Midway through the rugged patch of land, Lou Ella fell back, axe spiraling over the top of her head and cleaving the ground where it dropped. Fannie Lou caught up with her mother, whose hands clasped desperately over her eye—Lou Ella wailed. Fannie Lou brought water and struggled against her mother's impulse to shield the wounded eye, the young girl gasping as she saw the wood chip stuck directly in her mother's pupil. Fannie Lou plucked out the jagged splinter and doused both eyes with their water jug. Beyond her daughter's field-side triage, however, Lou Ella never received medical attention for her wounded eye.

Over the years, the deadening incident continued to erode Lou Ella's vision; she was completely blind in both eyes by the time of her death. With Lou Ella's capacity to labor severely impaired, the Townsends had hoped that their newly acquired mules might lighten their workload a bit and that Della's milk could help them nourish their hungry children. With those hopes now dashed, Lou Ella grew ever more desperate in her nightly outreach to God. As Fannie Lou listened to her mother's nightly lamentations, she realized what she had to do. Just before her thirteenth birthday, Fannie Lou dropped out of school to work full time and help support their family.

"The Spirit of the Lord is upon me," Fannie Lou's father declared from the pulpit.

"Yes, yes," responded the Strangers' Home Baptist parishioners. Fannie Lou looked around the old sharecroppers' cabin-turned-sanctuary to see a packed house, children nestled on their parents' laps near the back, elderly folks with bodies crippled from a life of unrelenting labor seated up front, all eyes fixated upon her father.

"He has anointed me to preach the gospel to the poor," Mr. Townsend attested.

Shouts of "c'mon now" and "tell it" encouraged her father to continue his sermon.

"He has sent me to heal the broken-hearted, to proclaim liberty to the captives, and recovery of sight to the blind, to set at liberty those who are oppressed, to proclaim the acceptable year of the Lord," Fannie Lou recognized that passage from the book of Luke and she knew just why her father chose it for this particular Sunday.

Nursing her own broken heart, Fannie Lou gave her father undivided attention. She listened on hopefully, believing God could speak through her father. God could sense and heal the hurt coursing through this room. The loyal Strangers' Home parishioners had long-supported one another as best they could, pooling their meager resources in hopes that one family's progress might spread more broadly across their community. As James Lee Townsend testified about what his family recently endured, the poisoning of their livestock, their inability to see a path toward a productive planting season, and their likely return to a life of exploitative labor on Brandon's plantation, Fannie Lou saw tears stream down the cheeks of those gathered, heads shaking, chests falling into deep sighs.

But her father didn't end his sermon with this relatable story of the black hopelessness that white supremacy sought to engender; rather, James Townsend shared the solace he found as he desperately searched for relief in scripture. Summoning the thirty-seventh Psalm, he implored: "Fret not thouselves because of evildoers, neither be thy envious against the workers of iniquity for they shall be cut down like the green grass and wither away as the green herb."

"Praise be to God!" the parishioners shouted, arms raised, hearts momentarily restored by this reminder of the right relationship they held with God.

Mr. Townsend looked into the crowd, trying to catch his youngest daughter's eye. With his loving look of encouragement, Fannie Lou rose where she was and sang out, slowly and quietly at first:

> *This little light of mine, I'm gonna let it shine*
> *This little light of mine, I'm gonna let it shine*
> *Let it shine, let it shine, let it shine*

By that third verse Mr. Townsend's daughter had gained confidence, the Strangers' Home parishioners were standing with her, clapping their hands in accompaniment to Fannie Lou's rich contralto voice.

Sunday after Sunday young Fannie Lou experienced the transformational power of the Black Baptist Church. Hamer's connection to the church ran deep. She was baptized in the Quiver River and her father served as the minister of their plantation parish. As the child of a Black Baptist preacher, Fannie Lou was not unlike scores of notable male civil rights orators who grew up learning lessons from the Bible in their home and hearing their fathers preaching the Word from the pulpit on Sunday morning. In communion with black families gathered from across the region, she listened to her father combine the images and idioms familiar to his sharecropping parishioners with scripture and song aimed toward comforting and inspiring his down-trodden audience. Fannie Lou took note of how he used this rare black-controlled space to proffer an alternative vision of their exploited existence.

When Fannie Lou Hamer reflected back on the church as an adult, she would often praise the communal space it provided—remarking that in light of all the things black sharecroppers did not have, the church was the one place that they "could really call their own." After leaving Professor Layne and her one-room schoolhouse in the sixth grade, in fact, Bible-study at the Strangers' Home Baptist Church became Fannie Lou's sole source of formal learning. And, in many respects, the church provided a training ground for her eventual activism. In this space, she learned how to research scripture for guidance in a chaotic world; she learned how to organize an engaging sermon, as well as how to comfort and challenge an audience; and she honed her natural talents as a vocalist, leading songs well-paired with her father's weekly sermons.

By the time James Townsend was taken from this world by complications from a massive stroke he suffered in 1939, Fannie Lou's father had shared with all of his children lessons of Divine justice, abiding love, and a commitment to testify. He had also modeled for them approaches to engaging with, relating to, and transforming oppressed audience members into an empowered collective. Several of Fannie Lou's brothers became ministers themselves. For her part, Fannie Lou parlayed this home training into what would become her human rights ministry.

As Fannie Lou grieved the loss of her father, she also mourned the departures of her brothers and sisters. One by one, her nineteen older siblings had come of age and left the Brandon plantation. Many moved North—to Chicago, Detroit, and Indianapolis—joining the Great Migration, which, by 1940, had carried more than 1.5 million black people from rural southern towns into northern cities. Other siblings married sharecroppers from surrounding plantations, leaving Fannie Lou and Lou Ella behind on Brandon's plantation. By the mid 1940s, Fannie Lou followed suit, moving from Brandon's plantation to the fields that W. D. Marlow owned and operated.

It is unclear exactly why Fannie Lou left the Brandon plantation, but it is likely that a man named Perry "Pap" Hamer played a central role in her relocation. A skilled tractor driver, Perry Hamer had moved from Kilmichael, Mississippi, to Ruleville in search of better paying work. In 1932, he found employment sharecropping, driving tractors, and repairing machinery on W. D. Marlow's plantation. Several years later, he also began a small juke joint, where black sharecroppers from the surrounding plantations gathered to dance, drink, and listen to music. Perhaps Fannie Lou first met Perry Hamer, who was five years her senior, at this social club he ran. And perhaps she was already a married woman when they met.

Although Fannie Lou never publicly mentioned a first marriage to a man named Charlie Gray, Monica Land, her great grandniece, found a record in the Sunflower County Courthouse of Gray's petition for divorce from a black woman named Fannie Lou. This petition bears a signature remarkably similar to Fannie Lou Hamer's and, in his petition, Gray alleged that the couple was lawfully wed in January of 1938, when Fannie Lou would have been twenty. The petition also noted that they bore no children, but lived together until February of 1943, at which point Fannie Lou allegedly "took up with another man, deserted [Gray] without any cause, and is now living in adultery with another man." Perry Hamer and Fannie Lou exchanged vows in July of 1944, which was also around the time she moved to the Marlow plantation. So, it is possible that the relationship between Perry Hamer and Fannie Lou began as an extramarital affair and that this affair is what brought Fannie Lou from the Brandon to the Marlow plantation in the mid-1940s.

Perhaps more important than the historical explanation that this divorce provides for Fannie Lou Hamer's move from E. W. Brandon's plantation to the W. D. Marlow farm is the insight it offers about both Gray and Hamer's eagerness to be recognized as citizens of the state. In 1930s rural Mississippi, most black sharecroppers had common law marriages—wherein couples lived together as husband and wife without formally filing marriage certificates at the county courthouse. If Gray and Fannie Lou Townsend did officially file for both marriage and divorce, these actions suggest a level of political engagement with the county that was quite rare among their contemporaries. Moreover, the suggestion that Fannie Lou broke her wedding vows with Gray to be with Perry Hamer intimates the deep connection, which their friends and family members all confirm, that existed between Fannie Lou and Perry Hamer.

"My life has been almost like my mother's was because I married a man who sharecropped," Fannie Lou Hamer would often contend. There were, however, some notable differences between the adult lives of Fannie Lou and Lou Ella. Unlike her mother, who began conceiving children at a young age, the Hamers struggled to conceive children together. Perry Hamer had been married before and he had several children from those previous relationships, so their inability to conceive probably had more to do with Fannie Lou's reproductive health challenges. While it was never confirmed, because the family lacked access to medical care, Fannie Lou likely suffered from a bout of polio as a child. As an adult, she attributed her persistent limp variously to either the injury she sustained when her brother dropped her from the bathtub or from a childhood polio infection. Post-polio syndrome could, therefore, be partly to blame for the two stillbirth children the Hamers mourned in the early years of their marriage. Conception itself was difficult for Fannie Lou, too, likely because she suffered from undiagnosed polycystic ovarian syndrome. She often complained of a "knot in her stomach," and the pain would eventually grow so severe that Perry Hamer insisted she seek medical treatment.

Fortunately, the couple—who shared a love of children—was able to rear two daughters entrusted to them from their community. Dorothy Jean, their eldest, was given to the couple by a single mother shortly after the Hamers wed. About ten years later, the couple took in Vergie Ree, a baby who was badly burned when she was five-months-old and whose biological parents had so many other children that they were unable to provide her with the care she required. Vergie's uncle noticed the severity of her condition and brought her to the Hamers in a desperate attempt to save the baby's life. The couple nursed Vergie back to health, and then her biological mother wanted her back. Not long after Vergie returned to her large family, however, the same uncle noticed the baby was being neglected yet again and returned Vergie to the Hamers— this time, the couple insisted, she would be there to stay. Vergie and Dorothy were well cared for by the Hamers. "My daddy was a provider," Vergie declared proudly. "He made sure we had plenty of food to eat. We raised our own garden, and daddy would raise hogs, chickens. They would make long sticks of bologna and potato salad that I could eat while they were working in the fields."

Through year-round labor and the leadership positions they held on Marlow's plantation, the couple was able to provide relatively well for their adopted children and for Lou Ella Townsend, whom Fannie Lou and Perry Hamer welcomed into their home in 1953. When Vergie reached the age of five, she began caring for her grandmother, who was now confined to a wheelchair, during the day. Vergie admitted that helping Lou Ella on and off the toilet, feeding and washing her, was hard work and she often resented it. But there were no other options. Her parents labored in the fields and her older sister Dorothy alternated between seasons of work and school. One time, Vergie recalled, her grandmother asked her to help her to the outhouse and the young girl refused. "Just go on yourself!" Vergie told her. Without Vergie's help, Lou Ella was eventually forced to urinate in her wheelchair. When Fannie Lou returned from work late that evening, she bathed her mother and punished young Vergie mightily for such neglect.

Fannie Lou made the most of the time Lou Ella Townsend spent living with the Hamers, using the opportunity to fulfill a promise she made to herself as a child. Witnessing her mother's self-sacrificing devotion to the Townsend family early in her young life, Hamer vowed that if she ever had the means to do so, she would make her mother's life more comfortable. To keep this promise, however, Hamer had to work so hard she "couldn't sleep at night." She explained, "I was determined to see that she did have something in her last few years. I went almost naked to see that my mother was kept decent and treated as a human being for the first time in all of her life." Lou Ella recognized her youngest daughter's devotion. Vergie remembered that Fannie Lou was "grandmama's *heart*, she didn't want to stay with nobody but my mama and my dad."

By working tirelessly Fannie Lou and Perry Hamer succeeded in making Lou Ella more comfortable during her final years on this earth, and the couple also succeeded in shielding Vergie from the harshest aspects of their impoverished and exploited existence. Looking back on her childhood, Vergie characterized their life on the plantation as "nice—everybody was family people," she remembered. "Back then everybody had enough food; you could leave your house unlocked. It was nice." Although "nice" was never a word Hamer used to characterize the eighteen years she spent on Marlow's plantation, the leadership positions she and Perry Hamer held did secure slightly better accommodations for the Hamer family. Marlow recognized Perry Hamer as a skilled tractor driver and frequently called upon him to run and repair the farm's machinery. What's more, Marlow also recognized that Fannie Lou had advanced reading and writing skills, gained during her several years of schooling and refined through years of Bible study. Marlow promoted Fannie Lou to the position of "timekeeper" on his plantation and moved the Hamers into a cabin near the river—the modest structure had a tin roof and cold running water, an indoor toilet (that didn't flush) and no electricity. Vergie explained that because her mother held this post, the plantation owner "made sure we was in a nice house." She described their living conditions: "We didn't have to worry about it raining inside. We had windows and doors, that kind of thing." She conceded that "it could have been better," but noted that "we had no need to complain because it was better than the house we had been living in" before Hamer was promoted.

As a plantation timekeeper, Hamer was a liaison between Marlow and the other sharecroppers; thus, Mrs. Hamer must have also had "trust on both sides," reasoned Dr. Leslie McLemore, a political scientist and personal friend of the Hamers. He explained that her position as a timekeeper reflected the confidence that Marlow had in her and it enabled her to help other sharecroppers, who were being cheated out of a fair measure for their harvest by the imbalanced measuring system Marlow used to determine the sharecroppers' payment. Hamer excelled in her role as timekeeper, McLemore posited, because of "her great ability to talk to both the white boss man and to talk to her friends and neighbors on the plantation."

Hamer's own reflections about her work as a timekeeper on the plantation support McLemore's contentions. To one interviewer Hamer explained how she transformed her responsible position into an outlet for her resistive desires: "I would take my p [a measuring device] to the field and use mine until I would see Marlow coming, you know, because his was loaded and I know it was beating people like that." Through the courageous act of providing sharecroppers with a fair measure for their harvest, Hamer worked to balance the scales that had been tipped against black people in Mississippi since her enslaved ancestors were forced to clear the densely wooded Delta terrain, sacred to the Choctaw people.

When not working in the fields or recording the workers' harvest, "I always had to work at white folks' houses," Hamer remembered. In this space, she created small moments of delight by secretively challenging daily assertions of white supremacy. "They would tell me that I couldn't eat with them or that I couldn't bathe in their tub," she explained to an audience later in life, "so what I would do was eat before they would eat and bathe when they was gone!" These subversive acts elicited wild applause from her listeners. Hamer continued: "I used to have a real ball knowing they didn't want me in their tub, just relaxing in that bubble bath." Similarly, "when they was saying that I couldn't eat with them, it would tickle me because I would say to myself, 'baby

I eat *first!*" Enjoying the warm food before she ever brought it to the table, Hamer explained, "I was rebelling in the only way I knew how to rebel."

Amidst the rare moments of pleasure that her resistance engendered, however, Hamer suffered painful indignities that shook her sense of self. Like the time Marlow's young daughter told Hamer not to worry about cleaning their smallest bathroom. "That one's just for Ole Honey," she explained with a giggle.

Anger boiled up inside Hamer. Year after year, Mr. Marlow refused to repair the toilet in Hamer's run-down timekeeper's cabin, forcing her family—her disabled mother—to relieve themselves in a ramshackle outhouse. And yet, Ole Honey, the Marlow's *dog*, had his own bathroom replete with functional facilities and warm running water, nestled comfortably inside the family home. In the Marlow's eyes, Hamer thought, we are less than dogs. "Negroes in Mississippi are treated *worse* than dogs," Hamer told a reporter years later, reflecting on how this incident wounded her.

While the Ole Honey incident stung, what the house cook told Hamer brought her to her knees. In her early forties, after years of suffering from severe menstrual cramping, Hamer sought medical treatment. The local doctor explained to Hamer that she would need surgery to remove a small uterine tumor, which was likely the source of her discomfort. After the surgery, word traveled fast across their small Delta town. The cook in the plantation house heard from W. D. Marlow's wife, Vera Alice, who likely heard from her cousin, who was Hamer's doctor: Fannie Lou had been given a hysterectomy—without her knowledge or consent. Hamer was devastated. "If he was going to give that sort of operation, then he should have told me. I would have loved to have children," she lamented.

Filled with anger, Hamer confronted the doctor, asking: "Why? Why had he done that to me? He didn't have to say nothing—and he didn't." Beyond a rage-filled confrontation, though, Hamer had no official recourse for this injustice. "Getting a white lawyer to go against a white doctor?" She mused, "I would have been taking my hands and screwing tacks into my own casket."

Hamer's resignation was both a sign of her lack of power, and perhaps also a recognition of how endemic such abuse was. The involuntary sterilization of poor black women "was so common" in the state, notes historian Danielle L. McGuire, "that blacks often called it a Mississippi appendectomy." In the late 1960s, in fact, the Mississippi legislature would introduce a bill that proposed sterilization for any "parent of a second illegitimate child." In support of the bill, State Representative Ben Owen was quoted in the *Delta Democratic Times* proclaiming: "This is the only way I know of to stop this rising black tide that threatens to engulf us."

When her beloved mother passed away in 1961, the Hamers buried Lou Ella Townsend alongside countless other sharecroppers, who rested in unmarked graves consolidated to a designated plot on the expansive Marlow plantation. Returning Lou Ella to the Delta soil upon which she labored for nearly a century, with nothing to show for the work—save total blindness, complete physical debilitation, and countless indignities—brought Hamer to a tipping point. This was not how she wanted her own story to end.

From an early age, Fannie Lou had been special in Lou Ella's eyes, capable of more than Hamer could even see in herself. During her formative years, young Fannie Lou struggled to make sense of the conflicting messages about who she was and what she could become. To the plantation owner, E. W. Brandon, who looked upon her six-year-old self, caught in a daydream on his dusty plantation path, she was nothing more than another set of hands whose labor could line his pockets. According to the Mississippi Department of Education, she and the other black sharecropping children in the Delta were not worthy of their investment; they became instead objects of their curriculum's ridicule. Even the Marlow family, whom Hamer once believed held a modicum of respect for her, let it be known that she and her family were inferior in their eyes—providing accommodations worse than their dog's; her body violated by their kin.

The overwhelming grief Hamer felt upon losing her mother, recognizing the wasted potential she buried along with Lou Ella Townsend, prompted reflection. She came to realize that those degrading visions were short-sighted; racism warped the perceptions of white supremacists, making them unable to see in Hamer what her strong mother, her God-fearing father, and her adoring husband recognized. And it wasn't just those closest to Hamer who saw her for what she could become. Professor Thornton Layne, who countered the state's derogatory curriculum with black artists' brilliance, also saw in young Fannie Lou potential for comparable greatness. The parishioners at Strangers' Home Baptist Church saw it too—rising to their feet, arms stretched up to Heaven whenever she sang out "This Little Light of Mine." Then there were the community members who entrusted her with their precious children—acknowledging her as capable of saving their little lives—not to mention her fellow sharecroppers on Marlow's plantation, who looked to Hamer as a fair and just leader among their ranks.

Hamer was transformed by recalling these visions of who she was, had been since her youth, and could become if she was given "a chance to really lash out, and say what she had to say about what was going on in Mississippi." She looked up from the fresh earth covering her mother's worn body and sensed that chance peeking over the Delta horizon.

· 2 ·

Putting Up a Life

"Though I walk through the valley of the shadow of death, I will fear no evil: for thou art with me; thy rod and thy staff they comfort me. Thou preparest a table before me in the presence of mine enemies: thou anointest my head with oil; my cup runneth over.

—Psalm 23: 4–5

Fannie Lou Hamer wiped the sweat trickling down her cheek with a crumpled handkerchief as Perry Hamer opened the door to Williams Chapel Baptist Church. Once inside, the couple cautiously approached the spirited scene. Congregants were on their feet, hands clapping to the rhythm of an unfamiliar call and response song:

> *Have you got good religion?*
> *Certainly Lord*
> *Do you hate segregation?*
> *Certainly Lord*
> *Do you want your freedom?*
> *Certainly Lord*
> *Have you been to the courthouse?*
> *Certainly Lord*
> *Certainly, Certainly, Certainly Lord*

Fannie Lou scanned the room in search of Mrs. Mary Tucker. She found her friend introducing long-time parishioners to the young kids from out of town. "Freedom Riders," thought Mrs. Hamer skeptically, as she and Pap settled into their usual pew. But this was no ordinary meeting at the Ruleville church led by Reverend J. D. Story. He'd made an announcement during yesterday's service that tonight, August 27, 1962, the church would be the first in the region to host what was being called—in hushed whispers across Delta plantations—a "mass meeting."

In the summer of 1962, members of the Council of Federated Organizations (COFO)—a coalition comprised of the major civil rights groups operating throughout Mississippi, including the Southern Christian Leadership Conference (SCLC), the Student Nonviolent Coordinating Committee (SNCC), and the Congress of Racial Equality (CORE)—traveled around the state holding gatherings in black churches to inform local people of their voting rights. These mass meetings were part and parcel of COFO's novel strategy to undermine segregation. Voting registration drives were nothing new in the state; nearly half a century before COFO began their campaign, the National Association for the Advancement of Colored People (NAACP) had been promoting suffrage as the key to black political, social, and economic advancement in Mississippi. COFO's efforts to activate voters weren't new, but their decision to work primarily with the poor was. The constituency COFO sought was fundamentally different from the target of past NAACP campaigns. Unlike the NAACP's emphasis on developing leadership among well-educated middle-class black people, COFO targeted the masses of poor black people living in vast rural areas like the Delta.

Although "Freedom Riders" was the catch-all label Deltans used to refer to out of town activists, COFO's political empowerment strategy was also distinct from concurrent direct action campaigns favored by young activists in the early 60s—such as lunch counter sit-ins and Freedom Rides. Bob Moses, one of the initial SNCC activists to enter the Magnolia state, followed the advice of Greenwood native and veteran organizer, Amzie Moore, who suggested expanding the NAACP's existing focus on voting rights to the masses. As SNCC soon learned, given the state's viciously racist and violently retaliatory climate, voter registration in Mississippi was, in fact, a form of direct action protest. Though highly dangerous, the focus on voter registration made strategic political sense, especially in places like Sunflower County, where black people outnumbered white people by two-to-one. And yet, of the more than 13,000 black people eligible to vote in this particular county, fewer than 200 were registered when COFO began their work. Black people had been barred from political activism since Reconstruction. They had been economically exploited since their ancestors cleared the Delta's flatlands. They had been systematically scared into submission through rape, lynching, and the landowner's lash. To ask them to now risk their lives and livelihoods for the vote was a formidable challenge, but one that COFO activists faced head on.

On this sweltering August evening in the summer of 1962, local leaders like Amzie Moore, Joe McDonald, and Hattie Sisson collaborated with national COFO activists James Bevel, James Forman, Bob Moses, and Reggie Robinson to accomplish the seemingly impossible: to convince black people in Ruleville to risk their lives by demanding their voting rights.

Fannie Lou reached for Pap's warm hand and gave him an uncharacteristically timid smile before catching Mrs. Tucker's eye. Hamer was grateful that Pap accompanied her to the meeting tonight, just as he said he would, as long as the couple could finish the day's work before the meeting started. On W. D. Marlow's plantation, Fannie Lou worked even harder than usual to ensure they would make it into town that night. She was a bit curious about the meeting, but she really needed to apologize to Mrs. Tucker, who was headed toward the couple now.

Fannie Lou's heart rate quickened, she took a deep breath and burst out with it: "Tuck, I come to beg your pardon. I never sassed you before in my life and it hurt me so bad when I thought about what I had said to you. I come to beg your pardon."

Mrs. Tucker's kind eyes and her outstretched arms indicated that all was forgiven. She was thrilled to see the Hamers at the mass meeting, and she said as much before darting off to welcome other nervous parishioners who were lingering in the back of the sanctuary.

In the year since Lou Ella Townsend's passing, Mrs. Mary Tucker—affectionately known as "Tuck"—had become like a mother to Fannie Lou Hamer. Between Perry Hamer's supportive companionship, Fannie Lou's steadfast devotion to their growing girls, and Tuck's guidance, Hamer's heart began to heal. And in the healing process, a fog seemed to lift from Hamer's mind. Throughout the 1950s, Hamer's thoughts were never her own, constantly clouded by the worry that accompanies caregiving with limited resources: Could the Hamers turn a profit from this year's harvest to provide the medical treatment her mother sorely needed? Would they be able to afford the clothing and school supplies their children so badly wanted? Would their small garden patch yield enough food to preserve and sustain all five of them through Mississippi's unrelenting winter months? With her mind racing in a loop of concern, Hamer's thoughts—as well as her time—strained against the trials of day-to-day survival. She tended to the crops on Marlow's plantation, cleaned his family's home, and measured the sharecroppers' harvest, all before returning to the Hamers' dilapidated cabin to care for her own children, to comfort her mother, to clean her own home, and to tend her small garden.

From discarded newspapers Hamer found lying around the Marlow home and through headlines blaring from the radio kept in their main kitchen, Hamer could sense a spirit of resistance spreading. She had likely heard about the *Brown v. Board of Education* decision, the Montgomery Bus Boycott, the desegregation of Little Rock High School, the sit-ins and Freedom Rides. But these black freedom movement advances all felt as far removed from her rural Deltan life as the paperback crime novels featuring Justice Department cases that Hamer relished before she fell asleep, exhausted from her whirlwind days of worry.

When Tuck first approached Hamer about voting rights, she said, "Fannie Lou, I want you to come to my home. I want you to come to a meeting. We're having a civil rights meeting. We're learning to register and vote so you can be a citizen."

"Tuck, they taught us that mess in school," Hamer said, waving her hand dismissively.

Hamer could tell by the fading smile on Tuck's worn face that her words had stung this kind woman in her late sixties, who had bravely opened her home to the young people from out of town.

Older people provided key points of entry for voter registration workers to gain broader access into the larger community. SNCC organizer, Sam Block remembered that after spending a good deal of time in Greenwood's "laundromats, grocery stores, pool halls, and juke joints," he discovered it was the "older people who were most receptive" to the topic of voter registration. Block explained that adults in their fifties, sixties, and seventies "were angry, they were looking for somebody who could give form and expression to ideas and thoughts that they had in their mind for years." What's more, they had slightly less to lose. By contrast, middle-aged professionals, whom the NAACP campaigns had traditionally privileged, became targets for economic retaliation whenever they dared engage with COFO. As COFO workers like Bob Moses and Charles McLaurin walked the unpaved streets of Ruleville's black quarter, they found residents like Herman and Hattie Sisson, Robert and Mary Tucker, Joe and Rebecca McDonald, who all welcomed them into the community. With the help of these local leaders, COFO organized a planning meeting at the Tuckers' home to prepare for the mass meeting that would be held at Williams Chapel.

Hamer was initially quite skeptical about the mass meeting idea, but the hurt she saw in Tuck's eyes compelled Hamer to reconsider her response to Tuck's invitation. Hamer now had the mental space to consider what Tuck was asking of her and, given the respect she held for her dear friend, Hamer changed her mind. Though she missed that initial planning meeting held at the Tuckers' Byron Street home, Fannie Lou convinced Perry Hamer to drive her into town for the mass meeting at Williams Chapel. Once there, the couple listened attentively as a man named James Bevel boldly led into his sermon with scripture.

From Luke chapter twelve, verse fifty-six, Bevel read: "You hypocrites! You know how to interpret the appearance of earth and sky, but why do you not know how to interpret the present time?" A native Mississippian and trained Baptist Theologian, Bevel used Jesus's admonishment of the Scribes and Pharisees, who were skeptical that he was the Messiah, to challenge the sharecroppers seated before him—those black Mississippians who had yet to recognize the winds of change blowing around them.

Bevel's "Discerning the Signs of the Time" sermon resonated with the Ruleville-area sharecroppers gathered that fateful evening. Following Black Baptist tradition, he made the abstract tangible, drawing connections between his political message and the congregation's lived experience. He knew they already lived their lives paying careful attention to the weather, for it determined how their crops—and therefore their families—would fare. People who had lived for generations off the Delta soil's produce understood weather patterns; now it was time to pay attention to the national climate, too. Years later, Hamer recalled the moral of Bevel's speech. "He talked about how a man could look out and see a cloud and predict it's going to rain, and it would become so; but still he couldn't tell what was happening right around him," Hamer said.

Many of the people at that mass meeting had heard murmurings of local and national events challenging segregationist laws, policies, and customs. What's more, the presence of national COFO members in their modest Delta sanctuary signaled a precipitous change in the nation's racial climate. But many congregants likely wondered what *they* could do about all of this? If they didn't have money enough to buy a bus ticket or eat at a lunch counter, let alone the educational background to integrate an institution of higher education, then why did COFO gather them here tonight? Why did it matter if Ruleville's sharecroppers "discerned the signs of the time"?

SNCC's Executive Secretary, James Forman, provided a compelling answer to the questions raised by Bevel's sermon. "Jim Forman got up, and he talked about voter registration," Hamer remembered. "That was the next strange thing to me. I never heard about that."

In several interviews, Hamer contended that up until this moment, as a forty-four-year-old woman, she was unaware of her constitutional right to vote. It seems somewhat unbelievable that anyone living in the United States in 1962 would be unaware that black Americans could vote. For Hamer, in particular, this seems quite unlikely. Several Mississippi movement activists and one of Hamer's biographers claim that during the 1950s she participated in at least one of the Regional Council of Negro Leadership (RCNL) meetings held in the all black town of Mound Bayou—less than twenty miles from Ruleville. The RCNL was founded by black veterans, including Dr. T. R. M Howard, who returned from World War II demanding the rights they had fought for abroad. The meetings organized by the RCNL would draw thousands of black Deltans, who enjoyed food, music, and speeches by politicians. In light of Fannie Lou Hamer's comment to Mrs. Tucker that she had learned "that mess" in school, given that she likely attended at least one of RCNL's meetings, and because Hamer was an avid reader—devouring newspapers, crime novels, and any other literature she could acquire—it is doubtful that Hamer first learned she had a right to vote in August of 1962.

Her comment does, however, speak to a larger cultural truth about the insular nature of plantation life. Charles McLaurin, a SNCC Field Secretary, explained that most black sharecroppers he met in the Delta during his years of voter registration work were surprised to learn that Mississippi even had a constitution. "All people knew about Mississippi was racism, brutality, harassment, violence, intimidation—they never thought about Mississippi being a state." He continued, "Because to them what was a state? The plantation owner owned them, in a sense." Because white landowners intentionally circumscribed their livelihoods and therefore their lives, it is, in fact, true that many black Mississippi sharecroppers were unaware of recourse outside the plantation's confines. Given the closed nature of plantation society within the larger closed society of Mississippi, it seems possible that some of Hamer's neighbors learned about black suffrage for the first time when Forman introduced the Williams Chapel parishioners to the power of the vote.

Perhaps it was also the *way* Bevel and Forman explained the franchise to Hamer that day—planting the idea that, through the vote, black Mississippians could transform the exploitative conditions surrounding them—that so deeply resonated deeply with Hamer. As she would often recall, Bevel's and Forman's messages seemed to Hamer, "like the most remarkable thing that could happen in the state of Mississippi." After these two civil rights workers finished speaking, she was among the eighteen people who raised their hands—in the mass meeting version of an altar call—indicating her willingness to try to register at the Sunflower County Courthouse that Friday.

When Friday came, Mrs. Hamer dressed in her Sunday's best. Ever the pragmatist, she tucked some comfortable shoes into a travel bag before Perry Hamer drove her four miles downtown to meet the bus. "If I'm arrested or anything, I'll have some extra shoes to put on," she explained to a curious Pap. Arrest was likely and perhaps the most moderate of all the consequences that COFO activists warned the would-be registrants about. Bob Moses, who accompanied the eighteen Ruleville residents twenty-six miles to the courthouse in Indianola, had first-hand experience with the ravages of white supremacist retaliation. A year earlier, Moses was helping register two black residents of Amite County, in southern Mississippi, and Moses himself was badly beaten by the sheriff's cousin right inside the courthouse.

When they arrived at the chapel parking lot, Fannie Lou kissed Pap's cheek. He was still skeptical of these "Freedom Riders," but supportive of his wife nevertheless. She climbed aboard the discarded yellow school bus, owned by a black farmer from the neighboring Bolivar County. The group of eighteen Ruleville residents, accompanied by several civil rights workers who rode both on the bus and trailed in cars behind, caravanned toward the county seat. Surprised by the outcome of their first mass meeting at Williams Chapel, Moses and Amzie Moore had scrambled to find transportation for the large group. Fortunately, they located a bus, which was used to transport migrant workers to and from Florida's orange groves during Mississippi's colder months. As the old bus sputtered along Highway 49, the registration hopefuls looked onto the fields lining either side of the roadway. They saw rows upon rows of white cotton bolls beginning to crack open out of thorny green plants. As the bus turned off the country road and into town, Hamer wondered if this registration attempt would be the beginning of a new life for her family, a new arrangement on the plantation, across the county.

Her rays of hope diminished the moment the bus rounded the corner and turned onto Indianola's Main Street. Momentarily disoriented, Hamer wondered what all the commotion was about. The concerned looks shared between COFO activists made it clear: the commotion was about *them*—this bus full of black Rulevillians and caravan of "outside agitators." A small town spectacle, they must have caught the attention of some white onlooker, who likely spread the word like wildfire across the county.

One by one the passengers warily exited the bus, sticking together in a pack and stalling in front of the courthouse doors. Six large pillars stretched across the entrance way of this formidable brick building, which held the county jail and embodied the white supremacist power structure. The courthouse appeared all the more foreboding on this August morning, as the mob of rifle-toting white men swelled. Indianola was the birthplace of the Citizens' Council—a white supremacist organization comprised of prominent farm managers, lawyers, bankers, and government officials, colloquially referred to as the "Klan in suits, not sheets." Historian Neil McMillen characterized the group as the "mouthpiece of southern defiance." The Citizens' Council not only broadcast their segregationist ideology nationally, the group also wove a dense web of internal communication facilitating resistive gatherings like the one that met Ruleville's black voter registration applicants at the entrance to the Sunflower County Courthouse. A sense of panic spread among the registration hopefuls, who became just as fearful of congregating outside the courthouse as they were of what awaited them inside the building.

Out of this morass emerged Fannie Lou Hamer. She stepped off the bus and through the crowd, head held high and eyes fixed on the courthouse door. Grateful for her bold direction, the seventeen other passengers and COFO activists followed closely behind.

"What do you want?" barked Circuit Clerk Cecil B. Campbell, visibly angered by the group's presence.

"We are here to register," Hamer said.

Campbell ordered the large group to leave the registration office, insisting that only two people could take the test at a time. The remainder of the group would have to wait outside, facing both the late summer heat and the white supremacist intimidation. Hamer and Ernest Davis were the first to try their hands at Campbell's registration test. He approached them with a resentful expression on his face and a large black book tucked under his arm. Given her success in school and the preparation that COFO fieldworkers had provided that week, Hamer felt fairly confident at the outset. The first part of the registration test contained basic questions: date, name, address, and employer. Hamer's heart sank as she recalled more of the repercussions the COFO activists had warned the group about: this information was gathered by the registrar and often shared with the applicant's employer. She thought of Pap and her girls, laboring in the fields today without her. She thought of the decrepit sharecroppers' cabin that they'd turned into a home. And she wondered if her action in this very moment was jeopardizing the life—rock hard as it was—they struggled to build together.

Campbell abruptly flipped open the large black book, pointing to Section Sixteen of Mississippi's State Constitution, and ordered Hamer to read, copy, and provide a "reasonable interpretation" of the passage. Since Hamer had only recently learned that Mississippi had a constitution, she characterized this portion of the exam as "rough." Because registrars administered the exam, moreover, the rigor or simplicity of the chosen passage as well as the acceptability of the interpretation was left up to Campbell's discretion—white applicants might be given simple questions or no test at all, black applicants were frequently given rigorous exams and their responses seldom met the registrars' approval. Literacy tests, like the Grandfather Clause, poll taxes, and the widespread practice of publishing registration applicants' names in local newspapers, were strategies that white leaders devised in an attempt to curtail the political advances made in the period following the Civil War known as Reconstruction. During Hamer's grandparents' generation, newly freed black Mississippians voted in droves and elected black leaders to such notable posts as Lieutenant Governor, Secretary of State, and Speaker of the House of Representatives. By the turn of the century, however, voter discrimination, combined with economic reprisal and widespread violent retaliation, effectively put an end to this period of black political advancement.

So, nearly one hundred years after President Abraham Lincoln signed the Emancipation Proclamation, here sat Hamer nervously copying down the Sixteenth Section of Mississippi's Constitution and struggling to interpret its meaning to Campbell's satisfaction. The constitutional passage he chose for Hamer that day dealt with *ex facto* laws. "And I knowed as much about a *facto* law," admitted Hamer, "as a horse knows about Christmas Day." On this, her first registration attempt, Hamer failed. She was ordered to exit the building.

As Hamer waited outside for the rest of the group to take the registration exam, she watched the crowd of angry white men with cowboy hats, rifles, and mangy dogs, pacing up and down Main Street. Illustrating the crowd's absurdity to audiences later in life, Hamer would say the men gathered in front of the courthouse that day resembled Jed Clampett of the CBS television show, *The Beverly Hillbillies*—only "they wasn't kidding," she said. Perhaps this humorous resemblance helped quell her fears and opened her mind to the realization she would soon share with fellow black sharecroppers across the region. "You know the ballot is good," she declared at mass meetings. "If it wasn't good how come he trying to keep you from it and he still using it?" She continued, "Now if it's good enough for them, I want some of it too!"

Back home at Marlow's plantation, Perry Hamer was arriving at a similar understanding. Around noon, he took the girls in from the field for lunch and Mr. Marlow came storming by their cabin. "Where's Fannie?" he demanded.

"I don't know. She gone to town somewhere," Mr. Hamer said.

"No, she ain't gone to town. She gone down to Indianola to register. We ain't going to have that now," Marlow insisted, and he instructed Perry Hamer to relay this message to his wife: "We're not ready for that in the State of Mississippi."

Over the course of the afternoon's work, this encounter loomed over Perry Hamer who thought, "Hell, there must be something to *it* or why would he want to raise hell *about* it?"

At the courthouse, registrants continued to file through the clerk's office in pairs. They endured Campbell's spite and the rigorous exam before exiting to the jeers of white supremacist onlookers. By 4:30 that afternoon, all eighteen registration hopefuls had failed the exam and were now on board the faded yellow school bus—bound for Ruleville. Spirits were low as the Ruleville residents grumbled about the futility of their day, the work that would meet them when they returned home, and the repercussions that would likely befall their attempt at civic assertion.

"From the back of the bus this powerful voice broke out in song," Charles Cobb, a SNCC fieldworker from Washington, D.C., remembered. "The voice was Mrs. Hamer's. . . . With the power of her voice alone she shored up everybody on the bus."

A loud gasp interrupted Hamer's song leading. A state highway patrolmen swerved in front of the car caravan following the bus. The patrolman was soon joined by a cadre of officer cars and motorcycles, lights on and sirens blaring.

With trembling hands, the bus driver slowly pushed up his right blinker and pulled off to the side of Highway 49. The passengers listened fearfully to the tense conversation between the bus driver and the policeman. The bus that had been used to transport migrant workers for years was suddenly the "wrong color," they heard the state highway patrolman say. "Too yellow, it resembled a school bus."

Once it became clear that the police officer intended to arrest the driver—this brave and patient man, who lent his vehicle to the cause, drove the Rulevillians to the courthouse, and spent the day waiting with them—the group decided that if the bus driver was going to jail, the police would have to book all eighteen of them. Their defiant act of loyalty worked. Whether the patrolman was concerned about the federal attention such an impromptu civil rights demonstration might elicit or whether he was reluctant to go through the hassle of arresting, transporting, and processing so many people on a blatantly fraudulent charge, the officer changed the consequence from arrest to a fine of $100. The group pooled their money and came up with a grand total of $30 between them, which the patrolman took and exited the bus. Hamer's strong voice belied her tangled stomach. She summoned the power of gospel music and sang all the way home.

The cicadas had just begun their high-pitched chirping by the time Reverend Jeff Sunny drove Mrs. Hamer back to Marlow's plantation. She noticed Pap unloading cotton trailers as she limped exhaustedly toward their cabin. Before Mrs. Hamer could set her shoe bag down on their rickety front porch, she heard her daughter Dorothy Jean shouting, "Mama, Mama!"

Dorothy and Pap's cousin were running toward her, breathlessly recounting their mid-day conversation with Mr. Marlow. Perry Hamer joined his family on the front porch and confirmed the girls' tale—Marlow was, indeed, "raising Cain" across the plantation over Fannie Lou's alleged registration attempt.

And soon there was the plantation owner himself, stark-raving mad as he approached the Hamers. "Fannie Lou! Did Pap tell you what I told him?" Marlow hollered.

"Yes, he did," Mrs. Hamer replied.

"Well, I mean it," continued Marlow, red-faced, spittle bubbling in the corners of his mouth. "You'll have to go down there and withdraw your registration. We're not ready for that in the State of Mississippi."

"I didn't try to register for you," she said. "I tried to register for myself."

Stunned by this brazen retort from the sharecropper he'd promoted to timekeeper, who cared for his family for well over a decade, and who had sent him baked goods while he served overseas, Marlow's face hardened and his voice lowered. "If you don't go down and withdraw your registration, you'll have to leave the plantation." Marlow said: "You have until the morning to decide."

Mrs. Hamer didn't wait until morning. She walked inside, talked it over with Pap, and they agreed—it was no longer safe for her to stay there. She made a phone call. Within the hour, James Bevel and Andrew Young of the SCLC arrived to load up Hamer's personal belongings and transport her to a late night meeting held at Williams Chapel. On the short drive from Marlow's plantation back to the downtown chapel, tears streamed down Hamer's cheeks. Her life had turned upside down in the course of one day—fired from her job, separated from her family, and left with no place to live. The moment she arrived at the meeting of COFO activists and newly initiated local leaders, who were analyzing the traumatic events of the day, Hamer testified about her troubled state.

"Don't say you ain't got nowhere to stay," Tuck said, interrupting Hamer's lament. "As long as I got a shelter—if I ain't got but one plank, you stick your head under there, too."

Joe McDonald chimed in next. "If you ain't got room, I got room," he assured them.

With gratitude, Hamer wrapped her arms around them both.

The next morning, when Marlow returned to the Hamer home to find Fannie Lou already gone, he informed Mr. Hamer that he, too, had a choice to make. If Perry Hamer followed his wife off the plantation, Marlow would have him arrested and would confiscate couple's belongings, including a car and all the furniture the couple had acquired over nearly two decades. If Pap stayed and worked the harvest, however, he could go freely and take their belongings with him. For Perry Hamer to stay behind on the Marlow plantation after Fannie Lou had been fired was cruel punishment indeed, but his position as a skilled maintenance worker on the plantation may have saved her life.

Less than two weeks after Fannie Lou's registration attempt, Perry Hamer noticed newly purchased buckshot shells in the plantation's maintenance shop. Fearing that the shells were intended to hunt down his wife and not meant for any game this early in the hunting season, he convinced Fannie Lou to take their two daughters, and flee from Tuck's home to their niece's remote cabin in Tallahatchie County.

The first shot startled Mary Tucker awake.

"Did you hear that?" she asked, shaking her husband, Robert.

Fifteen shots followed in rapid succession. The couple lay motionless, paralyzed with fear, as the buckshot blasts tore through the window into their guest room, landing above the bed where Fannie Lou Hamer had slept the night before. They heard the screech of truck tires and then more shots, not far in the distance. Their ears strained to place them. Had the nightrider moved on to the McDonalds' home? they wondered, whispering fearfully to each other.

Screeching tires, yet again, engine revving and then more shots. Now screams of terror echoed through Ruleville's black quarter. Moments later, the Tuckers' phone rang. Robert stayed low, away from windows, as he crept to answer it.

"They got the Sissons' granddaughters!" he screamed to Mary.

Marylene Burks and Vivian Hillet, Jackson State University students, were visiting their grandparents on the evening of September 10, 1962. When the white supremacist nightrider's shots were fired, the two young women were seated on the couch near the window in the living room of Herman and Hattie Sisson's house. The Sissons, like the Tuckers and the McDonalds, had encouraged and assisted with COFO's voting rights activism. Each of their three homes was shot into, but only the Sissons granddaughters were critically injured. Burks was shot in the head and Hillet was wounded in the arms and the legs. With help from their neighbors, the Sissons rushed Burks and Hillet to North Sunflower County Hospital. There, they were met by Ruleville Mayor Charles Dorrough, who approached the terrified family and said, "You done that yourself, trying to lay it on somebody else. You done that yourself, get out of here, go on out of here!" Dorrough's spiteful response echoed the common victim-blaming white supremacist refrain, which alleged black activists burned down their own churches, beat themselves up, and even inflicted one another with gunshot wounds to drum up publicity for the cause of civil rights.

The Sissons pushed past the mayor's attempt to deny their granddaughters' medical treatment and admitted the young women to the hospital. Thankfully, they both survived, but the shootings sent chills through Ruleville's black community, freezing COFO's budding registration campaign. Since COFO's Delta campaign began early in summer of 1962, SNCC activists Charles Cobb and Charles McLaurin had encouraged close to fifty local black people to try their hand at voter registration. But after the early September shooting, nobody wanted to be seen talking to COFO workers. It took months, remembered Cobb, until they could convince anyone to try to register again. To regain Black Deltans' confidence and to help overcome their fears of white retaliation, voter registration workers remained in the community and dug into local affairs. When they found that no one was willing to talk to them on their front porches or attend meetings at local churches, Cobb and McLaurin offered to take people to the store in town, to help them pick cotton, or to chop wood. By staying in the community and engaging in everyday activities with Ruleville's inhabitants, "gradually, very gradually," suggested black freedom movement scholar Charles M. Payne, voter registration workers won "back the town's confidence."

⁃ While Cobb and McLaurin were embedding themselves more deeply into the Ruleville community, Hamer was living in exile. Hamer and her daughters began picking cotton on the Tallahatchie County plantation where her niece worked. The Hamers' youngest daughter, Vergie, remembered how miserable the living conditions were there. By fall, the weather was growing cold and the remote cabin where they stayed was drafty. She would cry out in the middle of the night to her mother, "I want to go home. I miss my Dad!"

And though the separation from Pap was painful for Hamer as well, she tried to assure her homesick daughter that "it's going to be alright."

But the longer they stayed in Tallahatchie County, the angrier Hamer became. For Hamer, it wasn't the living conditions that caused her the most pain—she had grown up in worse—rather it was being forced to live on the run for acting well within her rights. Celebrating her forty-fifth birthday, separated from the man she loved, her home, and from her friends, Hamer wondered: Why should she have to live like a fugitive when she had done nothing wrong?

Shortly after Fannie Lou Hamer's birthday, Charles McLaurin set out to find the powerful woman who had inspired them all at the Sunflower County Courthouse. During the August 31, 1962, registration attempt, Hamer had emerged as exactly the kind of leader SNCC was searching for. SNCC adhered to long-time activist Ella Baker's model of cultivating grassroots leadership among locally respected community members. Baker, who Hamer later celebrated as "the most important black leader in the United States," challenged the black freedom movement's traditional racial uplift ideology, which was rooted in class and gender-based hierarchies. A cherished SNCC mentor, Baker taught the young, mostly college-educated, activists to recognize the collective wisdom of sharecroppers, maids, and manual laborers. Baker held the firm conviction that "the people should speak for themselves," often insisting "it was not urbane articulateness that was needed; the people who were suffering could say it better." Every COFO activist who had encountered Mrs. Hamer to date was convinced that she could offer a compelling account of Mississippi sharecroppers' plight. They knew she could relate to the masses of black people across the Delta and inspire them to register. SNCC's leadership was eager to enlist Hamer among the movement's leadership ranks.

So, in the pouring rain, McLaurin drove around Tallahatchie County for hours trying to locate Mrs. Hamer. He got lost several times, relying as he was upon uncertain tips and vague landmark directions, which might have been familiar to other Deltans, but which proved baffling to the Jackson native. On his circuitous route, McLaurin had plenty of time to contemplate how he would convince Mrs. Hamer to join him and to confront the dangers of civil rights activism head-on. He wouldn't need to marshal these arguments. Finally, McLaurin spotted smoke billowing from the center of a small run-down shack on the top of a grassy hill in a town called Cascilla. He parked and approached the dwelling warily. The door to the cabin was ajar and, peeking inside, he could see a stout woman crouched over a pot-bellied fireplace, stoking the flame.

"Mrs. Hamer?" McLaurin asked. The woman turned to face him, a smile spread across her face, reaching all the way to her tired brown eyes. Mrs. Hamer's girls quickly tucked themselves behind her, unsure of this stranger. They listened as McLaurin nervously explained that he was sent there by a man named Bob Moses to take their mother to a civil rights meeting in Nashville, Tennessee.

To the surprise of everyone in the house, Mrs. Hamer agreed to go and she took only a few minutes to make arrangements for the girls to join their father back in Ruleville before heading out into the stormy fall evening with McLaurin behind the wheel. They first drove down to Tougaloo College, in Jackson, and then back up to a civil rights workshop at Fisk University in Nashville.

On their drive, McLaurin remembered asking, "Mrs. Hamer, did you know I was coming?"

"Yes. God sent you," was her faithful response.

Her reply scared the hell out of him, McLaurin admitted. And he corrected her. "Bob Moses sent me," he said.

"Well, He told Bob to tell you to come," she explained.

Hamer had long believed that God was on the side of the oppressed. Her upbringing in the Black Baptist tradition paired with Bevel's recent sermon taught her to look for signs of God's will in her everyday life. To Hamer, McLaurin's ability to track her down at her niece's small cabin in the hard-to-find town of Cascilla, just as she had come to her own realization that she was sick of living on the run, was surely a sign that the time for exile was over.

The workshop McLaurin brought Hamer to was organized by SNCC for the local leaders that registration activists had discovered in communities across the South. In 1962, Andrew Young was working for the SCLC and as an administrator for the United Church of Christ. Young's duties as administrator included recruiting people for the citizenship training workshops developed by Septima Clark. To find trainees, Young would drive "across the South looking for people who had PhD minds, but who had never had an opportunity to get an education. There are people like that in every community," he said. "There are people who are really bright that everybody looks up to for their opinions, but they may not have had any formal training or schooling. Mrs. Hamer was that way," Young remembered.

Movement reports indicate that Hamer's singing and ability to communicate were what earned her an invitation to attend the Nashville workshop. Once she arrived at Fisk, Hamer did not disappoint. Young activists and older local leaders alike were eager to hear her sing, to listen to her testify about growing up as the granddaughter of enslaved persons in the Mississippi Delta, and to learn about the retaliation she endured after attempting to register. Beyond sharing her own story, Hamer learned from the other activists—later recalling that this was the first time in her life where she interacted on an equal plane with white people. She attended politics and voting workshops to learn more about the roles nonviolence, communications, and economics played in the movement. Hamer became so comfortable amidst this group of activists that immediately following the Nashville rally, she toured college campuses, speaking and singing to raise awareness and money for SNCC's voter registration campaign.

During her time on the road, Perry Hamer kept a close eye on their girls, who helped him work the harvest on Marlow's plantation. He was spared arrest, but when Mr. Hamer and the girls finally left Marlow's property in early December, the landowner alleged the Hamers owed him money. Marlow confiscated their car and furniture as payment against their debt. With nothing to their name, the Hamer family relied upon local friends and movement workers to rent a modest home at 626 East Lafayette Street, a small three-room white house near Williams Chapel with no indoor plumbing. But it did have a screened porch and a large pecan tree in the front yard.

Hamer was so grateful for the home provided to her family, which was her first home outside of a plantation, that she understood this gesture, too, as a sign from God. She encouraged other black Deltans to take the risks she had by testifying to God's protective grace. "It's a funny thing since I started working for Christ," which is how she characterized her civil rights advocacy, "it's been kind of like in the twenty-third Psalm when He says, 'Thou prepareth a table before me in the presence of my enemies. Thou anointed my head with oil and my cup runneth over.'" The house secured for her family and the ten dollars a week provided to Hamer by SNCC for her registration work were surely signs that she was on the right path, but having her life spared definitively signaled to Hamer that she was called by God to do this work: "I have walked through the shadows of death," she would frequently testify, "because it was on the tenth of September in '62 when they shot sixteen times in a house and it wasn't a foot over the bed where my head was. But that night I wasn't there—don't you see what God can do?" Hamer would ask audiences of black people who were skeptical of voting rights activism.

While in exile and during her time on the road fundraising for SNCC, Hamer grew determined to devote her life to the struggle for civil rights. She compared her devotion to the Apostle Paul, who risked his life to spread Christianity. Hamer explained: "as long as you know you going for something, you put up a life that it can be like Paul, say 'I fought a good fight.' And 'I've kept the faith.'" For her, there was now no turning back. She realized that protecting herself from white supremacists' violence by hiding away was futile and really no life to live. As she instructed her fellow Mississippians, "quit running around trying to dodge death because this Book said: 'he that seeketh to save his life, he's going to lose it anyhow!'"

Armed with this renewed sense of determination and supported by COFO activists, Hamer revitalized the voter registration campaign in Ruleville. She returned to the Sunflower County Courthouse in Indianola the day after she and her family moved into their home on Lafayette Street. "We moved in on the third of December," Hamer remembered, "and I went back on the fourth of December to take the literacy test again." This time Hamer was presented with Section 49 of the Mississippi Constitution, which describes the House of Representatives. Just as before, County Clerk Cecil Campbell asked her to read and copy the passage, as well as to provide a reasonable interpretation. Although Hamer was able to read and copy the selected passages well during both of her registration attempts, this second time she felt far more confident interpreting the text because she had been studying the Mississippi Constitution with SNCC activists. In some recollections, Hamer explained that the studying paid off as she passed the literacy test, becoming only the sixth black registered voter in the entire city of Ruleville, on this, her second try.

In other recollections, however, Hamer's account of her success is more realistically mindful of the fraudulent registration system that was set up to keep black people powerless, not to reward their competence. In these accounts, her successful registration attempt is linked to a promise she made to Campbell. "You'll see me every 30 days till I pass," she informed him with convincing determination, though she was never pressed to make good on that threat.

Regardless of the cause—whether the studying did indeed pay off or the registrar simply did not want to deal with Hamer each month—her eventual success at the Sunflower County Courthouse and her determination to use the ballot to challenge the white supremacist oppression surrounding her were contagious. The town saw a marked increase in registration hopefuls. "In February 1963 alone," observed historian J. Todd Moye, "400 Ruleville residents traveled to Indianola to take the registration test."

Motivating poor black Mississippians to risk their jobs and to put their lives and the livelihood of their families on the line was "really rough" and often "very disappointing" work, Hamer admitted. Hamer remembered truckloads of white men with gun racks circling the houses that held registration meetings. She also recalled white men walking the streets with large dogs, leering at her, while she tried to canvass small towns. She would travel around the Delta talking with black sharecroppers, who expressed interest in learning about their citizenship rights, only to return to their community days later to find that these people had been threatened by their bosses and warned not to talk to her. The consequences for those brave enough to continue talking with her, to attend a mass meeting, and to register were devastating. Well-connected members of the Citizens' Council would bar politically active black people from access to bank loans, or they would make sure those involved with the campaign were fired from their jobs. COFO would hold mass meetings at local churches one night and the next day those churches would be stripped of their tax-exempt status or firebombed. Hamer explained to historian Neil McMillen that the very rare people who were able to withstand this pressure and become registered voters "were punished to the fullest to keep other black people disgusted, to keep them from going" down to the courthouse and registering too.

As Continental Trailways run number 1729 headed West from Columbus toward Greenwood, Mississippi, on Sunday June 9, 1963, the voices of ten black passengers rose above the other bus travelers' chatter:

> Go tell it on the mountain, over the hills and everywhere
> Go tell it on the mountain, to let my people go
> Who's that yonder dressed in red?
>   Let my people go
> Must be the children Bob Moses led
>   Let my people go

Hamer initiated the singing of this Gospel song-turned-movement anthem after the bus driver, Billy Eugene Haithcock, ordered the group she was with to sit in the back of the bus.

The activists had been traveling all night, returning from a weeklong civic education and voter registration training session in South Carolina spearheaded by Septima Clark and Bernice Robinson. The ten activists aboard the bus that fateful Saturday morning were chosen to attend the workshop because of their dedication to the cause of black political advancement and their potential to engage their community. Inspired by their training and emboldened by their comradery, several activists attempted to integrate lunch counters at bus stations along the return route—declaring their legal right to do so given the Interstate Commerce Commission's (ICC) 1961 ban on segregated interstate travel facilities. These protests infuriated the bus driver, who began exiting the bus at each stop to use the phone. The activists rightly suspected that Haith-cock was reporting their bus station protests to Mississippi police along their route.

A mere thirty miles away from the group's final Greenwood destination, Haithcock pulled into the terminal adjacent to Staley's Café. This establish-ment, and the city of Winona in which it was located, was a hotbed of racial tension. Winona was now home to the organizational headquarters of the Citi-zens' Council, which had been operating for nearly nine years by this point and had spread its white supremacist ideology across the region, the state, and the South, boasting more than 200,000 members. Staley's Café had been the site of several attempts at desegregation since the ICC's 1961 ruling. Yet, the café and the bus terminal remained strictly segregated, in spite of the edict, the persistent challenges, and in the face of CORE's widely publicized Freedom Rides.

Haithcock informed the passengers they would have just twenty-five minutes at this particular stop. Six of the black activists with whom Hamer traveled hurriedly exited the bus. Two of the female passengers, Euvester Simpson and Ruth Davis, visited the designated "white" restroom, while Annell Ponder, James West, June Johnson, and Rosemary Freeman headed toward the lunch counter. At first, the wait staff ignored the group as they tried to place their food order, but after much persistence an aggravated server threw a wadded dishtowel against the wall and declared, "I can't take it no more!"

Her outburst caught the attention of Winona Police Chief Thomas Herod, Jr. and State Highway Patrolman John L. Basinger, who had received a tip about the group's previous protests and had been waiting for such provo-cation. Herod and Basinger quickly advanced upon the group.

"Get up and get out of here," Chief Herod ordered as he tapped the black activists' shoulders and jabbed their sides with his Billy club.

"According to the 1961 ICC ban on segregated interstate facilities, it is unlawful for this establishment to refuse us service," Annell Ponder, the thirty-one-year-old Georgia native and Clark College graduate, informed Herod.

"Ain't no damn law, you just get on out of here," he responded.

Scanning the diner, the group of activists noticed that, in addition to Herod and Basinger, two more policemen—Sheriff Earle Wayne Partridge and his deputy, Charles Perkins—were closing in on them. Partridge glared at the group as he shifted his own Billy club from hand to hand. In the two years since the ICC ruling, according to Mississippi State Sovereignty Commission reports, there had been at least three other instances wherein Partridge had taken the lead in arresting and torturing those who dared violate the now expressly outlawed racial customs. What's worse, Partridge and the police force he led did so with impunity. "And so on the morning of June 9, 1963, Sheriff

Partridge had good reason to believe that he and his fellow officers were above the law," wrote rhetorical scholar Davis W. Houck. Fearful, the activists complied. They left the counter and regrouped outside, now joined by Simpson, who had also been reprimanded for defying the segregated restroom custom.

Hamer, who stayed on the bus, spotted her anxious-looking friends and shouted from an open window, "What happened?"

"The policemen wouldn't let us order food from the counter," Ponder told her.

"Well, that's Mississippi for you," Hamer replied and settled back into her seat on the bus.

Ponder, however, was less resigned to the policemen's unlawful behavior. She copied down Herod and Basinger's license plate numbers and began jotting brief physical descriptions of the men, as their activist training had taught them to do. The officers, surveying the group from their perch inside the diner, noticed Ponder's scribbling and exited the restaurant. Once outside, they began placing the activists in handcuffs and ushering them toward their patrol cars.

Still inside the bus, Hamer rose to her feet. Looking at the frantic scene through her bus window, she was conflicted. The group made a pact to stay together on this return trip—no matter the consequences of their activism—and yet, they were so close to Greenwood. If she and the remaining activists on the bus could return to SNCC headquarters, they could get help for their friends.

Hamer shouted to Ponder, the group's acting leader, "What should we do?"

At that moment, Herod spotted Hamer. "Get that one there!" he shouted to Deputy Perkins.

In a flash, Perkins ran toward Hamer and yanked her off of the bus. He dragged her toward his vehicle, kicking the back of her limping leg as she struggled to walk at the brisk pace he set. "Hurry up, Fatso!" Perkins ordered.

When they reached his patrol car, Perkins spun Hamer around and slammed her face down against the hard metal exterior. He handcuffed her wrists together and shoved her in his backseat. The short drive to the Winona jailhouse was a blur of pain and confusion. What had she done to warrant *arrest*? The handcuffs were so tight her fingers grew numb. Who else had the Montgomery officials taken into custody? Her left leg throbbed from Perkins' kicks. Would help come from SNCC headquarters? Blood dripped down the side of her cheek.

In the booking room, Hamer accounted for Annell Ponder, Euvester Simpson, June Johnson, Rosemary Freeman, and James West. Hopefully, Bernard Washington, Ruth Davis, Mr. Palmer, and Ms. Ford had escaped notice and were well on their way to find help at the SNCC headquarters in Greenwood.

"What do y'all know about the Greenwood Voter Registration Project?" demanded one officer.

Ponder began to explain the group's involvement.

"Shut up, n—r!" shouted the officer before she could finish.

"Were y'all trying to demonstrate at Staley's Café?" asked another state official.

Again, Ponder tried to explain their right to service.

"Shut up, bitch!" another enraged officer spat at her.

"We were just returning from a voter education workshop," came the timid voice of fifteen-year-old Montgomery County native, June Johnson.

"What was this 'voter education workshop' all about? Did you meet Martin Luther King, Jr. there?" asked a patrolman, mocking them.

This time, James West opened his mouth to respond.

The newly arrived Officer William Surrell jabbed West in the side of his stomach with keys and slammed his own foot down on top of West's feet. Hard. West fell to his knees, writhing in pain as Surrell dragged the teenager by his arms to the designated black area of the jail, known as the bullpen. Once there, West saw three inmates—Roosevelt Knox, Sol Poe, and Willie Kidd—huddled in the corner furthest from the entrance. Meanwhile, Hamer and Simpson were roughly loaded into one cell. Ponder and Freeman shoved into another.

Johnson was left in the booking room. Perhaps they'll let the young girl go? Hamer thought. This hope was dashed by the unmistakable sound of a fist hitting flesh. And then a blood-curdling scream. Again, fist pounds flesh, followed by a piercing cry. Hamer turned to Simpson, eyes wide as they struggled to process the booking room scene where Basinger and Perkins were taking turns punching Johnson in the face.

"Are you a member of the *NAACP*?" Basinger jeered.

"Yes," replied Johnson. Not "yes, sir," but simply "yes." This admission of her activist ties, coupled with the omission of a courtesy title, incited Perkins to beat the young woman with a blackjack, a two-foot long leather baton loaded at both ends with metal weights.

He repeatedly shouted, "N—r!" at Johnson as the force of the blackjack tore open her clothes and battered her bare skin.

Hamer and Simpson trembled in their cell as a bloodied Johnson was dragged by an officer to the cell occupied by Ponder and Freeman. Shoving Johnson inside, the officers turned their attention toward Ponder. Chief Herod hissed, "You come on out here. You the boss of these people. We want to talk to you!"

Ponder's torturous investigation took place in the booking room where Johnson had just been assaulted.

"Why'd you copy down our license plate numbers?" Herod demanded.

"My job is to report civil rights violations to federal authorities," Ponder responded.

Enraged by her assertive response, Surrell, Basinger, and Perkins took turns attacking her, punching her in the face and stomach.

"*Sir!* Why don't you call us, *sir!* Dammit." Basinger spat at Ponder amidst blows.

"I don't know you well enough," was Ponder's muffled reply.

As the three men continued to beat her, Hamer could hear Ponder—between moans, speech slurred—praying for God to forgive her assailants. Minutes later, Hamer and Simpson watched in horror as Ponder passed by their cell, barely able to stand. She tried to stabilize her ravaged body by holding onto the jail walls, her clothes torn to scraps, her mouth swollen, and her eyes bloodied.

The officers took a momentary rest from assaulting the prisoners and ordered the black inmates Knox, Poe, and Kidd to beat their cellmate, James West. Herod, Partridge, and Basinger supervised as the frightened prisoners followed orders to "whip this n—r's ass." For over half an hour, the black inmates beat West with a blackjack until the nineteen-year-old lost consciousness. Basinger rewarded Knox, Poe, and Kidd with a pint of corn whiskey.

Then Basinger approached Hamer's cell. "Where you from?" the Mississippi State Highway Patrolman demanded.

"Ruleville," Hamer replied.

"Ruleville, huh?" Basinger said squinting. "I'm going to check that out."

One phone call to local officials and Basinger discovered that Hamer was now infamous among the white power structure in her hometown. Over the last six months, she had become an active voter registration worker and a despised agitator in the eyes of the white Ruleville establishment.

"The big shit," Basinger branded her, as he pulled her out of her cell and thrust her into the bullpen, where West had just been assaulted. "We're going to make you wish you was dead, bitch!" Basinger said.

The sour odor of corn whiskey mixed with the foul stench of sweat pervaded the windowless room. Hamer looked pleadingly toward the three black inmates, who were passing the pint between themselves, knuckles bleeding, clothes drenched. Basinger unclicked her handcuffs and ordered her to lie face down on a thin soiled mattress. Her stomach turned as more men crowded into the bullpen—three black prisoners and Basinger, then Surrell and Perkins, too. She closed her eyes and prayed, the lyrics of the song she led just hours before looped through her mind:

> *Paul and Silas bound in jail*
> > *Let my people go*
> *Had nobody come to post their bail*
> > *Let my people go*
> *Go tell it on the mountain, over the hills and everywhere*
> *Go tell it on the mountain to let my people go*

As she tried to mentally escape that cell, the shock expressed in the black prisoner's young voice brought her right back to the bullpen.

"You mean for me to beat *her* with *this*?" one of the three black prisoners cried out, staring at the leather blackjack Basinger thrust upon him.

"You damn right. If you don't, you know what I'll do to you," Basinger said.

Reluctantly, the young man raised the blackjack and let it fall on Mrs. Hamer's back. She recoiled.

"Again," the command came from an officer behind him, "harder."

Hamer braced herself as the weapon landed with a thud and a crack against her backside. She couldn't help from screaming out in pain.

"Shut up!" Surrell ordered as he lunged forward and hit her in the head.

"Again," he told the young black prisoner excitedly, "harder!"

Hamer could sense the titillation in Surrell's voice and in the contorted face of Perkins, who both gathered close to her body. The harder the blows, the louder Hamer screamed and the more worked up the officers became. As she turned her head from side to side in a desperate attempt to shield her body from the blackjack's force, a fist—Was it Surrell's? Or maybe Perkins'?—landed squarely on her left eye. She gripped the mattress with all her might in hopes of muffling the sound of her pain. Her legs must have started jerking involuntarily because Basinger ordered another black inmate to sit on her feet, even as he demanded that the first prisoner continue with the blackjack beating. The young man lifted the instrument of terror above his head, succumbing to exhaustion, his shaking arms gave out. Without hesitation, Basinger ordered the remaining black inmate to take over.

Through sobs, Hamer called out to the inmate, "You mean you would do this to your own race?" She pleaded with him to refuse Basinger's orders.

Basinger patted his holster and the final black prisoner could only reply with a small dose of humanity, directing Hamer to move her hands. He reportedly did not want to break the hands Hamer used to shield the left side of her body. The force of his first blackjack blow pulled her dress up high. Hamer's hands instinctively moved to pull her dress back down, mortified that her bare body was exposed to all the men in this room. Surrell pulled the dress back up over her head. She began to heave into the mattress. Sweaty hands moved roughly between her legs. Unable to see anything now, dress fabric shielded her from watching the scene unfold. Hamer could nevertheless acutely feel the rough fingers squeeze between her flesh and the mattress, between her underclothes and skin, calloused hands aggressively groping her bare breasts. With her legs pinned by a prisoner, she struggled in vain to free herself from this sickening touch, jagged fingernails roughly scraping her bare skin.

Crack. With this blackjack blow Hamer was gone. Spinning, floating, falling—first stars, then fireworks surrounded her. The faint smell of metal instantly replaced the pungent concoction of sweat, corn mash, and blood. And the deleterious sounds of men violently thrusting, shouting, cackling gave way to a low innocuous hum. She could no longer feel the force of the blackjack, Surrell's punches, the officer's predatory hands—she didn't move to shield the blows. The officers' excitement depleted.

"Get up, fatso!" Basinger's harsh voice, the lingering odor of his hot breath, and the proximity of his bristly face, brought Hamer back to the bullpen.

Disoriented, she found her body cold and damp, unable to move, her head feverish. Thud. Basinger rolled her off the cot and dragged her back to the cell where Simpson shook with fear. The room spun as Basinger pulled Simpson, screaming and clinging to the bars, out of the cell and into the bull pen. The abuse had grown methodical; the officers ordered Simpson to lie upon that filthy cot, metal frame bent from the force of the preceding blows. The black inmates ordered once again to ravage the cowering body laid prostrate before them, but in the distance, Simpson could hear a telephone ringing.

One hard hit and then an authoritative shout came from the booking room, "Stop! Stop!" That phone call spared Simpson from the beating Hamer, Johnson, Ponder, and West endured. Simpson returned to the cell to find Hamer, floating in and out of consciousness. Her fever continued to spike and Simpson rushed to retrieve cool water from the sink in their cell. For hours, she continually rinsed and reapplied a threadbare washcloth to Hamer's forehead. Simpson struggled in vain to comfort Hamer, who couldn't lie on her back because of the swelling and bruising; nor could she lie on her stomach because her face was so badly beaten. Hamer moaned and shifted, sweated and convulsed, as Simpson stayed by her side—tending as best she could to Mrs. Hamer's wounds, both women fearing the jailers' return.

Sometime after midnight, Hamer's fever broke and she regained consciousness. Parting her cracked lips and breathing deeply in and out of her bruised diaphragm, Simpson remembered, Hamer's low voice singing out:

> *Walk with me, now Lord walk with me*
> *While I'm on this Jesus journey*

> *I want Jesus to walk with me*
> *Be my friend, now Lord, be my friend*
> *Make a way for me, now Lord, make a way for me*
> *While I'm on this Jesus journey, I want Jesus to walk with me*

The phone call that spared Euvester Simpson opened the floodgates of messages sent directly to the Montgomery County Jail. Calls came first from local SNCC activists, then regional civil rights workers, then federal officials. The four remaining black passengers aboard the Continental Trailways Bus had escaped the notice of the Winona policemen, and they had traveled on to Greenwood. Once there, the group informed activists at SNCC headquarters about their traveling companions' arrest. SNCC workers immediately began calling all of the jails in the area searching for Hamer, West, Ponder, Simpson, Johnson, and Freeman. Lawrence Guyot, a Mississippi native and Tougaloo College graduate, was the first person to locate the activists at the Montgomery County Jail. He immediately traveled there in hopes of securing their release. Not only was Guyot unable to rescue the group, but the twenty-three year old was taken into custody, beaten, and ordered to disrobe while officers set his genitals aflame with a lit piece of paper.

By Monday, June 10, 1963, after Guyot failed to return to the Greenwood headquarters, SNCC registration workers escalated the matter. First, SNCC Communications Director, Julian Bond, sent a telegram directly to Attorney General Robert Kennedy, who enlisted FBI Director J. Edgar Hoover to pursue the case. Second, the SNCC activists reached out to the Reverend Dr. Martin Luther King, Jr. at the SCLC offices in Atlanta. By Tuesday, June 11, FBI special agents arrived in Winona to meet with the seven detained civil rights workers; that same day, all seven activists were tried at the Winona courthouse, each pleading "not guilty" to the spurious resisting arrest and disorderly conduct charges leveled against them by their assailants. And that same day, less than 200 miles to the east, Governor George Wallace of Alabama staged his infamous "Stand in the Schoolhouse Door." Wallace defied desegregation orders at the University of Alabama by personally blocking the entrance of black students, Vivian Malone and James Hood. President John F. Kennedy responded to Wallace's Stand by issuing Executive Order 1111, directing the Alabama National Guard to remove Wallace from the doorway of the Foster Auditorium. And further still, on the evening of June 11, 1963, Kennedy delivered his "Civil Rights Address," announcing the federal push to desegregate all public facilities and provide greater protection for voting rights.

In the early morning hours of Wednesday June 12, as NAACP leader Medgar Evers returned home from a late-night meeting, Ku Klux Klansman Byron de la Beckwith shot him in the back. Word of Evers' assassination on the front lawn of his suburban Jackson home, less than 100 miles south of Winona, prompted King to acknowledge the gravity of the situation faced by the civil rights workers, who were still being held in the Montgomery County Jail. He had learned of the group's arrest a few days earlier, remembered SCLC activist Dorothy Cotton, but now "after hearing about the shooting of Medgar Evers, he called from Atlanta advising some of us to go to Winona and see if we could get them out of jail." King phoned Andrew Young to inform him that the Greenwood SNCC leaders had been unable to secure the groups' release, in part, because they did not have access to the set bail of $1,400. On King's orders, the SCLC wired the necessary funds from their headquarters in Atlanta to Young, who was in Birmingham, alongside activists James Bevel and Dorothy Cotton. The three were there supporting the black students' entrance into the University of Alabama. Heeding King's request, Cotton, Young, and Bevel embarked on the 200-mile drive west from Alabama to Mississippi and made it to Winona by four o'clock in the afternoon on Wednesday June 13, 1963. They posted the civil rights workers' bail and helped carry the battered activists from their cells, remaining respectful to the officers they despised until each member of the group safely exited the Montgomery County Jail.

"I've got some sad news," Young said as they reached the jailhouse lawn.

He told the newly freed group about Evers' early morning assassination. The activists blinked away tears, squinting as the late afternoon sun stung the deep cuts crisscrossing their swollen cheeks.

With an FBI escort, Hamer and Ponder were rushed to Greenwood, where Dr. Mabel Garner examined and treated the women. She stitched up their deep lacerations and gave them medication to help with the swelling. Hamer still couldn't bend her fingers, so engorged were her hands. Her backside, discolored a deep navy blue, was hard as metal to Dr. Garner's touch. Garner also took color photographs of the women's battered bodies for the FBI's mounting case against their assailants.

Nothing would have brought Mrs. Hamer more comfort in the early days of her release than seeing her girls' sweet faces and losing herself in Pap's warm embrace, but she selflessly refused her family's visits. She didn't want to traumatize Dorothy and Vergie, and she worried not only about the retaliation Pap would desire, but also about his inability to avenge her abuse. She cringed as she considered the attendant feelings of powerlessness that would once again overcome Perry Hamer, a strong black man living in a white supremacist state. Although Hamer would not allow her family to witness the abuse, like generations of black activists before her, she felt compelled to use her ravaged body as evidence of white supremacy's brutality. "I was begging somebody. I told them, I wanted to go to Washington to show in person what had happened to us," she recalled. Movement activists listened to Hamer's pleas. After receiving immediate care in Greenwood, Ponder and Hamer traveled to Atlanta, where they were given additional medical treatment—Hamer's kidneys were badly damaged and she required advanced care. In Atlanta, Hamer and Ponder also met with King and other members of the SCLC, as well as leaders of the Voter Education Project. The SCLC then flew Hamer and Ponder from Atlanta to Washington, D.C., where they met with Justice Department officials including attorneys St. John Barrett and John Rosenberg, who filed suit against the Winona assailants. In a series of heretofore unprecedented injunctions, the Justice Department ordered the Montgomery County officials to overturn the spurious "resisting arrest and disorderly conduct" charges filed against the civil rights workers and to prohibit local police from blocking racial integration of interstate travel facilities. Furthermore, the Justice Department charged five Mississippi officers with "conspiracy to deprive Negroes of their civil rights," a federal offense.

The officers' week-long federal trial was held from December 2–6, 1963, in Oxford, Mississippi. Oxford was still reeling from white supremacist backlash to James Meredith's integration of the University of Mississippi "Ole

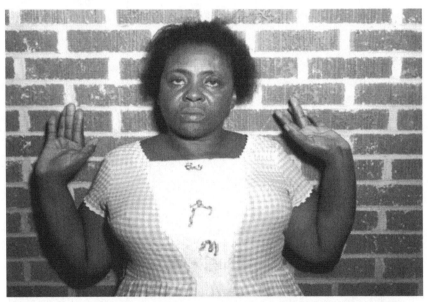

Figure 2.1 In June of 1963, after she was beaten in a Mississippi jail cell, Fannie Lou Hamer traveled to Washington, D.C. There, she met with Justice Department officials, who gathered evidence and brought charges against her assailants. Source: Federal Bureau of Investigation.

Miss." Just months before, in September of 1962, the black Air Force veteran's enrollment at the previously all-white institution incited riots among white supremacists, which resulted in the death of two people, the injury of hundreds more, and required 23,000 soldiers to restore order to the northern Mississippi town of Oxford.

By January of 1963, the segregationist angst had not subsided much—white supremacists attended the officers' trial brandishing Confederate flags and hurling insults at the prosecution. So hostile was the climate in Oxford that the seven civil rights activists, who were each called to testify about their abuse, did not feel safe staying in Oxford; they sought refuge with movement sympathizers in the nearby town of Holly Springs. In addition to testimony from all seven survivors, the jury heard from the black prisoners who beat West and Hamer upon Basinger's orders, from the FBI special agents who visited their cells, and from Dr. Mabel Garner, who treated Ponder and Hamer immediately following their release. Neither eyewitness testimony, nor photographic evidence, nor professional observation succeeded in convincing the all-white, all-male jury to acknowledge the guilt of their peers.

Flattering the jury, the defense positioned the verdict they controlled as a veritable bulwark against the tide of civil rights agitation that threatened to erode white dominance across the South. As the federal trial transcript indicates, time and again, the defense attempted to shift the blame, ostensibly placing the battered civil rights workers on trial, linking them to the national movement for racial equality, especially to King, who was reviled by white supremacists in the state. The defense went so far as to suggest that the civil rights activists' allegations of abuse were fictitious, a ploy to gain the country's attention and to vilify Mississippi before the eyes of the nation and the world. By the defense's twisted victim-blaming logic, acquitting the indicted Mississippi officials was the jurors' patriotic duty. The twelve jurors heard the case, *United States of America v. Earle Wayne Partridge, Thomas J. Herod, Jr., William Surrell, John L. Basinger and Charles Thomas Perkins*, deliberated from 4:29 pm until 5:45 pm on December 6, 1963, and found the Mississippi law enforcement officials "not guilty" on all counts brought before them.

As maddening as the "not guilty" verdict was, and as traumatizing as facing her perpetrators in that antagonistic courtroom must have been for Fannie Lou Hamer, by December 1963, she was fully committed to the cause of civil rights. Though initially skeptical of the difference voting could make in the trials of her everyday life, let alone the difference she could make in the movement, Hamer had come to see black political activism as divinely inspired. Prompted by Bevel's mass meeting oration to "Discern the Signs of the Time," Hamer began noticing what she interpreted as indications of God's will unfolding in her own life—escaping the nightrider's bullets, being found by McLaurin in her niece's remote cabin, and living to testify about her abuse in Winona. She interpreted these acts of deliverance as indications that, after being fired from the Marlow plantation, she was now "working for Christ." Far from deterring her activism, being fired from the plantation, harassed, and beaten within an inch of her life, deepened her resolve. "If them crackers in Winona thought they'd discouraged me from fighting," Hamer proclaimed, "I guess they found out different. I'm going to stay in Mississippi and if they shoot me down, I'll be buried here." By the close of 1963, Hamer was determined to put up her life for the cause of black political advancement and, in the coming year, the irrepressible force of Hamer's determination would send shock waves throughout the nation.

· 3 ·

"Sick and Tired of Being Sick and Tired"

"*I* want to run for Congress," Fannie Lou Hamer declared. She stood firm, gaze fixed on the Mississippi Secretary of State's receptionist. Charles McLaurin, the Student Nonviolent Coordinating Committee (SNCC) voter registration worker, was close by her side.

The receptionist looked up from her desk in disbelief, as if she hadn't heard Hamer's bold words correctly.

"I'm here to declare my candidacy for the Second Congressional District Democratic Primary," Hamer clarified.

A mocking smile spread across the receptionist's lips. She turned and sauntered toward the back of the office, inviting her coworkers to come view the spectacle. "Look! Two n—rs want to run for US Congress!" she squealed.

McLaurin cleared his throat and placed his hand on the small of Hamer's tensioning back. At least a dozen bemused onlookers gathered, pointing and chuckling. Hamer and McLaurin had expected that her candidacy would be met with resistance and ridicule. But they woke up early on the morning of March 20, 1964, and they drove over 100 miles from Ruleville down to Jackson anyway: they intended to register Hamer as an official candidate for the June Democratic Primary.

McLaurin cleared his throat once more and spoke. "First of all, I resent what you just called us. Second, we are here to qualify this lady to run for Congress."

The mocking dissipated and the bureaucratic obstacles began. "You'll need to fill out this paperwork," the receptionist said, shoving a form-laden clipboard across the front desk.

Mrs. Hamer took the clipboard and nodded. Eager to exit that hostile room, McLaurin and Hamer returned to the SNCC car they had borrowed that day and filled out the candidate registration paperwork together.

To the receptionist's thinly veiled surprise, McLaurin and Hamer promptly returned with the completed paperwork. "You'll need a $500 cashier's check made out to the Democratic Party Executive Committee to file your candidate registration," she said.

Hamer sighed. They were not expecting this. McLaurin and Hamer exchanged nervous glances—neither of them had access to *that* kind of money—they headed once again for the car to talk it over. On the way out, McLaurin spotted a pay phone and made a call to the Council of Federated Organization's (COFO) main Jackson office. "Don't move," came the instructions from the other end. "We'll meet you there with the check."

Sure enough, the check arrived from COFO within the hour. McLaurin and Hamer delivered it to the Secretary of State's receptionist, who now appeared more irritated than surprised by their return.

As the pair turned to leave, feeling relieved and a bit triumphant, she called out to them. "Hold it, there's one more step," she said. Their shoulders sagged as they returned to the front desk. "Your campaign manager will need to sign this page." She pointed to the clock on the wall with feigned sympathy. "It's now 4 o'clock. Our office will close promptly at 4:30 this afternoon, and today is the last day to qualify. So, if we don't receive the paperwork by the end of the day, I'm afraid you will be unable to run." The receptionist explained as she fanned herself with their $500 cashier's check.

McLaurin thought this was the end of the road, but Hamer tugged at his sleeve and gestured toward the door. The moment they reached the hallway, Hamer whispered hoarsely: "Mac, go put your name on those papers and let's go home."

"Me? Your campaign manager? What do I know about running a congressional campaign?" McLaurin replied.

"Mac, you know as much about being a campaign manager as I know about running for Congress. Now go sign those forms," she instructed.

Never one to argue with Mrs. Hamer, he returned to the office one final time. McLaurin signed the papers, and together they made history. On March 20, 1964, Fannie Lou Hamer became the first black woman in the state to run for US Congress and the first black person from the Second Congressional District to run since Reconstruction.

The harassment McLaurin and Hamer endured at the Secretary of State's office was just a small taste of the repercussions that awaited them back in the Delta. Hamer returned home from Jackson to find Perry Hamer drinking, which she knew meant that he was once again out of a job. Word traveled fast through the dense web woven by the Citizens Council's vast and well-connected membership. By the time Fannie Lou Hamer's candidate paperwork was filed, Perry Hamer had been fired from the local cotton mill. The family sorely needed his income. Their youngest daughter, Vergie Ree was now ten and in the fourth grade. Dorothy Jean, their oldest daughter, was nineteen and had left high school after her sophomore year. She worked odd jobs to help support the family, but Dorothy, too, was punished for her mother's activism. The last job interview she had ended abruptly when the manager said, "You sure talk like that Fannie Lou."

"Well, she raised me," Dorothy responded with pride, before realizing the manager's words were no compliment. She didn't get that job and she was hard-pressed to find another.

What's more, financial contributions to COFO from the National Voter Education Project (VEP) were drying up, in part, because of the slow progress SNCC field secretaries were making registering voters within the Magnolia state. Without the VEP's financial support, SNCC struggled to pay its Mississippi workers even the meager wage of ten dollars a week that the organization promised those who worked full time for the movement. SNCC's Mississippi field secretaries remained the lowest paid and most in demand of all the SNCC workers spread across the South. Rumor had it that by 1964 not only was SNCC unable to regularly pay its field secretaries in Mississippi, but the cost of transporting would-be registrants to county courthouses, supporting them when they were fired from their jobs, and often bailing their staff out of jail, had allegedly left the fledgling organization over $130,000 in debt.

The extensive 1963 Freedom Vote campaign organized by SNCC contributed to its dire financial situation as well. Fannie Lou Hamer's early voter registration work had been part of this blossoming regional campaign. During the spring of 1963, she frequently spoke at mass meetings in small churches and to large crowds gathered in the SNCC-headquartered town of Greenwood. In the summer of 1963, while she both convalesced from, and testified about, her Winona jailhouse beating, SNCC organized an extensive Freedom Vote campaign across Mississippi. Looking toward the state's fall gubernatorial election, SNCC saw both a formidable challenge and a great opportunity. Mississippi had the largest black voting age population in the country. But in a state with roughly 430,000 black people of voting age, only 28,500 black people were registered. That was a registration rate of just over 6 percent of the black voting age population compared to nearly 70 percent of the registered white voting age population. White supremacists explained to appalled national onlookers that the disparate figures indicated that black Mississippians were apathetic about the franchise. Well aware of the white supremacist intimidation and retaliation that kept black people away from the polls, COFO organized a mock election to demonstrate that if black Mississippians weren't viciously prohibited from the ballot box, they would cast their votes in droves. The mock election also provided experiential training for black communities, who had been systematically excluded from participating in the political process since Reconstruction.

COFO set up registration sites in black communities and ratcheted up their door-to-door canvassing efforts. As word spread that they could register safely for this mock election—without intimidation, discrimination, or recrimination—black people actually began seeking out field secretaries to add their names to COFO's voting rolls. COFO even held a statewide convention in October of 1963, where longtime black NAACP activist Aaron Henry was selected as the Freedom Vote candidate for governor and the white Tougaloo College Chaplain, Reverend Edwin King, was selected as lieutenant governor. Henry and King traveled across the state campaigning in black churches, neighborhoods, and parks to large enthusiastic crowds—one rally swelled to over 1,000 people.

To accommodate widespread interest in COFO's mock election, the organization enlisted the help of northern volunteers. Allard Lowenstein, a professor at Yale who had observed mock elections during his travels to South Africa, gathered student volunteers from Yale and Stanford to work with COFO on the 1963 Freedom Vote project in Mississippi. On November 2–4, with polling places set up in black churches, barbershops, beauty parlors, and pool halls, 83,000 black Mississippians cast ballots for Henry and King in the mock election. With an increase of over 50,000 "registered" black voters in just a few months' time, COFO's mock election demonstrated to state and national audiences that black Mississippians were, in fact, eager to participate in the political process.

Such a powerful display of black voting strength shook the white supremacist foundation upon which Mississippi's segregated society was built. The surge of civil rights activity in Mississippi corresponded with a national push for equality. As COFO ramped up its Freedom Vote campaign in Mississippi, the Southern Christian Leadership Conference (SCLC) was hard at work leading demonstrations in opposition to Birmingham, Alabama's segregated facilities. In May of 1963, the Supreme Court ruled Birmingham's segregation laws unconstitutional and in August of that year, Martin Luther King, Jr. captured the world's attention with his "I Have a Dream" speech delivered at the March on Washington for Jobs and Freedom. White supremacists in Mississippi, which was home to the country's largest black population, feared that equality for black people would mean "absolute extinction," in the Citizens Council's characterization, for white people. Their backlash to civil rights gains reflected this fearful zero-sum assessment of the local, statewide, and national push for black freedom.

Segregationists' retaliation to black civic engagement in Mississippi was as swift as it was cruel. All across the state, politically active black people lost their jobs. They were denied bank loans or forced to pay outstanding debts back immediately under threat of arrest. Black people who engaged with COFO were harassed and subject to surveillance. Their lives were threatened, as were the lives of their children. In the Delta, where the majority of the black population worked planting, tending, and harvesting crops, families relied on a federal commodities program that distributed surplus government food to those with low or no income during Mississippi's barren winter months. Following the November 1963 Freedom Vote election, white authorities in Sunflower and Leflore Counties opted out of the federal commodities program, which was specifically designed to feed regions of the country with the lowest family income levels.

Families that SNCC activists had encouraged to register to vote now faced starvation amid record freezing temperatures. Witnessing this, SNCC's appeals to the North for funds, clothing, and food became desperate. One impassioned letter came from Mrs. Hamer, who spoke directly to the dire needs she saw in her community. "We need a change in Mississippi," she wrote. "I'm sick of being hungry, naked and looking at my children and so many other children crying out for bread." Appeals like Hamer's were distributed throughout the "Friends of SNCC" network, which had been built over the past year from speaking and fundraising tours of northern college campuses, churches, and community centers. Friends of SNCC chapters from Seattle to Boston responded generously, sending thousands of pounds of food and clothing, in addition to cars and money, to support black Mississippians and to keep COFO's larger voter registration project alive. Ten thousand pounds of food and clothing arrived from the Friends of SNCC's Boston chapter alone. Most notably, in December of 1963, comedian Dick Gregory chartered a plane to Greenwood, filled with 14,000 pounds of canned food, cereal, powdered milk, and baby formula. Gregory's dramatic gesture and the steady stream of donations from Friends of SNCC chapters across the country helped forge the link between survival and voter registration by revealing to the nation the cruel recriminations black Mississippians faced for their civic engagement. These donations also suggested to black Mississippians that beyond Mississippi's white supremacist apparatus, the larger nation cared about them and supported their voter registration efforts. SNCC reinforced this message at distribution sites, passing out voter registration pamphlets along with warm clothes and food.

After a harsh winter enduring record low temperatures in threadbare clothes and drafty plantation shacks and subsisting on food donations sent from northern supporters, many black Deltans were eager for change. Chief among them was Fannie Lou Hamer. As the Delta soil began to thaw, Fannie Lou Hamer's congressional campaign took root. The Second Congressional District she campaigned to represent was made up of twenty-four counties in the North-west region of Mississippi, commonly known as the Delta. In terms of geographical expanse, the Second Congressional District is the largest, nearly 300 miles long and 200 miles wide. COFO recognized the Second Congressional District's potential to become a majority black voter district—black people made up 59 percent of the voting age population, yet, in 1964, less than 5 percent of black voters in the region were registered. In Hamer's Sunflower County, for instance, 114 black voters were registered, which amounted to less than 0.1 percent of the total black voting age population in this region. In that same county, 4,500 white voters were registered, constituting 51 percent of the total white voting age population. In Tallahatchie County, home to the incumbent Congressional Representative, Jamie L. Whitten, 4,334 white voters were registered—constituting nearly 85 percent of that county's voting age population—while only five black people were registered across the same county. COFO supported Hamer's candidacy in this region, establishing a Committee to Elect Mrs. Fannie Lou Hamer Congresswoman of the Second District of Mississippi, which was run out of their Jackson headquarters. Mrs. Hamer was one of four black candidates whom COFO supported in 1964, in hopes that running black people for Senate and for Congress in districts across Mississippi would not only inspire more black people to register in the short term, but that their candidacies would engender a more representative government in the long run.

With the slogan "Justice Today for All Mississippians," Hamer's campaign platform appealed to poor people—black and white alike. She recognized that farm mechanization and advances in chemical weed killers, as well as the advent of synthetic fibers, had made cotton—the Delta's primary export—less competitive in the global marketplace. "The conditions that prevail in Mississippi are horrible," Hamer contended on the stump. "Cotton, our chief product, has become an increasingly less profitable commodity. There is little industry and few towns. The dominant economic system is still sharecropping and we have the lowest family income levels in the nation. And we know we want to change those things."

Impoverished white people were also impacted by the lack of industry in the region, and, Hamer informed them, her opponent's policy decisions negatively affected poor white people too. Whitten, a white Tallahatchie County lawyer and chairman of the House Appropriations Subcommittee on Agriculture, was running for his thirteenth term, having served the Second District since 1941. He ran unopposed during his previous election, and he was known on Capitol Hill as the "permanent secretary of agriculture." In this post, argued Hamer, Whitten served the narrow interests of the Delta's planting and cattle-ranching class. He perpetuated this class's wealth by enforcing the racial segregation of the working class at all costs. During her speeches and campaign interviews, Hamer would commonly cite the example of a 1961 federal training program for tractor drivers that could have helped upwards of 3,000 Delta citizens learn a new trade with the potential to improve their wages. "About 2,400 of the workers to be trained would have been Negroes and the other 600 would have been whites. The classes would have been integrated. Negro and white workers would have the chance to get to know and understand each other," she explained.

But Whitten killed the interracial tractor training program in committee. "This is the entering wedge into the Labor Department's supervision of wage rates and hours in agriculture, which would upset the local economy," he said.

"What he meant was that he was afraid there'd be more money for the workers and less for the planters—that's what he calls 'upsetting the local economy'," Hamer told her audiences gathered at popular lakes, mass meetings, and COFO's Freedom Day rallies. During these gatherings, Hamer promised to "undo everything Jamie Whitten has done in Washington" and to "work for the development of all parts of the state," by representing the "entire community—regardless of race."

Hamer's campaign did, however, raise issues specifically relevant to the black majority. When speaking in Washington County in early May, for example, Hamer addressed staggering race-based disparities in public health. She drew her audience's attention to the fact that there were only six black doctors in this county where the black population totaled well over 40,000 people. With so few black doctors, black patients across Washington County were forced to see white doctors. "At the white doctor's office," Hamer lamented, "we're put in a little overcrowded room and made to wait all day until the doctor treats his white patients." Lack of access to care and segregated second-class treatment doubtlessly contributed to the death rate, which was twice as high for black people in the Delta as it was for whites. Hamer also informed her Washington County audience that infant mortality rates between white and black babies were astoundingly disparate—26.1 percent for white infants and 67.2 percent for black infants. "Poverty and poor health form an unbreakable circle," Hamer declared at her campaign rally in Washington County, "one which need attention from the people who are supposed to represent us."

COFO staff members drafted Hamer's campaign speeches during her three-month-long primary campaign. McLaurin remembers driving Mrs. Hamer around to small towns and remote rural areas rehearsing what she would call "the high points" of the texts sent from Jackson. Gifted as she was at the art of extemporaneous speaking, Hamer rarely spoke from a manuscript. So she and McLaurin would go over the speeches that COFO sent and decide which parts would resonate with other Deltans. She would then take these points and infuse them with her trademark wit, exposing the narrow interests of the wealthy planters and cattle ranchers that Whitten served and contrasting these interests with her own motivation to represent the poor and disenfranchised.

COFO also raised $38,000 for Hamer's congressional bid, which McLaurin stretched to meet the costs of printing campaign pamphlets, running radio, newspaper, and television advertisements, renting meeting halls for rallies, and fueling their drives across the vast Delta region. To save on food costs, the pair lived off of soda pop, bologna sandwiches, and hot dogs; Hamer's blood pressure went through the roof during the spring of 1964. She was also still suffering from the effects of the Winona beating, which caused her to miss a week on the campaign trail.

Eating poorly and traveling six days a week certainly contributed to her strained health, but so did the stress of white supremacist retaliation. Just as Hamer's landmark campaign inspired black people across the Delta, it alarmed the white segregationist power structure. Records from the Mississippi State Sovereignty Commission, which was a government-sponsored spy agency established in the wake of the *Brown v. Board of Education* decision to ostensibly protect state's rights from federal encroachment, indicate that the Commission closely followed Hamer and her campaign. Agents were sent to her rallies, where they recorded crowd sizes, license plate numbers of those in attendance, Hamer's major talking points, and press coverage of her historic run. The state-sponsored spy commission also worked in concert with local officials. S. L. Milam, the brother of J. W. Milam, who was one of the two men responsible for Emmett Till's lynching, was the night patrolman in Ruleville. Nicknamed the "sundown kid," S. L. Milam kept close watch on the Hamer household. Late one night, when Perry Hamer got out of bed to use the bathroom and relight their furnace, Milam began pounding on the Hamers' front door. The moment Mr. Hamer opened the door, Milam burst into their home, his flashlight invasively searching the three room structure only to find Mrs. Hamer and the girls trembling in their beds. Milam nevertheless demanded to know what Perry Hamer was doing out of bed at that hour. Ostensibly satisfied with Mr. Hamer's reasonable explanation, Milam left without further incident.

The first night Hamer announced her candidacy, however, two of her campaign workers were arrested in Ruleville for violating a constitutionally-banned curfew law. The Hamers' phone calls were also monitored. Their water service was cut off, and Perry Hamer was arrested when he tried to recover the damaged water supply. Using money earmarked for "harassment expenses," McLaurin bailed Mr. Hamer and the campaign workers out of jail, stretching their strained campaign budget to a snapping point.

Mrs. Hamer's campaign caught the attention of national onlookers as well. On June 1, 1964, the day before the Democratic primary, the *Nation* ran "Tired of Being Sick and Tired," a profile of Hamer written by Jerry DeMuth. In this piece, DeMuth introduced the rest of the country to Fannie Lou Hamer. He included large excerpts of her life story: growing up as a sharecropper in the Delta, being fired for trying to register, beaten for attending a voter education workshop, and harassed while running this historic campaign. DeMuth spotlighted her determination as well, capturing what would become her famous refrain: "All my life I've been sick and tired. Now I'm sick and tired of being sick and tired."

In the *Nation* article, Demuth wrote presciently that "until Mississippi stops its discriminatory voting practices, Mrs. Hamer's chance of election is slight." When the Democratic primary votes were tallied the following day, in fact, Hamer lost to Whitten by a considerable margin: 35, 218 to 621 votes. Despite COFO's valiant fundraising, speechwriting, and campaign-coordination efforts, neither the organization nor Hamer was all that surprised by the defeat. Victory wasn't the primary purpose of Hamer's candidacy. DeMuth acknowledged this as well. "She is waking up the citizens of her district," he wrote. "Fannie Lou Hamer won't be easily stopped."

"I'm showing people that a Negro can run for office," Hamer was quoted as saying within the *Nation* article. She then previewed COFO's long-range strategy: a second Freedom Vote in the fall of 1964, Freedom Schools for Mississippi's underserved black youth, nine federal voter discrimination lawsuits, and the formation of the Mississippi Freedom Democratic Party. Hamer's historic candidacy was but one tributary that flowed into a mighty river of black organized resistance to white supremacist rule in Mississippi.

> *We shall overcome*
> *We shall overcome*
> *We shall overcome, some day*
> *Oh, deep in my heart*
> *I do believe*
> *We shall overcome, some day*
> *We'll walk hand in hand*
> *We'll walk hand in hand, some day*

Fannie Lou Hamer's voice was low and strong. From time to time she skipped a word to draw in a deep breath that would fuel the remainder of the song's verse. One by one the college students gathered around her on the lawn. Their circle grew wider as young people from the West to the East Coast, from all across the Midwest and major southern cities, too, arrived at the Western

College for Women in Oxford, Ohio. Mrs. Hamer smiled at each one of these tentative volunteers, her tired eyes brightening a bit as she watched them climb off Greyhound buses and out of packed cars.

> *We shall live in peace*
> *We shall live in peace*
> *We shall live in peace, some day*
> *Oh, deep in my heart*
> *I do believe*
> *We shall overcome, some day*

This stocky black woman invited the students into her circle. Following her example, they joined hands with the strangers surrounding them—some offering a friendly smile, others seeming less inviting. All the while Hamer's song of welcome continued.

> *We are not afraid*
> *We are not afraid*
> *We are not afraid, today*

The strength in Hamer's voice, the way she threw her head back and stared up to the heavens when she sang, convinced even the most fearful recruits that they were brave enough to challenge white supremacy in the most fiercely segregated state of the union.

Fannie Lou Hamer often primed her pupils with song. Of the several pivotal roles Hamer played within the civil rights movement, welcoming the 1964 Freedom Summer volunteers to the training session that COFO organized in Oxford, Ohio, is among the most memorable. COFO enlisted Mrs. Hamer to teach the student volunteers about Mississippi—its viciously enforced segregated customs and its white supremacist political apparatus.

"How bad could it *really* be?" wondered the more naïve Freedom Summer recruits.

Some marched off buses and out of crammed cars insisting, "First we'll solve the problem of racial segregation in Mississippi, then it's on to the oppression of American Indians!"

To counter this naiveté, SNCC field secretaries and COFO voter registration workers rolled up their shirtsleeves and pant legs to display bruises, broken limbs, and burns—physical evidence of the white supremacist terror they had already endured.

"If you don't get scared," the more seasoned activists would say, "pack up and get the hell out of here because we don't need any people who don't know what they're doing!"

Hamer took a slightly different tack. She inspired the newly arrived Freedom Summer volunteers and quelled their anxieties by sharing gospel music infused with contemporary lyrics, relevant to the struggle for freedom they would soon join. Hamer also testified, sharing her lifelong experiences living under white supremacist rule, and she explained to the young college students the ever-present danger of segregationist retaliation. Hamer's personal narrative of losing her job, being forced into exile, narrowly escaping nightriders' bullets, enduring life-threatening abuse in the Winona jail cell, and facing starvation amid constant harassment gave meaning and force to the ubiquitous warnings Freedom Summer volunteers received.

To be part of this movement, the Freedom Summer volunteers had to forego summer jobs. They were also not paid for their ten weeks of labor, and they had to cover their own bailout expenses. As a result, economically privileged students predominated. Nearly 90 percent of the 1,000 student volunteers that COFO enlisted in the summer of 1964 were white. Recruited through Friends of SNCC networks, CORE (Congress of Racial Equality) campus chapters, and NAACP youth groups, these volunteers applied to become Freedom Summer volunteers in the early spring of 1964. They were then interviewed and carefully screened to weed out unstable white savior-type personalities. Nevertheless, it was challenging to convey to privileged college students what it meant to face arrest at the hands of Mississippi law enforcement, what day-to-day life would be like living in the homes of the black struggling class, and why it was so pivotal that the highly capable students follow the leadership of local black people, rather than jump in and take over the Mississippi Project.

Many SNCC field secretaries were so worried about what the influx of privileged white students would do to the Mississippi movement that they vehemently opposed the very concept of Freedom Summer. Yet, Bob Moses, who was among the first SNCC activists to enter Mississippi back in 1961, believed the influx of privileged students would help support Freedom Schools. These schools were pivotal in a state where education was a requirement for the franchise and yet quality education was systematically withheld from black Mississippians. Moses hoped the students would also help the mass voter registration project, by not only registering voters, but also by drawing federal attention to Mississippi's voter discrimination practices. Playing directly upon the nation's racist tendency to care more about economically privileged white youth than impoverished black people, Moses insisted that the Freedom Summer volunteers—and their influential families—would shine a national spotlight on terror in Mississippi.

Charles Cobb was one of many voter registration workers who firmly opposed the influx of white volunteers. He worried that "to bring a whole lot of outsiders in felt like we had failed." Cobb was also concerned that "if you have a whole lot of presumably mostly white outsiders coming into Mississippi they would trample on the very fragile grassroots we were trying to cultivate." On the other hand, Hamer and "*all*, I say *all* of the local people like Mrs. Hamer were very much for the Summer Project because, in their experience, people coming from the outside was a good thing," Cobb recalled.

In fact, Hamer would later characterize the presence of COFO voter registration workers, SNCC field secretaries, and Freedom Summer volunteers as "the beginning of the New Kingdom in Mississippi." Praising the young people who opened up her viciously guarded state, she said, "They did something in Mississippi that gave us the hope that we had prayed for for so many years. We had wondered if there was anybody human enough to see us as human beings instead of animals."

During a Freedom Summer planning meeting, in fact, Hamer effectively resolved the SNCC staff's heated dispute over inviting Freedom Summer volunteers into Mississippi. Looking fondly over at Charles Cobb, who had been in the state for two years, but was originally from D.C.. Hamer said straightforwardly: "Well, Charlie, I'm sure glad *you* came to Mississippi."

After that, remembered Cobb, there was no argument left to make. "Who is going to argue with Mrs. Hamer about the Summer Project?" Cobb asked rhetorically. To quash a program that the local people characterized as the answer to their prayers would undermine SNCC's guiding "Let the People Decide" philosophy. "You can't, on the one hand, say that people have a right to participate and make decisions that affect their lives and then turn around and say, 'Well I don't like your decision,'" Cobb explained. He attributed Mrs. Hamer's intervention into the debate as holding as much influence and contributing "as much to there *being* a Summer Project as any proposal Bob Moses put forward."

Hamer's contributions to Freedom Summer were, in fact, manifold. Fannie Lou Hamer—among other local people—convinced COFO to recruit northern volunteers. At their two-week training session in Ohio, she warmly welcomed those volunteers, who relished her southern Christian hospitality as respite from the resentment of the SNCC field secretaries. Hamer also prepared these volunteers for what they would face in Mississippi, even as she tried desperately to protect them. Hamer's most broad-ranging attempt to secure the safety of SNCC field secretaries and Freedom Summer volunteers came on June 8, 1964, when she testified about Mississippi's climate of racial terror at the National Theatre in Washington, D.C. A prestigious board of lawyers, psychologists, professors, college presidents, and government officials convened to hear firsthand, from black Mississippians and war-torn COFO activists, about the hostile racial climate awaiting the Freedom Summer volunteers.

As this board soon learned, the white segregationist apparatus in Mississippi had assumed a siege mentality in response to announcements about Freedom Summer. Police forces across the state swelled and precincts purchased military equipment, including caged trucks, armored vehicles affixed with searchlights, rifles, and even a tank, which the Jackson Police Department named "Thompson's Tank," after the fiercely segregationist mayor, Allen C. Thompson. The state legislature passed a series of bills designed to criminalize the protest of students they were now branding as "outside communist agitators."

From the landmark 1954 *Brown v. Board of Education* decision up until 1964, the Ku Klux Klan had relatively little presence in Mississippi. "The Klan was unnecessary," argued William K. Scarborough, an outspoken leader of the Citizens' Council. The Klan, a well-known terrorist organization, fostered "bad publicity," reasoned Scarborough. The Council had effectively quashed civil rights uprisings in more insidious ways. But on the heels of the statewide 1963 Freedom Vote and in anticipation of what white segregationists characterized as the 1964 "N—r Communist Invasion," Klan activity and Klan membership surged. Elected officials framed resistance to the project in warlike terms. "It was us against them," Scarborough recalled, "and I hated them."

Hoping for federal protection for the Mississippi Summer Project, Hamer spoke during her National Theatre address not only about the specific acts of discrimination she endured, but also about the larger invasions of privacy and unconstitutional recriminations that were commonplace throughout the state. "Well, I can say there will be a hot summer in Mississippi and I don't mean the weather," she predicted.

Beyond seeking federal protection from white supremacist retaliation for the Freedom Summer volunteers, Hamer attempted to protect the students by teaching them about deeply entrenched and lethally enforced southern racial customs. "You got to spell out the rules for them," she told McLaurin. "All of this just ain't real for them yet."

As one white female volunteer put it: "White Mississippians were obsessed with sex." The widespread (and generations-old) fear among white men that black civic empowerment would lead to sexual relationships between black men and white women was a driving force behind the lynching epidemic that cost over 5,000 black lives and curtailed the hard-won political advances made during Reconstruction. These racist fears resurfaced following the *Brown v. Board of Education* decision, and by Freedom Summer they had reached hysteric heights. The idea that white women would be working alongside black men in Freedom Schools, COFO offices, and as fieldworkers registering black voters, not to mention living with black families, enraged white people across the state.

Hamer knew the history of white supremacists' projection well—after all, it was white men who had raped enslaved black women for centuries. Her own grandmother spoke about the sexual abuse she endured at the hands of white slaveholders. And, less than ten years before Freedom Summer, fourteen-year-old Emmett Till had been lynched for allegedly wolf-whistling at Carolyn Bryant, a white woman who still lived in the Mississippi Delta. Mindful of this hysteria, Hamer went to great lengths to warn the volunteers about white Mississippians' obsession with interracial sexual relations—before the students ever entered the Magnolia state.

But once the young white women arrived, Hamer complained to McLaurin, "It's just as if I never said nothing to them at Oxford! They sit out under the trees in the back yard playing cards with the Negro boys. Or they stand around in the front in groups, chatting and laughing! Some even wave at cars as they drive by!"

Hamer was rightfully concerned about the young women's safety. White female volunteers were soon arrested. One woman was detained and questioned by police, who asked her to "describe the size of black men's penises." Another white female volunteer was accosted by a truck filled with white men. The men tied a rope around her neck and dragged her behind their moving vehicle shouting "N—r lover!" before they released her and drove away cackling.

Hamer also fretted over the young women's safety out of a concern for the lives of black men, who were who were routinely scapegoated for white men's crimes. "If some whites laid hands on one of those young girls, every Negro man in Ruleville would be in trouble. That kind of trouble kills people in Mississippi. And what would become of the movement then?" she confided in McLaurin.

Even the presence of white male volunteers living in the homes of black people violated Mississippi's strict codes of segregation. Tracy Sugarman, a World War II veteran and gifted illustrator, was among the cadre of older Freedom Summer volunteers, including approximately 150 lawyers, 300 ministers, and 100 physicians, nurses, and psychologists who lent their skills to the project. Sugarman characterized the Hamer home as a "nerve center" for the project. The Hamers' Lafayette Street home became a veritable way station, where field secretaries set up makeshift offices and volunteers passed through on the way to their assigned homes that were intentionally spread out across the state.

The constant activity at the Hamers' home infuriated Ruleville Mayor Charles Dorrough, also a leader of the local Citizens' Council chapter. Durrough roared up to 626 East Lafayette Street one hot summer afternoon and eyed a white male volunteer. "How do you feel having white men sleeping in your house?" he demanded of Perry Hamer.

"I feel like a man," Sugarman recalled Mr. Hamer's calm and confident response, "because they treat me like a man."

The rage felt by white supremacist Mississippians fueled a spate of violent retaliation to Freedom Summer projects. White supremacists bombed and burned churches where mass meetings and Freedom Schools were held. They shot into the homes where Freedom Summer volunteers slept and into restaurants that served them. Mississippi law enforcement officials arrested field secretaries on spurious charges, set their bail at astronomical rates, and mercilessly beat them while in prison. Klansmen ran cars driven by movement activists off roads, burned crosses on the front lawns of homes housing volunteers, and threatened the lives of the local black people who owned or rented the homes where volunteers stayed. COFO kept careful track of this retaliation, listing each incident—including the date, location, and details of the report—in a document entitled "Mississippi Summer Project: Running Summary of Incidents." During the 1964 Freedom Summer in Mississippi, there were 1,000 arrests, 65 buildings bombed, 35 churches set aflame—including Williams Chapel where Hamer worshipped—and there were over 100 recorded beatings of civil rights workers.

Haunting sketches of the three slain civil rights workers James Chaney, Andrew Goodman, and Michael Schwerner hung across the Atlantic City boardwalk, just above their burned-out blue station wagon. The car's remains were flanked by the Mt. Zion church bell, cracked from the bombing in Philadelphia, Mississippi, that they were sent to investigate. Out in front of the sketches and the artifacts of Mississippi's deadly Freedom Summer, at least a hundred of the state's farmers, day-laborers, and maids stood in solidarity. In the center of the crowd stood Fannie Lou Hamer, her contralto voice belted out freedom songs that pierced through the boardwalk chatter.

> *Which side are you on, now*
> *Which side are you on? Everybody!*
> *Way down in Mississippi*
> *No neutrals have I met*
> *You either are a Freedom Man*
> *Or a Tom for Ross Barnett*

The MFDP's demonstration disrupted Atlantic City's jovial atmosphere. In late August of 1964, the boardwalk was otherwise abuzz with patriotic fervor. Democratic National Convention (DNC) attendees donned "All the Way with LBJ" t-shirts. Rickshaws carried delegates past ice cream shops and vendor booths pawned flags, donkey figurines, and oversized Uncle Sam hats.

Most delegates had heard murmurings of the Mississippi challenge throughout the summer. Media coverage of white supremacist retaliation to Freedom Summer dominated the airwaves, especially after Chaney, Goodman, and Schwerner disappeared in late June. News stations followed the month-long search for the three activists, replaying footage of search parties combing bayous and raking thick forests. The search was first carried out by local authorities, then—after Michael's wife, Rita Schwerner, met with President Johnson—it was led by federal officials. In early August, the FBI found the three civil rights activists' battered corpses, which had been buried deep in an earthen dam outside Philadelphia, Mississippi. Their bodies discovered just three weeks prior to the DNC and their funerals recently covered in the national news, delegates to the 1964 Convention likely knew the slain civil rights activists' story well.

Perhaps some delegates also understood the larger significance of the civil rights workers' deaths. From the moment of her husband's disappearance to the discovery of their burned out blue station wagon and the eventual recovery of Michael's corpse, Rita Schwerner was trailed by the national press. Reporters hoped to craft a broken widow narrative that might tug at the heart strings of national audiences, but Rita Schwerner refused to play the part. Later recalling that she couldn't stand to let the disappearance of her three fellow civil rights activists deteriorate into a "poor white girl" tragedy. Instead, she refocused the national gaze on racialized terror in the state, suggesting that even the national attention this very case garnered was evidence of racial bias: had her husband and Andrew Goodman been black, making this yet another story of three *black* men killed in Mississippi, Schwerner insisted, there would be no national interest.

Longtime black freedom movement activist Ella Baker extended this logic when she spoke before the statewide convention of the newly formed Mississippi Freedom Democratic Party (MFDP). Addressing an enthusiastic crowd of MFDP delegates and supporters on August 6, 1964, just two days after the bodies of Chaney, Goodman, and Schwerner were discovered, Baker expressed the MFDP's *raison d'être*: "Until the killing of black men, black mothers' sons becomes as important as the killing of a white mother's son, we who believe in freedom cannot rest."

The MFDP was formed in the spring of 1964 as a parallel political party to the exclusive all-white Democratic party in the state. Open to all, the MFDP adhered to the National Democratic Party's rules as they organized along the precinct, county, and statewide levels. They amassed an interracial delegation to challenge the all-white delegation at the 1964 DNC. The MFDP also set up an office in Washington, D.C., headed by Ella Baker, and they enlisted Washington-insider Joseph Rauh as the head of their legal counsel.

Together Rauh and Baker orchestrated a lobbying effort to clear the way for the MFDP delegates' historic DNC challenge.

By the MFDP's August 6 statewide convention, Baker, Rauh, and MFDP leaders had developed a multi-tiered strategy to demonstrate the illegitimacy of the segregated delegation and to support their request that the interracial MFDP delegation replace the all-white delegation. First, the MFDP elected a slate of sixty-eight delegates, and thirty-four alternatives, out of 800 candidates from across forty counties who participated in the MFDP's landmark political gathering. Hamer was chosen as vice president of this delegation. Second, Rauh and Baker secured a hearing before the DNC's credentials committee. MFDP witnesses, including local Mississippi leaders such as Hamer, Reverend Edwin King, and Dr. Aaron Henry, as well as nationally known figures like Martin Luther King, Jr.. executive director of the NAACP, Roy Wilkins, and Rita Schwerner, would testify about the white supremacist apparatus that kept black people from participating in Mississippi's political process. Third, Rauh, the MFDP lawyer, would reason that given this discrimination, the all-white delegation sent from Mississippi should be replaced by the interracial MFDP delegation. At the convention, Rauh explained the DNC's bylaws to the nearly 2,000 MFDP supporters, who excitedly waved American flags and held signs proudly bearing their counties' names. According to the bylaws, the MFDP needed eleven credentials committee members' votes, 10 percent of the panel, to bring their challenge before the larger convention. Once there, the challenge would need eight states to officially support bringing their challenge to a convention-wide roll call vote. Rauh was hopeful that a nationally-televised roll call vote, forcing state delegations to publicly choose between a segregated or an integrated delegation, would swing the MFDP's way.

"Eleven and eight, Eleven and eight!" Mrs. Hamer chanted, summarizing the complex strategy Rauh outlined and inciting enthusiastic support among the delegates. The national news caught glimpses of Hamer's zeal on camera and President Lyndon B. Johnson watched this coverage with trepidation.

Paranoid that Attorney General Robert F. Kennedy, brother of the recently assassinated President John F. Kennedy, would use any convention disturbance to usurp his nomination, Johnson declared: "We won't have any of that eleven and eight bullshit on the floor of the convention!" And he began devising plans to ensure that nothing would stand in the way of his nomination.

This was the woman they had seen along the boardwalk belting out movement anthems—old gospel songs and labor union medleys imbued with fresh meaning for the current civil rights struggle. This was the woman whose harrowing story was shared over breakfast and lunch meetings, as MFDP supporters lobbied delegates to support their convention challenge. And this was the woman on whom the MFDP's lead lawyer built his case during the nationally televised credentials committee hearing on August 22, 1964.

"Will the remaining witnesses please focus their testimony on the problems with the election machinery, rather than on problems with general life in Mississippi," instructed credentials committee chairman and Pennsylvania governor, David Lawrence.

"It is the very terror that these people are living through that is the reason Negroes aren't voting. They are kept out of the Democratic Party by the terror of the Regular Party," Rauh proclaimed. "What I want the credentials committee to hear is the terror that the regular party uses on the people of Mississippi, which is what the next witness will explain—Mrs. Fannie Lou Hamer."

Slow and low, in the Black Baptist tradition she learned from her father's weekly sermons, Hamer's testimony began. "Mr. Chairman, and to the credentials committee, my name is Mrs. Fannie Lou Hamer, and I live at 626 East Lafayette Street, Ruleville, Mississippi, Sunflower County, the home of Senator James O. Eastland and Senator Stennis."

In the eleventh hour, Rauh had secured a large ballroom for the credentials committee hearing. By moving the public testimonies out of a small boardroom and into a ballroom, Rauh created the space necessary for legions of camera crews to broadcast Hamer's testimony across the three major networks—ABC, CBS, and NBC. Back home in Mississippi, Freedom Summer volunteers and local people marveled at Mrs. Hamer's bravery. Stating her full name and her home address did more than establish her credibility as a resident of Mississippi, it defiantly directed the Klan and the Citizens' Councils right to her front door. Clearly, she refused to be intimidated. Hamer also specified her county and the names of influential US senators entrusted with the power to make decisions that affected all Americans.

Seated at the center of a long rectangular table, directly across from the regular party whose legitimacy she challenged, Hamer continued to tell her story. As she moved from her encounter with Marlow, the plantation owner who fired her for trying to register, to the sixteen bullets shot into the Tuckers' home and aimed at her, the bustling room fell silent. Cameras scanned the audience and revealed conversations stopped midsentence, necks craning to catch a glimpse of Hamer, jaws hanging in disbelief.

"We interrupt this live television broadcast to bring you the president, who is addressing a gathering of governors in the East Room of the White House," explained news reporters on each major network channel. With that, the national broadcast traveled from the ballroom in Atlantic City to Washington, D.C., where it was rumored Johnson would announce his running mate.

But the networks were duped by the Commander in Chief. Johnson

Figure 3.1 On behalf of the Mississippi Freedom Democratic Party, Fannie Lou Hamer testified before the Credentials Committee at the 1964 Democratic National Convention. Source: Associated Press.

made no newsworthy announcement. Rather, his goal had been to divert national attention away from Hamer's damning testimony of the nation he led. He managed that by noting that today—August 22, 1964—marked nine months since President John F. Kennedy's assassination.

Fortunately, the cameras in Atlantic City kept rolling, and once the networks caught on to Johnson's game, they replayed Hamer's testimony during their prime time nightly news coverage of the convention—reaching an estimated three million viewers. American families, eating their dinner on television trays in living rooms across the nation, witnessed Hamer recount the horror of her Winona beating. She spoke of the physical abuse and alluded to the sexual assault she endured as punishment for attending a voter education workshop. The credentials committee, too, heard Hamer describe the official positions of those who harassed, kicked, and ordered her brutal beating. These weren't rogue hooded Klansmen, as the country might imagine; Hamer specified eleven times within her eight minute testimony that those who incited terror in her state were policemen, state highway patrolmen, city police, and even the chief of police. Tears streamed down her cheeks as she built from the abuse in Winona to her climactic conclusion: "All of this is on account of we want to register, to become first-class citizens," Hamer declared with disgust, her voice cracking as she held back sobs:

> And if the Freedom Democratic Party is not seated—now—I question America. Is this America, the land of the free and the home of the brave, where we have to sleep with our telephones off of the hooks because our lives be threatened daily, because we want to live as decent human beings, in America? Thank you.

Back at the rundown Gem Motel, where the MFDP delegates slept five and six to a room, Hamer first learned that President Johnson had diverted national attention away from her testimony. She was angry and exhausted. The whole afternoon had been harrowing. As soon as the eight witnesses for the Freedom Democratic Party shared their heart-wrenching experiences, the Mississippi regulars worked to discredit their testimonies and undermine their challenge. Led by State Senator E. K. Collins and Mississippi attorney general, Ruble Griffin, the regular party constructed their defense by criticizing the MFDP's case as "all emotion and no evidence." They claimed that the Freedom Democrats represented "no one" because there was no way of verifying if they had, in fact, followed the proper procedure for founding a political party. The regulars referred to themselves as the only "lawful party," and they appealed to the Johnson administration's fears of a southern walkout when they pleaded with credential committee members not to "kill our party."

Hamer was confident that her testimony had moved committee members. She could see it in their rapt attention, furrowed brows, and tear-filled eyes, but would their sympathy be enough to override threats that all of the southern delegations would abandon the Democratic Party? Hamer seethed. Rauh wanted the news stations to catch those testimonies so the American people would put pressure on their delegates, especially if the MFDP challenge came to a floor vote.

"You're on! You're on TV!" Shouts of excitement interrupted Hamer's worry, and fellow delegates crowded around her as they turned the volume nob up. There she was, telling her story—without interruption—in prime time. She felt validated by this, even a bit proud, her friends remembered.

"It shocked them all," Hamer told an interviewer two years later. "This testimony turned the tide of the convention."

She was right. After the major networks broadcast Hamer's credentials committee address, telegrams of support flooded into DNC delegates urging them to seat the interracial MFDP in the place of the segregationist party sent from Mississippi. Johnson received correspondence, too—some from southern white people, who threatened to support the Republican nominee, Barry Goldwater, if the MFDP was seated. Amid threats of a southern walkout and fears that Bobby Kennedy would somehow abscond his nomination, Johnson doubled down on his resistance to the MFDP.

Johnson had already ordered the FBI to tap the hotel rooms where Martin Luther King, Jr. and other well-known movement activists deliberated, as well as the Union Baptist Temple in Atlantic City, where the MFDP set up their convention headquarters. Now he ordered his potential running mate, the Minnesota Senator Hubert Humphrey, to settle the conflict or forfeit the vice presidency. To ensure Humphrey delivered, Johnson also called in Walter Reuther, president of the United Autoworkers' Union. Johnson would not, in his words, permit "that illiterate woman to speak from the convention floor!"

Publicly, Johnson refrained from commenting about the challenge that Hamer now symbolized. Recorded telephone conversations between Humphrey, Reuther, and Johnson indicate that he wanted to maintain a facade of "benevolent neutrality," precisely what Joseph Rauh, head of the MFDP legal counsel, had publicly and repeatedly requested of the president.

Johnson cautioned Humphrey and Reuther not to "let people know I'm making you do this. I've never heard of it," he instructed.

Privately, the challenge tore Johnson apart. Threats that the southern delegations would abandon the party, pressure from northern groups allied with the MFDP, and the media's fixation on the challenge kept him up at night and put him on the verge of giving up the office entirely. His closest advisors confirm that Johnson considered quitting rather than resolving this conflict that brought to the fore the divisive issues of race, representation, and power politics.

Immediately following the official credentials committee testimonies, and in anticipation of the committee's vote, which would determine whether or not the MFDP challenge was brought to the convention floor, the backdoor dealing began. Credentials committee members were lobbied by both high-ranking Johnson administration officials and leading civil rights activists like King, Roy Wilkins, of the NAACP, and US Congressmen Adam Clayton Powell and Charles Diggs. One delegate, Vera Canson, from California was decidedly on the side of the MFDP until the Johnson administration threatened her husband's federal judgeship appointment. Other delegates were interested in sparking a compromise to avoid a convention floor showdown. Edith Green, a congresswoman from Oregon, floated the idea of seating half of each Mississippi delegation, but requiring a loyalty oath to the Democratic Party from any delegate seated upon the convention floor.

Hamer was dismayed. "When we went to Atlantic City," she told one interviewer, "we didn't go there for publicity, we went there because we believed that America was what it said it was—the land of the free. And I thought with all of my heart that the people would have been unseated in

Atlantic City." Hamer couldn't stomach the idea of sitting alongside delegates who had literally locked black people out of their statewide proceedings. She couldn't imagine why the two delegations were being given equal consideration, in light of the terror to which she and others testified. In her mind, the choice was clear: the MFDP swore loyalty to the party, followed its rules for organizing, and opened its doors to all Americans, whereas the regular party excluded black people from its membership, drove to the convention with Goldwater bumper stickers pasted on the backs of their vehicles, and threatened to foment a southern walkout should the MFDP be recognized. There was no room for compromise, Hamer insisted. But more seasoned leaders thought they knew better.

Shuttling between closed door meetings at a hotel much nicer than the one she and the other MFDP delegates crowded into, Hamer spotted NAACP executive secretary Roy Wilkins. His tie was loosened, his cheeks speckled with stubble, and dark circles lined his eyes. He, too, had been steadily lobbying since the hearing yesterday afternoon. Even in his disheveled state, something about his mohair suit and his shined shoes made Hamer nervous. But she was a southern woman and that hospitality traveled with her. "How you doing, Mr. Wilkins?" she asked, limping toward him.

He let out a long exhale and clenched his jaw. "Mrs. Hamer, you people have put your point across. You don't know anything, you're ignorant, you don't know anything about politics."

Instinctively, she recoiled. Hamer wasn't expecting this from the man who had testified on behalf of the MFDP's challenge. Perhaps she should have been more suspicious of the head of an organization that had spent decades working in Mississippi, never reaching out to the likes of her. Instead, she was stunned into a rare moment of silence.

"I been in the business over twenty years," Wilkins continued. "You people have put your point across, now why don't you pack up and go home?" he said, moving away from her before she had a chance to respond.

Hamer's blood boiled as she considered Wilkins' hurtful words. Hadn't her testimony meant something to the movement? She had a right to be here. Weren't they on the same side—NAACP, SNCC, SCLC, CORE—all bound together as the Council of Federated Organizations, working for a representative democracy in Mississippi? She had every right to speak up.

There was little time to ruminate, however. Her next scheduled meeting had already begun, and it was an important one. Hubert Humphrey, the likely nominee for vice president of the United States, wanted to talk with her and the MFDP leadership. Hamer remembered feeling "delighted to even have a chance to talk with this man." In a closed door meeting, with his vice presidency hanging in the balance, Senator Humphrey tried to persuade the MFDP toward accepting a compromise. Rauh, their head legal counsel, kept pushing back against the very suggestion of compromise. He was still confident that a floor vote would force the party to live up to its creed. Rauh was also confident that Humphrey, who had been instrumental in the 1948 DNC push for a civil rights platform, which had indeed resulted in a southern walkout, would be supportive now. Rauh miscalculated.

Humphrey tried another tack. He turned to Hamer, his round eyes filled with what she later described as "crocodile tears," and said, "If the MFDP doesn't stop pushing for a vote to come to the floor, then I won't be nominated for vice president of the United States."

"Well, Mr. Humphrey, do you mean to tell me that your position is more important to you than 400,000 black people's lives?" Hamer replied. This time it was Humphrey who was stunned into silence. Hamer continued, "I've been praying for you. You're a good man and you know what's right, but the trouble is you're afraid to do what's right. I'm going to pray for you again, Mr. Humphrey."

Hamer recalled being stunned by Humphrey's indifference toward the 435,000 black people of voting age in Mississippi, who were being barred from the franchise by state-sanctioned terror. "You see, this was blows to me," remembered Hamer, who left that crowded smoke-filled hotel room in tears herself. After the exchange with Humphrey, Hamer was not invited to join anymore backroom, closed door meetings.

She returned to the makeshift MFDP headquarters at the Union Baptist Temple to find additional pressure regarding a compromise. By this point, the details of the deal were ostensibly settled. To bypass a committee vote and a convention floor showdown, the Johnson administration offered the MFDP two delegate seats. And those seats came with stipulations. First, the delegates could not be seated in the Mississippi section, nor could they cast votes for the Magnolia state. Instead, the MFDP delegate seats would be positioned at-large and the so-called regular party would be permitted to keep all sixty-eight of their convention floor seats and attendant votes. Moreover, the Johnson administration named the at-large seats' inhabitants: Dr. Aaron Henry, the black pharmacist and NAACP activist from Clarksdale, and Reverend Edwin King, the white chaplain from Tougaloo College.

"Oh, hell no!" was the immediate reply from MFDP member Hollis Watkins, who, like Hamer, was unpersuaded by the abounding false equivalence arguments.

The MFDP came to Atlantic City to unseat a party that used terror to perpetuate its power. The MFDP came to represent the people of Mississippi. What ground was there to compromise? Further still, what right did the Johnson administration have to handpick the delegates who would occupy those seats? Henry was chair of the delegation, sure, but Fannie Lou Hamer—not Reverend Edwin King—had been elected as the delegation's vice-chair.

A steady stream of seasoned movement activists coursed through Union Baptist Temple urging the Freedom Democrats gathered there to accept the Johnson administration's compromise. Martin Luther King, Jr., who had been threatened by Walter Reuther that the United Autoworkers Union would rescind their financial support to the SCLC if King opposed Johnson, now outwardly promoted the compromise. So, too, did Rauh, whose position on the United Autoworkers' legal counsel was also threatened by Reuther. Even US Congressman Adam Clayton Powell now lobbied the MFDP to support the two-seat compromise. Powell, an ordained Baptist minister offered a sermon about moral victory, the nature of politics, and the art of compromise. As Powell preached, Hamer sat stone-faced, arms crossed, livid.

After his message to the MFDP, the congressman approached Mrs. Hamer directly, "You don't know who I am, do you?" said Powell, the first black person to ever be elected to the US Congress from the state of New York.

"I know who you are. But I wonder, how many bales of cotton have you picked? How many beatings have you taken?" she asked the congressman from Harlem, making it clear to Powell that he lacked the lived experience required to lead the MFDP's decision-making processes.

Dr. Henry, chair of the MFDP and one of the two delegates named in the compromise, was in favor of the deal. He, too, tried his hand at persuading Mrs. Hamer. "Mrs. Hamer," Henry said, "we going to have to listen to some of them leaders that know much more about politics than we know."

"Tell me the leaders you're talking about," demanded Hamer.

"You know we got some great leaders," Henry said, gesturing toward the likes of Wilkins, King, and Powell.

"That's right," she said in ironic agreement. "All those people from SNCC are some of the greatest leaders I ever seen. But now don't go telling me about somebody that ain't been in Mississippi two weeks and don't know nothing about the problem, cause they're not leading us. And that's the truth."

She was firm in her conviction that to compromise would be to sell out—or, in Hamer's more pointedly evocative words, to "auction off" the people in Mississippi whom she came to represent. How could the MFDP compromise in the face of the lost, threatened, and terrorized lives of black Mississippians upon which the challenge was based? Doing so, to Hamer's mind, would be akin to profiting off of their pain.

But she was human. Hamer, too, experienced moments of self-doubt, which were compounded by the barrage of insults hurled her way during the negotiation process. So Hamer turned to those trusted SNCC leaders—Ella

Baker, who mentored SNCC activists and lobbied for the MFDP in D.C., and Bob Moses, who saw Hamer's great potential during her first registration attempt in Indianola. She approached both of them separately and admitted, "I believe I'm right, but I might be wrong. I respect you and I will respect your decision. Whatever you say, if you think I'm wrong, even though I feel like I am right, I will do what you think."

Hamer remembered both Moses and Baker, independently, telling her the same thing, "Mrs. Hamer, you're the people living in Mississippi and you people know what you've experienced in Mississippi, we don't have to tell you nothing. You make your own decision."

The faith Baker and Moses had in Hamer restored her conviction. The MFDP took a vote and decided—unanimously—to reject the Johnson administration's compromise. As chair of the delegation, Henry was responsible for delivering the verdict to the news media surrounding their headquarters. His earlier hedging made Hamer suspicious. Before Henry exited the Union Baptist Temple, she informed him that if he didn't accurately convey the MFDP's will—reject the compromise—she would slit his throat.

After the MFDP's rejection of the Johnson administration's compromise, negotiations ceased. Members of the segregationist delegation sent from Mississippi were also offended by the two-seat compromise and appalled by the suggestion that they would be required to sign a loyalty oath. Mississippi Governor Paul Johnson, former Governor Ross Barnett, and Mississippi Supreme Court Justice Thomas Brady all referred to the loyalty oath as the breaking point between white Mississippi Democrats and the National Democratic Party. Justice Brady, founding member of the Citizens' Councils, went so far as to suggest that the National Democratic Party treated the segregationist delegation as "second-class citizens," and he promised not a "white backlash" to the Democrats, but a "white tornado" in response to the party he and his fellow Citizens' Councilors now dubbed the "National Negro Party." While President Johnson's backroom dealing did succeed in averting a mass southern walkout, the majority of the Mississippi regulars left Atlantic City before the official convention proceedings began.

True to their pledge of loyalty, the MFDP stayed in Atlantic City for the remainder of the four-day convention. They led a march down Pacific Avenue and many of the Freedom Democrats eventually made it onto the convention floor, where they occupied the Mississippi seats left vacant by the regulars.

"Where did you get the credentials to come into the building tonight?" asked one reporter. "Do you have any credentials to sit in these seats tonight?"

"No, we don't, only as American citizens," Hamer replied.

Another reporter asked Bob Moses how he felt about the compromise, to which the characteristically calm Moses responded with anger. "What is the compromise?" he asked, his voice rising and his rate of speech quickening. "We are here for the people and the people want to represent themselves. They don't want symbolic token votes. They want to vote themselves."

Moses conveyed more widespread feelings of anger and disappointment shared by the MFDP. While Hamer's friends and fellow activists insist that she was no idealist, her own descriptions of, and memories regarding, Atlantic City suggest that she believed the challenge would succeed. Unlike her congressional campaign against Jamie Whitten, the MFDP challenge was not a symbolic gesture to motivate black civic participation; it was a plea for the National Democratic Party to follow its bylaws and enact its espoused values. When the party failed to do so, favoring backroom dealings over bringing the challenge to an open floor vote, the Freedom Democrats did not consider this a moral victory—as many media outlets and better-known national civil rights leaders referred to the outcome.

The twenty-hour bus ride from the East Coast back to the Mississippi Delta was far more subdued than the hopeful trip out to the convention had been. Following Freedom Summer's frenetic pace, the civil rights activists were both disappointed and utterly exhausted. For some MFDP members, the 1964 DNC was also their breaking point with the party. They could no longer work within its convoluted structures to bring about the change they sought. Rather than retreat to the Republican Party, as the majority of disgruntled white Dixiecrats did following Atlantic City, a contingent of the MFDP's disillusioned membership began to grow more global, more radical, and even more leftist in their politics. Fannie Lou Hamer, however, was just getting started on her work within the Democratic Party. She had her sights set on another national challenge. But this time, Hamer would lead the Mississippi Freedom Democratic Party straight to the floor of the United States Congress.

· 4 ·

Revelations

The most disrespected person in America is the black woman, the most unprotected person in America is the black woman, the most neglected person in America is the black woman.

—Malcolm X, Speech in Los Angeles, 1962

America is Mississippi. There's no such thing as a Mason-Dixon line. It's America. There's no such thing as the South. It's America.

—Malcolm X, Speech in Harlem, 1964

"*Y*'all got to go someplace where there's no chance for them to tap into you," Harry Belafonte, the famed performer and black freedom movement activist, suggested. "You're going to Africa."

It wasn't easy to convince the devoted civil rights activists to go, but Belafonte had the means to persuade. When he saw the rough state of the Student Nonviolent Coordinating Committee (SNCC) members after the 1964 Democratic National Convention (DNC) in Atlantic City, Belafonte knew they needed rest. He described the activists as "really stressed," even war-torn. "They were saying silly things, and making silly moves," he recalled. "I saw this behavior as the expression of total exhaustion." Belafonte proposed a retreat, a respite from the violent and demanding work of voter registration and direct action campaigns spread across the South. At first SNCC's leadership dismissed Belafonte's suggestion. Once he mentioned Africa, however, they became interested. The suggestion seemed to flow from him with little forethought. To Belafonte, the idea of Africa—"a faraway place, black countries, alive with independence and governments still shaping and forming themselves"—was the right place to go.

Yet the civil rights leaders remained reluctant to suspend the momentum of their voter registration campaigns, fundraising efforts, and preparations for the Mississippi Freedom Democratic Party's (MFDP) forthcoming congressional challenge. Belafonte knew the only thing SNCC's members needed more than rest was money. In fact, the Sovereignty Commission reported that in the wake of Freedom Summer, SNCC's Mississippi voter registration workers were no longer being paid and that local people had stopped housing and feeding volunteers. Those Freedom Summer volunteers who remained committed to fighting for black voting rights into the fall of 1964 piled into small houses—seven or eight to a residence—and subsisted on vitamin pills, reported one informant for the Sovereignty Commission, Mississippi's state-sanctioned spy agency. Belafonte raised $60,000 cash from his wealthy acquaintances, and he secured an official invitation from Guinean President Sékou Touré, who offered to sponsor SNCC's trip. Belafonte told the activists to choose the African delegation among their membership and, if they accompanied him Guinea, he would donate the $60,000 cash directly to SNCC.

It worked. On September 11, 1964, Belafonte accompanied James Forman, John Lewis, Bob Moses, Dona Richards, Prathia Hall, Julian Bond, Ruby Doris Smith Robinson, Bob Hansen, Donald Harris, and Fannie Lou Hamer on a flight bound for Conakry, Ghana. When the group touched down on African soil, they were greeted by a joyful crowd waving signs of support. This heroes' welcome continued once they made it to their final destination in Guinea, where the activists were treated as dignitaries.

For Hamer, the trip to Guinea provided respite and stimulated an awakening. Traveling to Africa revealed to Hamer a more empowered sense of self. The trip also inspired a vision for what might be possible in American politics. During their three-week stay, the group rested comfortably in a lavishly furnished villa provided by the Guinean government. The activists attended a Guinean Independence Day rally as the president's honored guests. They toured rural areas of the country, a match factory, a newly constructed sports stadium, and a printing plant named after the Congolese freedom fighter, Patrice Lumumba. President Sékou Touré visited the Americans at their villa, and he held galas for the activists at his palace. This black-led socialist society—which had won its independence from France just six years before—astonished Hamer. "It was quite a revelation to me," Hamer confessed. "I was really learning something for the first time."

Hamer's revelation ran counter to what she had been taught about Africa by America's media and educational institutions. "In Africa, I learned that I sure didn't have anything to be ashamed of from being black," she said. "One thing I looked at so much was the African women," Hamer remembered. "They were so graceful and poised." From attractive black flight attendants to strong women in rural areas carrying pails of water atop their heads, Hamer observed breathtaking similarities between the Guinean women and her own family. Witnessing this beauty inspired Hamer to take pride in her African heritage, even as the connections she observed left her heart with a hollow ache.

"It got to me," Hamer recalled. "I cried over there. If I'm living here, I just might have some people over there. I probably got relatives right now in Africa, but we'll never know each other because we've been separated. I'll never know them and they'll never know me."

The Transatlantic Slave Trade, which lasted for nearly four centuries and involved the continents of Europe, Africa, and America, separated approximately 25 million African men, women, and children from their families and from their homeland. Millions of African people died during the Middle Passage from Africa to America—inhumanely cramped into cargo ships with little to no food or medical provisions. The enslaved African people who arrived on American shores were further separated from one another. Babies were torn from their mother's breasts and husbands were separated from their wives through slave auctions, which dispersed people across the vast and growing American territory.

The separation wrought by the Transatlantic Slave Trade was compounded, in Hamer's mind, by the continued lies circulating throughout America about her African ancestors. "Being from the South," Hamer said, "we never was taught much about our African heritage. The way everybody talked to us, everybody in Africa was savages and really stupid people." The more Hamer thought about the forced separation and these false characterizations of African people, the angrier she became. "I felt the anger of why this had to happen to us. We were so stripped and robbed of our background; we wind up with nothing. And you know that was a real crime," she told one interviewer.

Hamer realized the shame she was taught to feel about her African heritage was part of a much larger anti-black ideology that extended far beyond the state of Mississippi. Just as witnessing the beauty, power, and potential of the African people dispelled this shameful ideology that had clouded Hamer's self conception, learning about anti-colonial movements for African liberation informed her activist sense of what was possible in the United States. In fact, by the mid-1960s, connections between civil rights struggles in the United States and African liberation movements were forged in the minds of many activists. "Liberation was in the air," SNCC leader Stokely Carmichael said about this period. Similarly, SNCC member Cleveland Sellers recalled, "We're beginning to expand our horizon, we're beginning to talk about the similarities between the struggle for independence in Africa and the struggle for the right to vote in Mississippi."

Following their travels in Guinea with the larger SNCC delegation, John Lewis and Donald Harris fatefully encountered Malcolm X at the airport in Kenya. Just as these SNCC leaders were primed to take a closer look at Black Nationalist, Internationalist, and Pan-African thought, Malcolm was undergoing his own ideological transformation. He had recently broken from the National of Islam, traveled to Mecca, and founded the Organization of Afro-American Unity (OAAU). After Lewis, Harris, and Malcolm's chance encounter at the Nairobi airport, the OAAU and SNCC began to collaborate for the cause of racial advancement within the US. By the winter of 1964, SNCC and the MFDP were focused intently on the forthcoming congressional challenge. Malcolm offered his support for this campaign and arranged for MFDP members and SNCC Freedom Singers to travel to Harlem to promote their cause.

At another Williams Chapel, this one a thousand miles from her humble Delta sanctuary that shared the same name, Fannie Lou Hamer sat next to Malcolm X. This Williams Chapel was much larger than the one in Ruleville, but on that late December afternoon in 1964, the Williams Institutional Christian Methodist Episcopal (CME) Church in Harlem sure sounded like home to Mrs. Hamer. Malcolm glanced over his notes for the address he would soon deliver, and he tapped his foot along to the beat of the SNCC Freedom Singers' a cappella anthems.

> *Oginga Odinga, Oginga Odinga*
> *Oginga Odinga of Kenya – who?*
> *Oginga Odinga, Oginga Odinga,*
> *Oginga Odinga of Kenya*

Malcolm lifted his gaze and set his notes to the side. The mention of Jaramogi Oginga Odinga, the Mau Mau freedom fighter, who had just become Kenya's first vice president, captured Malcolm's attention.

> *Uh-huuuuuuru – ha! Haaa!*
> *Freedom now! Oh-ooohh haaa!*

To hear the SNCC Freedom Singers demand "Freedom now!"—first in Swahili and then with such tonal force and conviction—brought Malcolm to his feet. He turned to offer Mrs. Hamer a hand, and soon they were both swaying to the rhythm and singing the words of SNCC's new freedom song.

In front of an interracial crowd of three hundred attendees gathered at Williams CME Church in Harlem on December 20, 1964, Hamer shared her renewed vision for socio-political change. As she had during public addresses over the last two years, Hamer testified about her experience of being fired, evicted, and shot at for trying to vote in Mississippi. She described her experience with police brutality in a Winona jail cell before declaring, "It's time for *you* to wake up!" She'd been critical of Mississippi politics for years, but Hamer now insisted change was needed not only in her home state, but all over the country. "Not only do we need a change in the state of Mississippi, but we need a change here in Harlem," she said. "And it's time for every American citizen to wake up because now the whole world is looking at this American society." Hamer's trip to Africa showed her the importance of drawing inspiration from liberation struggles across the globe, and it also revealed to her that in the midst of the Cold War the world was watching to see what democracy looked like in practice.

Hamer's own political experiences and her travels had taught her that racism extended throughout the nation. Her involvement in the MFDP's 1964 credentials committee challenge in Atlantic City and her national fundraising trips for their 1965 congressional challenge demonstrated that anti-black discrimination was not limited to the South. In the summer of 1964, for instance, race riots erupted throughout northern cities. In Harlem, specifically, the community waged protests after a police officer shot and killed James Powell, an fifteen-year-old black adolescent. "You are not free in Harlem," Hamer told her audience. "The people are not free in Chicago, because I've been there, too. They are not free in Philadelphia, because I've been there, too. Some of these places is *Mississippi in disguise*. And we want a change!" The change Hamer advocated included holding the nation accountable to its principles and recognizing the interconnection of struggles for equality.

As Hamer returned to her platform seat next to Malcolm, he ascended to the podium. Her vision was blurry. MFDP colleagues in D.C. had recently taken her to see an ophthalmologist, who had informed Hamer that she had a blood clot in the artery of her left eye—permanent damage from the Winona jailhouse beating. Hamer squinted to bring Malcolm into focus and her heart rate began to slow a bit. She dabbed at the sweat above her brow. Speaking before large crowds came naturally to her, but it exhausted her all the same. And since the beating in Winona, she had to dig even deeper to find the physical strength necessary to deliver orations that would move people to support SNCC and MFDP's campaigns politically and financially.

"We don't deserve to be recognized and respected as men as long as our women can be brutalized in the manner that this woman described," Malcolm said, gesturing toward Hamer. "And nothing's being done about it, but we sit around singing 'We Shall Overcome.'" He shook his head. "I watch you, those of you who are *singing*—are you also willing to do some *swinging*? If they don't want to deal with the Mississippi Freedom Democratic Party," he threatened, "then we'll give them something else to deal with. If they don't want to deal with the Student Nonviolent Coordinating Committee, then we have to give them an alternative."

Hamer relished opportunities to hear great speakers within the movement—Prathia Hall, Martin Luther King, Jr., and especially Malcolm X. Malcolm's addresses embodied the alchemy of anger, exhaustion, and resolve that boiled inside Hamer. "Malcolm X was one of the greatest men that I ever met in my life," Hamer later told an interview team from Stanford University. She held Malcolm in such high regard because "he told exactly how every Negro in this country feels and didn't have the guts to say it." Hamer noticed that Malcolm frequently constructed himself and the Nation of Islam (NOI) as an alternative to King's Southern Christian Leadership Conference (SCLC). Since Malcolm had parted ways with the NOI and traveled to Mecca, his advocacy of Black Nationalism had grown more expansive to include, as he told the crowd gathered that afternoon in Harlem, "anybody who's for freedom. I'm for anybody who's for justice. I'm for anybody who's for equality." But unlike Roy Wilkins, Adam Clayton Powell, Martin Luther King, Jr., and the other well-known black leaders, who had urged Hamer to compromise in Atlantic City, Malcolm told the Williams CME audience that he wasn't "for anybody who tells me to sit around and wait for mine." Hamer heard members of SNCC urging him on as Malcolm gave voice to their frustration, "I'm not for anybody who tells me to turn the other cheek when a cracker is busting up my jaw." She thought of the white chaplain from Tougaloo College, Reverend Edwin King, and his now disfigured face. "I'm not for anybody who tells black people to be nonviolent while nobody is telling white people to be nonviolent," Malcolm said.

After feeling sold out and disrespected by prominent black leaders at the Democractic National Convention in Atlantic City, hearing Malcolm refer to Hamer in his speech as the "country's number one Freedom Fighting woman" was as heartening as the radical view of Christianity he espoused. Hamer often described Jesus Christ as a "revolutionary person" and praised the son of God for his work among the people. Malcolm reminded the congregation gathered at Williams CME in Harlem about the description of Christ in the Bible's Book of Revelations. "In the Book of Revelations, they've got Jesus sitting on a horse with a sword in his hand, getting ready to go into action," Malcolm said. "But they don't tell you or me about that Jesus. They only tell you and me about that peaceful Jesus. No, go read the *whole* book," he instructed, "and when you get to Revelations, you'll find that even Jesus' patience ran out. And when his patience ran out, he got the whole situation straightened out. He picked up the sword."

Hamer nodded her head and raised her arms to the heavens when Malcolm talked about an enraged Jesus driving out the moneychangers, turning the tables over in the temple where thievery had replaced worship. And by the time he got to the revolutionary Jesus of Revelations, the Jesus whose patience ran out, Hamer was back on her feet shouting, "Tell it!"

"As Mrs. Hamer pointed out," Malcolm said by way of conclusion, "brothers and sisters in Mississippi are being beaten and killed for no reason other than they want to be treated as first-class citizens." Stipulating an alternative to SNCC's nonviolent philosophy, Malcolm said, "There's only one way to be a first-class citizen. There's only one way to be independent. There's only one way to be free." The audience leaned in closer anticipating Malcolm's instruction. "Freedom is not something that someone gives to you. It's something that you take. Nobody can give you independence. Nobody can give you freedom. Nobody can give you equality or justice or anything. It's something that you take."

This type of actualized freedom that comes from demanding one's rights, coupled with Malcolm's advocacy of empowered self-defense, likely reminded Hamer of Joe Pullum—the Delta folk hero who so inspired her as a child. The tale of Pullum standing up and speaking back to the exploitative landowner, taking the money he was due for years of unremitted labor, and defending himself with lethal force from would-be lynchers, reminded Hamer, as had her recent trip to Africa, that the power to demand the freedom she deserved was already within her.

America's freedom fighting woman responded enthusiastically to Malcolm's vision for black empowerment. "*Uhuru*," Hamer exclaimed: "Freedom Now!"

The 1965 March from Selma to Montgomery—the violence of Bloody Sunday, the determination of grassroots and national activists to secure first-class citizenship for black people in Alabama—is commonly cited as *the* impetus for the passage of the Voting Rights Act. As significant as the demonstrations in Selma were, there's much more to the story of how and why this landmark legislation came to be. As nonviolent protestors gathered from across the country in Alabama, the MFDP spearheaded another radical campaign right in Washington, D.C. The MFDP's campaign, dubbed the congressional challenge, unfolded along the same time line as the better-known Selma to Montgomery March. And the pressure from these two major civil rights demonstrations combined to force President Johnson and the US Congress to take decisive action against widespread voter discrimination.

The MFDP's congressional challenge began on January 4, 1965, the opening day of the eighty-ninth session of the United States Congress. That day, temperatures in Washington, D.C. hovered around freezing. Congressional representatives buttoned their overcoats, grabbed their briefcases, and took the stairs down to the indoor tunnel connecting the Cannon House Office Building to the basement of the US Capitol. They chatted with their aides and colleagues as they descended the stairwell. Midway down, they sensed something was amiss. The usual in-session bustle from below had been replaced by silence. The sound of heels clicking against the cement floor was the only noise echoing up into the stairwell.

Once the representatives entered the tunnel, many instinctively averted their gaze. But avoiding the faces of black Mississippians who stared directly at them became increasingly difficult the further the representatives walked along the pathway. The people lining the tunnel were evenly spaced, one person on each side, every ten yards, their hands clasped behind their backs. The searing eyes of the black Mississippians standing against the tunnel's white-tiled walls confronted the congressional representatives on their way to the opening session. These MFDP supporters—farm workers, domestic laborers, and teachers—came to D.C. by the busloads. On that January morning, they held no signs and sang no songs; instead, they stood silently. Their statuesque presence made a notable impact on the representatives. "I looked into the legislators' faces as they passed," remembers protest organizer, Stokely Carmichael. "Most could not take their eyes off those careworn, tired black faces. Some offered a timid greeting, a smile, or tentative wave. Others flushed and looked down. All seemed startled. Some clearly nervous, even afraid. All seemed deeply affected in some way."

Obligation rose like a lump in the representatives' throats and responsibility began to press heavily upon their chests. One congressman recalled, "When I started into the tunnel, I knew I was going to vote to seat the white Mississippians. The farther I got, the more I weakened. Finally I had to say to myself, 'What kind of person are you?'" By the time this representative made it to the basement of the US Capitol Building, he informed House majority leader Carl Albert, "I'm not going with you on Mississippi. I can't vote against those people out there."

The MFDP's silent tunnel protest was not the representatives' first introduction to the 1965 congressional challenge. Throughout the fall of 1964, the challenge's front-women, Fannie Lou Hamer, Annie Devine, and Victoria Gray, had been working with longtime movement organizer, Ella Baker, SNCC-members Michael Thelwell and Jan Goodman, and the Washington-insider legal team of Arthur Kinoy and William Kunstler. The MFDP had set up a D.C. office, and Hamer, Devine, and Gray shared a small apartment in town so they could devote themselves to lobbying representatives.

"We were absolutely persona non grata and the pariahs of beltway politics," Thelwell recalled. The MFDP's uncompromising stance in Atlantic City burned their bridge to the liberal political establishment in D.C., so the MFDP sent Hamer on a seven state speaking tour to rebuild relationships with influential representatives. Within states like New York, Illinois, and Wisconsin, Hamer visited districts represented by members of Congress whom the MFDP felt they had a fighting chance to enlist in their challenge. By building support among those representatives' constituents, Hamer eventually garnered the interest of the representatives themselves.

Meanwhile, the MFDP's legal team visited the new congressional representatives' orientation to describe the challenge in detail. As they explained to the incoming congressmen and women, the MFDP's congressional challenge began when the Democratic Party's candidates, who ostensibly lost in the spring 1964 primaries, attempted to run again as Independents in Mississippi's general election. But a Mississippi law stipulated that if a candidate ran and lost in the primary, that candidate could not then run again in the general election. As a result, MFDP candidates (including Hamer, Gray, Devine, Aaron Henry, and Harold Ruby) were barred from running. The MFDP suspected, however, that if black people had been free to register and vote in Mississippi, then their party's candidates would have won the initial primaries. To prove this, the Council of Federated Organizations (COFO) orchestrated another Freedom Vote mock election. This election was a three-day event that ran from October 31-November 2, 1964. Unlike the official fall elections in Mississippi, COFO's election was open to all, and registration and voting were made easy with polling places set up in churches, pool halls, local stores, and community centers. Given the lack of intimidation and the widespread accessibility of this mock election, the results differed markedly from the state's official primaries. In COFO's mock election, for instance, Hamer received 33,009 votes to Whitten's 59—a stark contrast to the primary held in the spring of 1964 when Whitten appeared to beat Hamer handily—35,218 to 621 votes. Just as its 1963 mock election had demonstrated, COFO's 1964 mock election revealed that black people in Mississippi were eager to vote and that when they were allowed to vote, the election results were considerably different.

Motivated by the outcome of the mock election, the MFDP officially launched its congressional challenge. This challenge was spearheaded by Hamer, Devine, and Gray; Ruby and Henry, bowing to political pressure, had withdrawn their support. The crux of the MFDP's congressional challenge was that rampant voter discrimination in Mississippi invalidated the results of the 1964 congressional elections. Hamer, Gray, and Devine were barred from running against Jamie Whitten, Thomas G. Abernathy, and William Colmer, respectively (Ruby had also been barred from running against John Bell Williams, and Henry prohibited from opposing Prentiss Walker). The MFDP reasoned further that even if their candidates had been permitted to run as Independents in the general election, widespread voter discrimination would have kept black people from the polls and from electing candidates who represented their interests. Not only did such voter discrimination violate the Fourteenth and Fifteenth Amendments to the US Constitution, but voter suppression in Mississippi also defied the Compact of 1870. The Compact of 1870 was the agreement by which Mississippi was readmitted into the Union, and it specified, as a condition of the state's re-admission, that Mississippi could not bar or intimidate black people from voting. Given these violations, argued the MFDP, the elections were fraudulent, the five Mississippi congressmen should be unseated, and new federally protected elections should ensue. Throughout the fall of 1964, the MFDP sought support for their challenge among a largely unsympathetic Congress; in the beginning, they even had difficulty finding a representative willing to bring their challenge to the floor of the House.

While the MFDP supporters lined the Capitol tunnel pathway, Hamer, Devine, and Gray, accompanied by their lawyers, attempted to enter the floor of the House of Representatives.

"You may not enter here," Carl Schamp, the Chief of the Capitol Police, said. He was flanked by a dozen additional Capitol policemen who formed a human barricade.

"But we are attempting to enter as contestants," Gray said.

Hamer brandished the affidavit, drafted by the MFDP's legal team, indicating that she, Gray, and Devine had come to officially challenge the Mississippi representatives' seats.

"I see that," Schamp said, acknowledging the document, "but you cannot come on the floor of the House. You do not have floor privileges."

Before Schamp could finish his explanation, Hamer gasped and pointed behind the row of officers, all of whom turned swiftly in the direction of the chamber—hands on holsters.

"*I'se de Mississippi delegation,*" mocked a tall white man in a stovepipe hat with a long black monkey tail and a blackened face. The man danced around the chamber in a minstrel performance, eliciting raucous laughter from some representatives and looks of dismay from others. Three Capitol policemen broke the barricade they had created to keep Gray, Devine, and Hamer out of the chamber and apprehended the man, who was later identified as a member of the Neo-Nazi Party.

Hamer, Gray, and Devine narrowed their eyes, glaring at the scene. "They didn't see him because they was watching us," Hamer said, shaking her head.

The three women turned away from the Neo-Nazi, who smiled menacingly, lit cigar dangling from his lips as the Capitol Police escorted him out of the House chamber. Hamer locked arms with her fellow challengers and together they ascended the marble staircase. They made their way onto the balcony, where an eager group of MFDP supporters had gathered to witness this historic challenge. By the time Gray, Hamer, and Devine were settled in their seats, Speaker John McCormack was pounding his gavel and calling the session to order. The swearing-in process was about to begin. Hamer held her breath.

"Mr. Speaker," came the voice of Congressman William Fitts Ryan. McCormack proceeded, undeterred. "Mr. Speaker," Ryan, repeated this time more loudly, successfully gaining McCormack's attention on his second try. "I object to the oath being administered to the gentlemen from Mississippi," he said. "My objection to the seating of Jamie Whitten, John Bell Williams, Thomas G. Abernathy, Prentiss Walker, and William Colmer is based on facts and statements about civil rights abuses, which I consider to be reliable."

Hamer exhaled and exchanged relieved glances with Devine and Gray. Ryan, a third-term Democrat from Manhattan's Upper West Side, hadn't been their first choice to bring the challenge before the House. MFDP lawyers Kinoy and Kunstler worried that Ryan was unpredictable, but few other representatives were willing to take this controversial stand, so they went with Ryan. And, as he addressed the House now, a wave of support washed across the chamber. Over seventy other congressional representatives stood in a demonstration of solidarity with the MFDP and in support of Ryan's objection to seating the Mississippi congressmen. The representatives from Mississippi, who just moments before had been pointing and laughing at the Neo-Nazi as he mocked the MFDP challengers, now seemed humiliated themselves. Their cheeks flushed as they witnessed their colleagues' judgment.

Speaker McCormack asked Representatives Whitten, Williams, Abernathy, Walker, and Colmer to temporarily step aside while the oath was administered and Congressman Ryan's objection to their seating was debated.

The MFDP members in the balcony could not help but smile as they watched the disgraced men hastily gather their belongings and vacate their congressional seats. Following the oath, which was administered to all but the five congressmen sent from Mississippi, arguments in favor and opposed to the MFDP challenge were considered. At issue on this opening day, was whether or not the Mississippi representatives should be seated and sworn-in while the full details of the MFDP challenge were considered. As deliberation began to wane, Oregon representative Edith Green initiated a roll call vote. 276 representatives went on the record, voting in favor of seating the men from Mississippi, and 149 representatives officially opposed the legitimating act of administering the oath to them.

"We did it," whispered Gray, clutching the hands of Hamer and Devine. "Even if just for *this* moment, we did it!" Because over a third of the representatives opposed seating the Congressmen sent from Mississippi, the MFDP's challenge moved to the House Subcommittee on Elections. Each side was given forty days to gather evidence in support their position. The MFDP's extensive lobbying efforts had, indeed, paid off. But because the MFDP's challenge did not receive a majority of votes, the representatives from Mississippi were allowed to retain their seats while the challenge was considered.

To gather the necessary evidence for their hearing, the MFDP recruited nearly 100 lawyers to travel the state of Mississippi taking depositions. This group, which became known as the "Legal Peace Corps," interviewed more than 600 black Mississippians who had been barred from registering or voting in the 1964 elections. The lawyers were also given federal authority to subpoena Mississippi election officials and state leaders who had expressly carried out or otherwise permitted the alleged discrimination. The Legal Peace Corps put the white supremacist power structure of Mississippi on the defensive, deposing the state's former governor, the present secretary of state, and the attorney general. The MFDP compiled their findings into 3,000 single-spaced pages of testimony and submitted that document to House Speaker McCormack. A subcommittee hearing was set for September 1965.

While the Legal Peace Corps, led by MFDP lawyers Kinoy and Kunstler, continued to compile evidence for the hearing, veteran organizer Ella Baker led Hamer, Gray, and Devine in further lobbying efforts. Enlisting the representatives' support for a floor-wide debate over what became known as the "Fairness Resolution" was no easy task. Opposition to the MFDP's congressional challenge now came from all corners. The most ardent opponents were representatives from southern states. Some southern representatives flatly denied that voter discrimination existed. Others acknowledged the discrimination that was painstakingly cited in the MFDP's 3,000-page report, but insisted that the five congressmen from Mississippi played no direct role in the specific acts of voter discrimination cited by the MFDP. Perhaps most persuasive was the slippery slope argument that the southern representatives popularized— warning that if the Mississippi congressmen were unseated, activists in other states would be motivated to bring similar challenges, creating sheer chaos in the House of Representatives.

Truth be told, the MFDP did little to allay fears of congressional upheaval. When interviewed about the challenge, Hamer suggested that its very significance was the precedent it set. "I think this is very important because if we have success with this challenge," she reasoned, "it won't only bring a change in Mississippi, but it will bring a change all across the South. And they'll get the message and I think they'll begin to let the people register and let them vote, and give them a chance to have a voice in the government."

President Lyndon B. Johnson offered the MFDP a compromise. MFDP chairman Lawrence Guyot remembered the president saying, "Look, if you just go after John Bell Williams, I will do everything I can from the White House to help you get the congressional votes to unseat him." Guyot took President Johnson's proposal to the MFDP Executive Committee, but they agreed with Hamer's view of the important precedent their challenge would set. They refused Johnson's offer. "Our position is that we understand that we're fighting to establish a precedent that could be applied throughout the South," MFDP leadership insisted. "If we win the challenge in Mississippi, we carry other states."

The precedent of unseating congressional representatives from districts with a demonstrated track record of voter discrimination would have fundamentally reconfigured American politics. And perhaps that was precisely the MFDP's purpose. The prospect of impending chaos, however, fed conspiracy theories that linked civil rights activists to alleged communist plots to undermine the US government during the Cold War. Such theories were not just expounded by extremist organizations; linking civil rights activism and communism justified state sponsorship of both Mississippi's Sovereignty Commission and the FBI's counter intelligence program (COINTELPRO).

Opposition to the MFDP's 1965 congressional challenge even came from those organizations ostensibly allied with the cause of civil rights. At issue among these more sympathetic organizations was a fundamental confusion surrounding what action the MFDP wanted Congress to take in response to their challenge. In their official correspondence, the MFDP explained that their challenge was geared toward unseating the representatives, invalidating the prior elections, and ordering a federal investigation that would result in re-elections. Through the optics of protest, however, it seemed that the MFDP was suggesting Hamer, Devine, and Gray literally be seated in the place of the illegally elected congressmen. This strategy would have extended the logic that the interracial MFDP delegation used when they demanded to be seated in place of the all-white "Regular" Party delegation at the 1964 DNC in Atlantic City. Certainly the image of Hamer, Devine, and Gray presenting their affidavit to the Capitol police chief as they requested to enter the floor of the House made it appear that they sought to replace the congressmen. Yet, in an interview just weeks before the official hearing, Hamer explained, "We didn't go there to be seated because we knew from the beginning that we wouldn't be seated, but we wanted to explain our side."

In light of this confusion, and perhaps because of the MFDP's refusal to compromise at the 1964 DNC in Atlantic City, national organizations wavered in their support of the 1965 congressional challenge. The National Council of Churches' (NCC) Commission on Religion and Race, for instance, issued an official statement in support of challenging the five prospective congressmen, but remarked that the appeal for Hamer, Devine, and Gray to replace the congressmen "clouds the clear issue of the legality of the present election system in that state." The NAACP was also in favor of getting "rid of the Mississippi Congressmen," but did not "endorse the method proposed by the MFDP." The Americans for Democratic Action (ADA), led by the MFDP's former lead lawyer, Joseph Rauh, warned of the "dangerous implications" of such replacement, given that the women were "not elected in any regularly constituted state election." the *New York Times* went further and referred to the appeal for replacement as a "preposterous gesture." The NCC, NAACP, the ADA, and the *Times* all suggested that the MFDP's case for unseating the representatives had merit, but they firmly objected to the idea of seating the challengers in their place.

Beyond the obstacles the MFDP challengers faced from white supremacists, anti-communist conspiracy theorists, and allies confused about the finer points of their unprecedented protest, the 1965 congressional challenge also fought for relevance alongside the concurrent voter registration campaign in Selma, Alabama. SNCC, the organization working with local activists on the ground in Selma, fully supported the MFDP challenge, and Hamer remained on SNCC's staff as a voter registration worker and frequent fundraiser throughout 1965. The SCLC also supported the congressional challenge; Martin Luther King, Jr. personally sent a letter of endorsement to be read on the floor of the House during congressional deliberations.

Hamer, however, was not entirely supportive of the SNCC and SCLC efforts in Selma. Years later, Hamer cast her tepid support within the frame of America's limited attention economy. "Dr. King is dead now, and I wouldn't want no strikes against him. But one of the things that diverted the attention from the challenge was his march, from Selma to Montgomery," Hamer told an interviewer. She recalled being in "the middle of the congressional challenge, drumming up all of this support," and King "turned their attention away." It's unclear from the interview during which Hamer made this statement whether she is referring here to the way King turned the media's attention away or to how he diverted the attention of the representatives themselves, but both were true at the time. And in the years that have passed since 1965, public memory continues to privilege the Selma voting rights campaign to the 1965 MFDP congressional challenge.

Why has the congressional challenge fallen away from the popular narrative of civil rights progress? MFDP member Dorie Ladner surmised that because their challenge "went straight to the heart of the government," popular commemorations of the civil rights movement refuse to include it. "They don't mind showing the horses that's going over John Lewis and others in Selma," Ladner reasoned, "but they don't show you going straight and asking for those seats. They would never show that." As a result of this erasure, which foregrounds nonviolent social protest and obscures radical confrontational politics, the 1965 Voting Rights Act is a victory attributed primarily to the Selma campaign. This version of political history not only overlooks the pressure that the MFDP placed on President Johnson and the US Congress, it also discounts the pivotal role that Hamer played at the 1964 DNC in Atlantic City.

The Reverend Jesse Jackson, Sr. worked to reclaim Hamer's centrality to the well-worn story of how the Voting Rights Act came to be. "If we just had the 1964 Public Accommodations Act and didn't have the right to vote, we still would be nowhere," he explained. "The absence of barbarism is not the presence of franchise. Hamer fought for the franchise. And the liberal democrats didn't want to grant it. Many liberal civil rights leaders even went along with the deal at the convention, but she wouldn't." Jackson argued that Hamer's "uncompromising stance" in Atlantic City was what "laid the groundwork for Selma."

Ironically, Selma's success was then used to undermine the MFDP's congressional challenge. Once President Johnson signed the Voting Rights Act into law on August 6, 1965, congressional representatives, supposed liberal allies on the Hill, and civil rights organizations across the country, pointed to that legislation as protection against the well-documented discriminatory acts of voter suppression upon which the MFDP had built their case. Hamer, however, was not satisfied with the promise of future protection. "This voting bill that the President passed last week it doesn't mean anything," she remarked. "I'm not looking for a voting bill in 1965 when they're not enforcing our voting rights with the Fifteenth Amendment." Hamer knew firsthand that rights on paper did not translate to rights in practice for black people in Mississippi. Hamer was seeking more than protection against future voting rights violations; she was demanding official recognition of past injustices. So even after President Johnson signed the Voting Rights Act into law, Hamer pushed forward with the MFDP challenge—taking her grievances back to the US Capitol for a formal hearing before the House Subcommittee on Elections.

On September 13, 1965, Hamer, Devine, and Gray were once again met by the Capitol Police, whom Hamer recalled treated them "as though we was carrying a bomb or something." After the three women showed their identification cards and their belongings were thoroughly searched, they were allowed into a small room on the third floor of the House. The door closed behind them and police stood guard. Hamer's nationally televised testimony before the credentials committee at the DNC a year earlier had left no question about her ability to stir the nation's conscience, so the media were barred from entering this hearing. In this enclosed space, Hamer, Devine, and Gray sat across from the congressmen they were challenging. Flanked by their legal team, the

MFDP leaders testified before a twenty-four person subcommittee, chaired by Robert T. Ashmore, a Democrat from South Carolina. Although the media were barred from recording the testimonies, the entire hearing was read into the congressional record. The transcript indicates that the MFDP held fast to their arguments about the specific ways in which voter discrimination violated constitutional principles, as well as the Compact of 1870, and thereby invalidated the election of the congressmen from Mississippi. The MFDP argued pointedly that the congressmen should be suspended while further investigation and potential re-elections occurred.

In her testimony, Hamer gestured subtly to the more radical layer of the congressional challenge. "You gentlemen should know that the Negroes make up 58 percent of the potential voters of the Second Congressional District," she told the subcommittee. "This means that if Negroes were allowed to vote freely, I could be sitting up here with you right now as a congresswoman."

William Colmer, dean of the Mississippi House delegation, represented the five congressmen from Mississippi. The congressmen's response emphasized the unofficial and illegitimate nature of the challengers' mock election. Suggesting that the Freedom Vote was "held without any sanction of law" and simply used to "dramatize injustice," Colmer's strategy for responding to the MFDP's 3,000 pages of legally documented injustices included suggesting that the five congressmen, specifically, did not play any direct role in the discrimination cited. Therefore, reasoned Colmer, they should not be held accountable for its effects.

Remarking on Colmer's rebuttal, Hamer later told CBS that "the congressmen from Mississippi couldn't even prove to theyselves that they was telling the truth!"

Without truth on their side, they appealed to fear. In response to the MFDP's allegation that the widespread voter discrimination in Mississippi violated the Compact of 1870, the challenged congressmen reminded the Subcommittee on Elections that all of the Confederate States were readmitted to the Union under similar provisions. Unseating the representatives sent from Mississippi would set a dangerous precedent, they contended, encouraging challenges waged on behalf of black people living in all seven Deep South states. This final argument, which became known throughout the beltway as the impending "Dixie Rebellion on Capitol Hill," was the most persuasive.

"We won't say that you Negroes are not right," Hamer remembered the committee members conceding behind closed doors, "but if you get away with this type of challenge, they will be doing it all over the South." Ultimately, the subcommittee voted against unseating the Mississippi congressmen by a 19–5 margin.

Hamer burst from the small room and spoke directly to the media waiting in the hallway. "You know, the congressmen said they represented the people of Mississippi. And 42 percent of the people we know, as well as they know, can't register and vote!" She distilled the complexity of this months-long protest into that straightforward truth. "And that's why I had to tell the congressmen there, and the chairman, and the committees that it's now time for America to wake up!"

Four days later, on September 17, 1965, the question of whether to dismiss the MFDP challenge or keep debating was brought before the House. Representatives were surprised to see three black women seated on the floor of the Congress that morning. Speaker McCormack had invited Fannie Lou Hamer, Annie Devine, and Victoria Gray to watch the debate unfold from within the chamber, which made these three women the first black women in United States history to be seated on the floor of the US Congress and the first black people from Mississippi to be seated in the House since Reconstruction. In the midst of this historical moment, 143 members voted to continue deliberating about their challenge. The 228 representatives who favored dismissing the MFDP's congressional challenge, however, were victorious.

With that floor vote, the MFDP had ostensibly lost another attempt to compel America to live up to its democratic values, to enact its own laws, and to protect its own citizens. But the MFDP had succeeded in placing Mississippi's white supremacist power structure on guard. "It shook them," remembered lead challenger, Victoria Gray. "It really shook them. That vote just really turned things upside down."

Just as important, Hamer, Gray, and Devine's challenge inspired people who had been intimidated for centuries. "That trio of women was just *awesome*," MFDP supporter, Dr. L. C. Dorsey recalled. "They represented all of us with our weaknesses, our strength, our future, our hope for the future of our children, and generations gone and generations to come."

The sun was setting as the old battered car that SNCC field secretaries shared turned down East Lafayette Street in Ruleville's black quarter. On this late September evening in 1965, the car carried Mrs. Hamer home from the airport after yet another national defeat. Looking out the car's dusty window, she could see her home. Outside her front door a line of people, wrapped around her front porch and stretched out to the formidable pecan tree. Hamer sighed heavily. She knew this was no hero's welcome. She hadn't made it home much during the congressional challenge. Between lobbying representatives for support in Washington and raising funds through national trips across the country, Hamer's time was strained as her health. When she did return home, it was never to rest because this was the scene that commonly greeted her: neighbors

Figure 4.1 Fannie Lou Hamer, Victoria Gray (Adams), and Annie Devine challenged the all-white congressional delegation sent from Mississippi to the United States House of Representatives in 1965. Getty Images, photo credit: Bettman.

in desperate financial need, local organizations eager for advice, and reports of tensions brewing between and among the remaining civil rights groups in Mississippi.

As Hamer ambled toward the front door, she offered those who had likely waited all afternoon a weary smile. She searched the crowd for her eldest daughter, Dorothy Jean. When Hamer returned home last April, Dorothy had hid behind Pap. Hamer had pulled Dorothy toward her for a warm embrace and stopped suddenly at the sight of her swollen belly. A flood of emotion washed over Hamer during that unforgettable April afternoon; she loved children dearly and was quite eager to become a grandmother, but Dorothy had been a sickly child and was not a healthy young woman. Could her body bear this pregnancy? Where would they live? How would she provide for the baby? Hamer blamed herself, as she wrote to her confidante, Rose Fishman, "Rose, my daughter that's 21 is going to be a mother. I can't say anything, but do all I can for her because I be away from my family so much."

But in that charged moment of revelation, Hamer didn't give voice to her worries. She simply pulled her eldest daughter close and relished the details that Dorothy shared about the baby's due date—early November—and the

Figure 4.2 Fannie Lou Hamer with Rose Fishman, a woman Hamer referred to as her "mother" and "one of the greatest friends I ever had," circa 1965. Photo courtesy of Larry Fishman.

baby's father, Sylvester Hall. Hamer had little time to dote on Dorothy during that trip in April of 1965, however. Among the people who lined her front yard on that return visit were members of the MFDP's Legal Peace Corps. To Hamer's surprise, the lawyers weren't there to talk with her about the congressional challenge. They had another route to securing political representation for black Mississippians in mind, and they requested Hamer's support.

In 1963, just months after Hamer and eighteen other Ruleville registration hopefuls had failed their registration exams administered by Sunflower County registrar Cecil Campbell, the Justice Department filed suit against Campbell for a pattern of routinely turning away black citizens. By April of 1965, the Justice Department's case, *US v. Campbell,* had worked its way to the high court that Federal Judge Claude Clayton oversaw. Clayton ordered Campbell to make it "no harder for blacks to register than it was for whites." The MFDP's legal team wanted to seize on this historic ruling by urging Judge Clayton to postpone the upcoming municipal elections in Sunflower County. This way, black citizens would have a chance to benefit from the court-ordered equality in registration practices. The Legal Peace Corps had come to Hamer's home to ask if she would be the named litigant in this motion to postpone elections. Without hesitation, Hamer agreed to the lawyers' request and *Hamer v. Campbell* was filed on April 23, 1965.

When Hamer returned to Ruleville in early June, her family time was cut short once more. On this visit, members of the newly formed Mississippi Freedom Labor Union (MFLU) requested her support. Moved by the personal testimony she shared across the Delta region and on national television, a group of black farmworkers in the Delta organized to demand a living wage. The MFLU, in partnership with SNCC, the MFDP, the Delta Ministry, and the Council of Churches, organized the first agricultural strike in the Mississippi Delta's abundant farm country since the 1930s.

Founded in January of 1965, the MFLU's first major stand took place in the small town of Shaw, just twenty miles to the west of Ruleville. The Shaw day-laborers had walked off of the fields, demanding $1.25 an hour and an eight-hour work day. By June, the MFLU had expanded further south to A. L. Andrews' 1,300 acre plantation in Leland, Mississippi. On Andrews' plantation, twelve families—eighty people in total, including skilled mechanics, tractor operators, as well as field workers—staged a walk out. The strikers railed against the six dollars that Andrews paid skilled workers for ten-hour days and they also objected to the three dollars paid to field hands and to the fact that neither group received pay for days missed due to bad weather or illness. The Andrews' plantation walk-out spurred several other strikes on adjacent farms and the MFLU built upon this momentum, planning rallies in eight additional agriculturally rich counties across the state. On Mrs. Hamer June trip home, therefore, the union's leadership sought advice, inspiration, and the national publicity her endorsement would engender.

As her own family struggled to make ends meet, the cause of economic justice remained close to Hamer's heart. She agreed to support the fledgling MFLU. Hamer visited striking workers, who stayed at Delta Ministry Shelters after being evicted from plantations for refusing to work. She delivered stirring speeches to the strikers, which caught the attention of newspapers from the *Delta Democrat-Times* to the *New York Times*. In one speech, of which only excerpts quoted in the *Times'* coverage remain, Hamer reportedly "exhorted the strikers to stand firm" and lambasted those who were not supporting MFLU efforts. Specifically, Hamer called out the "bourgeoisie Negroes" and "chicken-eating preachers," which was a frequent insult she lobbed against religious leaders who were well-taken care of by their congregations, but did little to advocate on behalf of their parishioners. Just as she'd threatened Aaron Henry with violent retaliation should he sell out the MFDP by taking the compromise President Johnson offered at the 1964 DNC, Hamer advised the strikers to threaten the "nervous Nellies and the Toms"—those black workers who allied themselves with white landowners and worked on the plantations in the striking workers' absence. "I don't believe in killing," Hamer instructed the striking Deltans, "but a good whipping behind the bushes wouldn't hurt them."

Unfortunately, the MFLU's efforts were undermined by day-laborers who crossed picket lines, by economically secure black people who refused to support this historic uprising among the laboring class, and by the massive restructuring of the Mississippi Delta's economy. Between 1950 and 1960, as Hamer biographer Chana Kai Lee reported, 50 percent of the jobs in Sunflower County were lost to advances in farming. As the use of cost-effective chemical weed killers and mechanical pickers became more widespread across the region, the need for human labor shrank considerably. By the time Hamer returned to Ruleville in the fall of 1965, in fact, she wrote to Rose Fishman, "I don't know what will happen next. All the workers are gone from this area [;] they are in other places in the state but not here in Ruleville." In this dire economic climate, the MFLU had all but abandoned their prospects of negotiating with white landowners and instead sought Hamer's expertise regarding appeals to the federal government for assistance in the form of relocation and retraining programs for the displaced workers.

Upon her return to Ruleville that late September evening, however, Hamer spotted Dorothy through the crowd and went straight to her. Unlike the sprightly Vergie, who came running to her mother the moment she exited SNCC's dilapidated vehicle, Dorothy remained seated on the front porch chair. Her large stomach, protruding from her otherwise wispy frame, covered her lap. Hamer choked back tears as she witnessed the toll this pregnancy had taken on young Dorothy. Her skin was dry, her eyes sunken and rimmed with dark circles, and she was unsteady on her feet, too—dizzy, as she rose to embrace her mother.

Yet, the crowd refused to dissipate.

Hamer sighed once more. After she gently settled Dorothy back in her chair, Hamer reached into her purse for her pocketbook. She averted Perry Hamer's disapproving glare and returned to the front lawn, listening as her neighbors described their pressing needs and doling out what support she could provide. When the little money that the MFDP insisted Hamer take for her extensive work on the challenge ran out, the crowd finally cleared.

October of 1965 was a particularly challenging month in the Hamer household. Shortly after Fannie Lou returned home from the congressional challenge, Perry Hamer was hospitalized for two weeks with a slipped and compressed disc. While he was in the hospital, Fannie Lou took over caring for their daughters—devoting special attention to Dorothy, who was in her final month of pregnancy. "She has been a wonderful child, so I'll stand by her now," Hamer penned to Fishman, asking her friend from Massachusetts to send "any used baby clothes" she could find.

Hamer confessed to Rose that throughout all of this—her husband's hospitalization and Dorothy's high risk pregnancy, not to mention Vergie just entering her teen years—Hamer herself had also "been very sick." To make matters worse, Hamer's national notoriety not only drew the attention of those seeking assistance for local causes, it also continued to draw the ire of white supremacists. Hamer described the late-night phone calls she received, people calling her names and threatening to blow up her home. She told Fishman that while Perry Hamer was in the hospital, cars driven by leering white people, "stopped in front of their house."

No doubt Hamer privately confided about her own ailments and the harassment she endured to Fishman because she was tired, sick, and scared; she sought comfort from a dear friend. And yet, publicly Hamer conveyed a fearlessness when describing her strategy for dealing with harassment. "I keep a shotgun in every corner of my bedroom and the first cracker even look like he wants to throw some dynamite on my porch won't write his mama again," she explained in her autobiography.

"One night somebody come calling up," she recalled.

"We're coming by tonight," the caller said.

To which Hamer responded, " 'Come on. I'll be waiting for you.' Guess you know that cracker ain't showed up yet. White folks may act like they're crazy, but they ain't that crazy. Ain't no man going to bother you if he know you going to kill him," she boldly reasoned.

By the end of the harrowing month of October, however, the Hamers had cause to celebrate. Dorothy's baby, Lenora Aretha, came early. She arrived on October 29, 1965—just weeks after Hamer marked her own forty-eighth birthday. Fannie Lou devoted herself to caring for Dorothy and baby Lenora full time. Dorothy's lifelong battle with anemia had intensified during her pregnancy and this iron deficiency also led to complications during childbirth. An already weakened Dorothy hemorrhaged following Lenora's delivery. To regain her strength, Dorothy required more iron-rich foods and supplements than were available to the cash-strapped Hamers in the economically destitute Delta, where health care for black people remained woefully inferior to the care available to their white neighbors. Recovery was, therefore, slow, incomplete, and heartbreaking for Hamer to witness.

The heart-wrenching experience of caring for Dorothy with limited resources impressed upon Hamer the interconnection between her personal struggles and her political work. As she would commonly explain to her neighbors, there's "no need of running around saying, 'Honey, I'm not going to get in the mess,' because if you were born in America with a black face, you were born in the mess." Political activism was the way out of the mess, as Hamer understood it. Further countering black Deltans reluctance to become involved with politics, Hamer would exclaim: "What we eat is politics!" Reasoning that whether or not one became active in determining the course of social and political change, all were swept along in its current.

By March of 1966, Lenora was nearly five months old, Dorothy, who had become pregnant again in January of 1966, was now several months into her second pregnancy, and the MFDP was celebrating a rare political victory. Less than a year after Federal Judge Claude Clayton denied the MFDP's request to postpone municipal elections, the motion filed under *Hamer v. Campbell*, a federal appeals court overturned Judge Clayton's opinion and ordered reelections. This reversal was indeed historic, marking the first time a federal appeals court had thrown out an election because black citizens did not have a fair opportunity to participate. Nevertheless, the US Court of Appeals clarified that the decision did not necessarily set a precedent for throwing out elections all over the South. In the particular case of *Hamer v. Campbell*, the appellants had tried to delay the election, which proceeded with approximately 80 percent of the white residents of Sunflower County registered and less than 10 percent of the county's black citizens on the rolls. On the basis of this marked suppression and because the appellants had filed a motion to delay the election, these specific results were invalidated. What's more, the circuit court ordered Clayton to set a date for reelections in the communities affected by his initial decision to permit the elections. The State of Mississippi appealed the Circuit Court's reversal, but the US Supreme Court ultimately denied their appeal and reelections in the small Sunflower County towns of Moorhead and Sunflower were scheduled for May 2, 1967.

Wasting no time, the MFDP reached out to national figures like Martin Luther King, Jr., Harry Belafonte, A. Philip Randolph, Franklin D. Roosevelt, Jr., Eugene McCarthy, and William Fitts Ryan. Together, Mississippi activists and their influential allies drawn from across the country formed the National Committee for Free Elections in Sunflower County, Mississippi. This organization would help raise national awareness and funds for the historic reelection campaigns, and they wanted Hamer to headline the Committee for Free Elections' fundraising effort.

As she considered another round of national travel, Hamer felt deeply divided. Hamer relished her time with Lenora and she was gravely concerned about the toll another pregnancy would take on Dorothy's already weakened body. More than the financial necessity of her work, more than even the pull of a career she enjoyed and excelled at, however, Hamer saw political activism as her family's and her community's most promising bulwark against the high tide of white supremacy. Hamer understood her unique speaking and song-leading abilities as God-given gifts to be used to carry out his will on earth. As Hamer declared to Fishman, "I'm going to do all I can for [Dorothy] and the Baby if it's the Lord will." Within the same letter, however, Hamer shared that, "We lost the challenge [;] it was dismissed. That just show how much hard work we have to do."

As Hamer was wont to do, she prayed to discern the Lord's will—was she called to stay at home caring for Vergie, Dorothy, and Lenora or should she return to movement work, which was itself a form of familial and community care? By the summer of 1966, Hamer had her answer. She was filled with the conviction expressed in an old spiritual, which she would soon adapt to present circumstances and share with civil rights movement activists. In June, Hamer led a large group of activists, gathered from across the country to participate in the 1966 Meredith March Against Fear, in song:

> *I'm going to do what the Spirit say do*
> *I'm going to do what the Spirit say do*
> *Now when the Spirit say do, we going to do, oh Lord*
> *We going to do what the Spirit said do*
> *We going to march when the Spirit said march.*
> *We going to march when the Spirit said march.*
> *Now when the Spirit said march we going to march, oh Lord.*
> *We going to march when the Spirit said march.*

· 5 ·

"Nobody's Free Until Everybody's Free"

Sunday June 8, 1966, was a balmy day in northern Mississippi. Temperatures reached into the nineties as James H. Meredith, the thirty-two-year-old Air Force Veteran and Columbia University law student, marched down Highway 51. Meredith clutched a Bible in his right hand and rested his left palm on an African walking stick. By the afternoon, Meredith was drained not only from the heat and the steady pace he kept, but also from onlookers' disdainful taunts. There were cheers of support, too, and he listened hard for those good sounds. As the first black person to integrate the University of Mississippi four years prior, Meredith was no stranger to controversy. The 1962 demonstrations that his integration of Ole Miss incited devolved into deadly riots that spilled out of the campus and flooded the city of Oxford. In the fall of 1962, President John F. Kennedy called on the National Guard to restore order and enforce Meredith's constitutional rights. But on this sweltering June afternoon, only a few local policemen dotted the crowd. Meredith had pledged to march from the Peabody Hotel in Memphis, Tennessee, through the Delta and end at the Capitol Building in Jackson, Mississippi. Reporters and photographers trailed Meredith along the route he dubbed a "Walk Against Fear." His goal was to "challenge the all-pervasive overriding fear" that still kept black Mississippians from exercising their constitutional rights. "I was fighting for full citizenship for me and my kind," Meredith remembered.

On that June afternoon, James Aubrey Norvell was crouched in the bushes and drenched with sweat. The weight of his rifle bore down on his shoulder. Norvell, a white out-of-work hardware clerk, was angry. He had not anticipated all the people gathered around Meredith; they were blocking his shot.

"I just want James Meredith!" Norvell shouted as he charged toward his target.

Meredith's Bible soared into the air and crashed onto the pavement. The clatter Meredith's walking stick made as it hit the ground was drowned out by the sound of buckshot blasts. Three rounds of buckshot shells blasted in Meredith's direction, riddling his head, neck, and upper legs with pellets. He collapsed instantly. The stunned onlookers took cover, some shielding themselves behind parked cars, others leaping into the bushes. Local law enforcement officials apprehended Norvell at the scene, his rifle still smoking. Meanwhile, Meredith lay alone, writhing on the pavement.

"Isn't anyone going to help me?" he cried.

A few clergy from the crowd rushed toward Meredith, praying with him as they waited for an ambulance to arrive. That ambulance carried Meredith back the way he had come, out of Mississippi and back into Tennessee, in search of a hospital that would treat a black freedom movement activist.

Within hours, Martin Luther King, Jr. of the Southern Christian Leadership Conference (SCLC), Roy Wilkins of the National Association for the Advancement of Colored People (NAACP), Stokely Carmichael, the newly-elected chair of the Student Nonviolent Coordinating Committee (SNCC), Whitney Young of the Urban League, and Floyd McKissick of the Congress of Racial Equality (CORE), arrived at Meredith's bedside. Once they learned that Meredith's injuries were not fatal, these black freedom movement leaders sought his blessing to continue the march. Meredith granted it.

Under the banner of COFO—the Council of Federated Organizations—these organizations had once collaborated on voter registration projects in Mississippi. But much had changed since the early 1960s. By the summer of 1966, political and ideological divisions among the groups seemed insurmountable. The men convened at Memphis's Lorraine Motel to strategize about what became known as the "Meredith March." Several key points of tension between the organizations kept the male leaders deliberating well into the night. Carmichael proposed a local focus for the march, during which marchers would encourage voter registration and provide a platform for local leaders. He also insisted that the Louisiana-based Deacons for Defense provide security. CORE's McKissick supported Carmichael's suggestions, but Young of the Urban League and Wilkins of the NAACP envisioned instead a national march that would draw white liberal allies and focus federal attention on the injustices that remained in Mississippi. They wanted to demonstrate that the 1964 Civil Rights Act and 1965 Voting Rights Act were not enforced in the state. Young and Wilkins also opposed enlisting the Deacons' participation, arguing that the presence of an organized group of armed black men would undermine what should be a nonviolent march. They also suspected that Carmichael's insistence on a locally focused march was a subterfuge for the exclusion of white people. Since much of Wilkins' and Young's financial and political support hinged on the multiracial nonviolent values that their organizations espoused, they refused to compromise and withdrew their support before the Meredith March began. Carmichael remembered that King had played the role of neutral mediator throughout the negotiations, but ultimately he pledged his support to Carmichael's vision of a locally focused march, protected by the Deacons.

As the SCLC, SNCC, and CORE took the lead in planning what would become the largest march in Mississippi's civil rights history and the last major inter-organizational march of the civil rights movement, Carmichael knew what mattered most: "We should do voter registration in every town with a courthouse. Urge local leaders to run for office. The local communities should be the entire focus. Local leaders should speak on every platform." And so, without a moment's hesitation, they called upon Fannie Lou Hamer.

During the summer of 1966, Hamer was working to secure Office of Economic Opportunity (OEO) funding for Head Start Centers across the state. She was a key spokesperson for the Committee for Free Elections in Sunflower County. And her own home was bustling with activity. Perry Hamer began driving a school bus for a local Head Start Center. With his steady income and financial contributions from northern supporters, the Hamers were able to purchase a larger home. They desperately needed the extra space. Dorothy Jean married Sylvester Hall, baby Lenora's father, in the spring of 1966. Their growing family now resided with Perry, Fannie Lou, and Vergie Ree—all living together in the small home on Lafayette Street that SNCC had helped the Hamers acquire back in 1963.

At age twelve, Vergie Ree had recently integrated the local middle school and was straining against the near-constant harassment not only of her peers, but also of administration officials who accused her of lying, cheating, and failing to meet grade standards—all in an effort, Hamer believed, to push her daughter out of what was previously an all-white school. Dorothy was reportedly doing "fine," months into her second pregnancy. Hamer's friend and confidante, Rose Fishman, sent Dorothy maternity clothes. In a letter dated April 11, 1966, Hamer wrote to thank her: "You should see Dorothy in some of those clothes! I told her the baby is almost as big as she is, just not as tall!" Dorothy's first-born, Lenora Aretha, had quickly become the Hamers' pride and joy. In a letter dated June 25, 1966, Fannie Lou gushed about the nine month old: "Rose, you should see this Baby . . . She is the most beautiful child. She is so friendly to anyone, she can pat-a-cake, try to dance. She is a short little fathead, look like a little doll. Rose, I love her so much."

In the same letter that Hamer gushed with grandparent adoration, Hamer also confessed, "All are ok, except me. Rose, I don't feel well at all." Three years after Hamer was assaulted in the Winona jail cell, the effects lingered. She wrote, "My kidneys are giving me trouble, and my head too." And, in the very next sentence, Hamer penned: "Rose, I have marched until my body and soul is tired. We taken up where James H. Meredith taken off."

Hamer's weariness showed. On June 12, 1966, Hamer donned a straw hat, a blue cotton dress, and comfortable shoes as she limped a row behind King, Stokely Carmichael, and Andrew Young. Together, they led the thick stream of marchers across the Delta. Hamer had been invited by the organizers to address the crowd set to gather at Enid Dam, about seventy miles northeast of Ruleville. Even in her worn state, Hamer pulled no punches during her address that afternoon. Hamer's experience in the Winona jail cell was likely top of mind not only because the physical pain plagued her as she marched in the mid-June heat, but also because the marchers would soon cross right through the city of Winona on their path to Jackson.

As Hamer looked out into the crowd—local black people, white support- ers drawn from across the country, reporters, and law enforcement agents—she explained why she had joined the march. "I'm on 51 Highway, not only because of James H. Meredith, but I'm on 51 Highway, because it was on 51 Highway where we was beaten and jailed by State Highway Patrolmen and beat till our body was hard as metal." Her strong, clear voice, rising above the crowd's murmur belied her weakened body yet again. She contrasted black Mississippian's motivation for marching with what Carmichael and McKissick feared would motivate out-of-state marchers. "You see, this march is some- thing deeper than people have any idea it is. So if you on this march to just march to Jackson, so the television can show your picture, you get off now. Because there's people's destiny is at stake in Mississippi." The crowd's chatter ceased.

The marchers shouted, "Talk! Talk!"

Hamer responded to their encouragement, filling her less than four- minute address with sweeping and incisive political analysis. Demonstrating the larger significance of the Meredith March, for instance, Hamer connected their protest to the resurgence of the Ku Klux Klan and to what she described as the hypocritical war in Vietnam. She pointed out that the war was backed by the two US senators from Mississippi, James O. Eastland and John C. Stennis. Hamer, an early critic of US involvement in Vietnam, clarified that she was "concerned about democracy, but she's sick of so much hypocrisy." She said, "It's ridiculous, for us to say that we are fighting for the rights of other peoples in other countries, to free these people, when we are enslaved in Mississippi!" To prove her point, she referenced Senator Eastland's exploitative plantation and described the recent midterm election during which poll watchers, secured by the 1965 Voting Rights Act, were thrown out of polling places by local police. In the absence of trained poll watchers, local policemen were entrusted with securing fair elections. "It was a State Highway Patrolman that had my body beat till it was hard as metal," Hamer reminded her audience. In light of these injustices, Hamer urged marchers to revise their route, to abandon the main Highway 51 thoroughfare and instead cut across Highway 49 W. She urged the crowd to march into the heart of the "Delta area and get some people registered. Because you don't march across Mississippi and leave people homeless, leave people hungry, leave people without food."

The marchers heeded Hamer's instruction, winding their way through the core of the Delta, inspiring the registration of sixty-nine black people in the region, and drawing the ire of local law enforcement officials along the way. The marchers attempted to set up camp on the grounds of Stone Street Elementary School in the Delta town of Greenwood. Three march organizers, including Carmichael, were arrested for trespassing. This arrest along the Meredith March marked the twenty-seventh time Carmichael, a twenty-four-year-old Howard University graduate, had been imprisoned during his activist career. Earlier in the decade, Carmichael spent time in Mississippi's notorious Parchman State Penitentiary for attempts to integrate public facilities. More recently, he suffered the brutal consequences of black voter registration work in Alabama, where the Lowndes County Freedom Organization adopted a Black Panther as its symbol and the phrase "Black Power for Black People" as its slogan. After his release from prison on June 16, 1966, Carmichael addressed the crowd of 1,500 marchers now gathered in Greenwood. The crowd in this SNCC-headquartered town was reportedly "explosive" as Carmichael rose to speak.

"We've been saying 'Freedom' for six years," Carmichael shouted. "And we ain't got nothing. What we going to start saying now is 'Black Power! Black Power! Black Power!'"

Willie Ricks, who worked alongside Carmichael as a SNCC field secretary in Lowndes County, joined him on the platform. Facing the crowd, Ricks shouted: "What do you want?"

"Black Power!" The crowd responded.

"What do you want?" Ricks asked again.

"Black Power!" the Greenwood crowd thundered.

From this pivotal moment forward, the press fixated upon Carmichael and the "Black Power" refrain, effectively whipping Mississippi's white supremacist power structure into a paranoid frenzy. By the time the Meredith March reached Canton, Mississippi—seventy-five miles south of Greenwood and just thirty-five miles north of their final Jackson destination—police descended upon the marchers, releasing tear gas, swinging their Billy clubs, and butting men, women, and children with the blunt end of their assault rifles. Likening the attack to Selma's Bloody Sunday, one reporter contended, "They were not arresting, they were punishing." Even in the face of this violent retaliation, or perhaps because of the injustice it presented, supporters clamored to join the last leg of the protest. By June 26, when the Meredith March Against Fear concluded at the Mississippi State Capitol in Jackson, Meredith himself was well enough to join the crowd—which had grown to 15,000 supporters.

The Black Power chant generated far more media coverage than the 4,000 newly registered voters the Meredith March inspired across the State of Mississippi. The Black Power chant also drew more press attention than the tear gas, Billy clubs, and rifles the police used against nonviolent marchers. And though Carmichael continually and carefully explained the concept of Black Power as "the power to affirm our Black humanity; to defend the dignity, integrity, and institutions of our culture; and to collectively organize the political and economic power to begin to control and develop our communities," many white Americans heard only "black supremacy" and "reverse racism." More conservative civil rights organizations also criticized Carmichael's promotion of the phrase. What's more, SNCC lost the financial and political support of many of its white liberal backers. Hamer explained to Rose Fishman in a letter sent in late June 1966, "Rose, SNCC don't have any funds because they call us Black Nationalists and we don't get any substance at all. Plus, they are trying to smear us any way they can."

At every turn, Hamer, like Carmichael, provided context for and added nuance to the Black Power slogan. Along the Meredith March, for instance, Hamer clarified the concept for reporters:

> What we mean by "Black Power" is we mean to have not only black political power, but black economic power, to have a voice in the educational system that our kids will know—not only the black kids, but the white kids should know—the kinds of contributions that have been made by black people throughout this country. We want to determine some of our destiny and that is what "Black Power" means.

And yet, overly simplistic understandings of "Black Power" predominated, driving people, in Hamer's characterization, "stark-raving mad."

A week after the Meredith March, Carmichael and Hamer were featured speakers at CORE's twenty-third annual convention. In front of the press and approximately two-hundred CORE members, Hamer again explained the concept of Black Power in both racial and economic terms. She chastised black preachers, the "Negro Bourgeoisie," and the "PhDs," who sold out their poor brothers and sisters to the white power structure. Hamer doubtlessly had in mind the struggle raging over Head Start Centers in Mississippi and federal OEO funding as she criticized middle-to-upper class black sell-outs and championed, instead, the "Black people in the United States [who] are starting to move for Black Power."

When it was Carmichael's turn to speak, he reiterated claims he had made all along the Meredith March when he had insisted that Black Power is "patently not about either hating or loving white people." In fact, "it really has nothing to do with them." In this same vein, Carmichael told the CORE attendees that integration was an irrelevant question and that it was futile to engage in nonviolent protest with a white power structure that supported the war in Vietnam. Instead, Carmichael said, "We will define our own tactics whether they like it or not." The definition of those tactics, unfortunately, drove a formidable wedge between Hamer and SNCC, the organization responsible for her political awakening.

During a December 1966 meeting at the famed black performer "Peg Leg" Bates's Catskill Mountains resort, SNCC gathered to redefine itself. Carmichael's election as chair of SNCC earlier that year marked a clear ideological transformation in the organization John Lewis had led since 1963. Carmichael not only had a charismatic star-quality that attracted media attention and new members to SNCC, he also gave voice to the frustrations shared by many existing members. In particular, Carmichael's more confrontational style embodied the frustration of those SNCC members who had grown weary of appealing to the hearts and minds of white people through Christian-based nonviolent direct action campaigns. Similarly, some SNCC members began to see grassroots voting rights campaigns as pointless, dependent as those campaigns were on making change within what they perceived to be a fundamentally corrupt political system. Furthermore, a slim majority of SNCC's black membership no longer favored an integrated solution to bringing about social and political change. These members proposed expelling white people from the organization, arguing it would be more beneficial for SNCC's white members to work within their own communities than to assert influence over what should be black-led programs for change.

Hamer disagreed. On the one hand, Hamer had great respect for leaders like Stokely Carmichael and sympathized with the turn to more militant ideologies like Black Nationalism. In a 1972 interview, for instance, Hamer was asked to reflect back upon black freedom movement activists with whom she had worked over the years. Carmichael was among the small list of activists Hamer mentioned by name. "I respected Stokely Carmichael. I knew Stokely Carmichael when he was one of the kindest people I had ever met, but I watched what society can do to a man that just keeps pushing him back." With similar understanding, Hamer told an interviewer in 1968:

> See, I think that every person regardless of their skin color should have a chance to participate in their own destiny because politics deals with everything, you

know. And I can understand why we have militants. I can understand why we have what they call [Black] Nationalists . . . You know, they don't say it's the black man's problem, they say it's America's problem, because if America treated people right we wouldn't have to have . . . [Black] Nationalists.

On the other hand, those closest to Hamer confirm that "she was not in favor of division," and contend that "Mrs. Hamer didn't share the bitterness that existed within SNCC."

Instead, she continued to advocate for a multiracial solution to social and political change. "She could have gone with the new thing," explained Reverend Edwin King, "but she didn't, that's evidence of her integrity. From her religious perspective, blacks had a right to share in the power of the democracy, but it was going be done together in America."

Lawrence Guyot, Mississippi Freedom Democratic Party chair, pushed King's assessment even further: "Fannie Lou Hamer was a religious fanatic in the most positive sense. I heard her say: 'If I hate white people, I can't see the face of Jesus.' So, she was very anti-hate, very pro-non-violent. She took her religious beliefs and she parlayed them into politics."

Though Hamer practiced love and understanding in the face of the ideological differences she encountered within the increasingly militant SNCC, newer members within the organization deemed her "no longer relevant" and "not at their level of development." And they said as much at the Peg Leg Bates' summit in December of 1966. There, the motion to expel white people narrowly passed in a nineteen to eighteen vote, with twenty-four members (mostly white) abstaining. While SNCC member Charles Cobb suggested that the "expulsion of whites is a bit over done," he nevertheless acknowledged that this 1966 meeting was a turning point for the organization and for Mrs. Hamer's role within it. In Cobb's assessment, "SNCC was more northern in 1966, than in 1962," when Hamer had become the organization's oldest voter registration worker. Cobb explained further that "northern people didn't have much interest in rural southern people like Mrs. Hamer, except as sort of symbols, who put their bodies on the line, but their thoughts were not revolutionary enough."

Hamer was dismissed not only by newcomers to SNCC, but also by middle-class black and white power brokers in her home state. During this middle phase of her activist career, Hamer virulently protested the displacement of poor black people, who were pushed out of leadership roles within poverty programs and burgeoning political parties alike.

"The fourth chapter of St. Luke and the eighteenth verse say: 'The spirit of the Lord is upon me because he has anointed me to preach the gospel to the poor.' Not to the rich," Hamer said.

As she amended this scripture, which she had often heard her father preach in their humble Strangers' Home sanctuary, Hamer scanned the faces of the mostly black women seated before her at the Oxford, Mississippi, grant writing workshop. Some stared back in admiration, urging her on. Others glanced at their watches, whispered to friends seated next to them, and tried to hide their yawns behind cupped hands.

"I hope I don't hold you up too long," Hamer said, eyes now set on the professional-looking black women in attendance. "But I want to tell *you* some of the things that *you* have failed to do to make this a better place for all of *us*."

Annie Devine, Hamer's friend and fellow MFDP activist, invited her to address this group of women gathered in Oxford in January of 1967. Hamer intended to speak her piece.

"I have been greatly shocked for the past few years at what I have watched in the State of Mississippi," Hamer said. She went on to describe the deadly struggle for black empowerment, recounting the names of civil rights movement martyrs: Herbert Lee, Medgar Evers, Andrew Goodman, Michael Schwerner, and James Chaney. Hamer contrasted those who "gave their lives for a cause" with "the people that we couldn't get to say a word." She remembered how, early in the struggle for black freedom, church doors were closed in their faces, and how people who had means were not willing to stand in solidarity with the poor. Hamer described their attitude as "We got it. So what is we got to worry about? . . . We got ours." Once the most dangerous phase of the movement had passed, and federal poverty money began flowing into the nation's poorest state, Hamer observed, these same professional people were all-too-eager to join the cause and take the lead in dispersing funds.

Opposing these Johnny-come-latelies, Hamer advocated empowering impoverished people to run the federally sponsored programs intended for their benefit. "Give them a chance to have a head start in life," she pleaded, "not only for their children, but for themselves, too." But this plea, Hamer recognized, had gone unheeded by middle class power brokers—black and white—whom Hamer accused of forging alliances against the poor. "The professional Negro got with the power structure—*white*—and they have done everything to drag us down," Hamer told her Oxford audience.

In contrast to the present class division, Hamer offered the women gathered in Oxford an alternative pathway—built by multiracial cooperation across class lines and rooted in her Christian faith:

> I'm not just fighting for myself and for the black race, but I'm fighting for the white; I'm fighting for the Indians; I'm fighting for the Mexicans; I'm fighting for the Chinese; I'm fighting for anybody because as long they are human beings, they need freedom. And the only thing we can do, women and men,

whether you white or black, is to work together. Because, you see whether you got a degree or no degree, all wisdom and knowledge come from God.

The National Council of Negro Women (NCNW) had organized the January 1967 workshop to teach black women in Mississippi how to write federal grant proposals. Grant-writing was an increasingly sought-after skill in the years since President Lyndon B. Johnson had declared a "War on Poverty" in his 1964 State of the Union Address. Buoyed by a landslide victory over Barry Goldwater in the 1964 presidential election, Johnson introduced a sweeping set of legislation under the banner of the Great Society he envisioned. The Great Society could be realized, according to Johnson, through an extensive War on Poverty, which included initiatives he intended to "not only relieve the symptoms of poverty, but to cure it, and above all, to prevent it."

Oppressed as they were by interlocking systems of sexism, racism, political, and economic discrimination, black women in Mississippi felt the symptoms of poverty acutely. Just as black people in the Delta were making significant political progress, the economy changed. By the late 1960s, thousands of Delta sharecroppers were unemployed. Their labor was no longer needed; chemical weed killers and mechanical pickers became far cheaper alternatives. Synthetic fibers were growing in worldwide popularity, too, and so the US government awarded subsidies to farmers who slashed their cotton acreage to avoid a surplus. Without access to low-skill agricultural jobs—the only jobs for which the majority of black Deltans had ever been trained or hired—people in the region faced malnutrition and even starvation. A mid-decade Department of Agriculture study noted that the majority of Sunflower County residents "received less than two-thirds of the minimum dietary allowances recommended by the federal government." A reporter visiting the region observed, "Children with the great swollen bellies that mark the protein deficiency disease called kwashiorkor dot the countryside . . . these children live in Mississippi on a diet of cornbread, grits and Kool-Aid."

After hearing Marian Wright Edelman, the first black woman admitted to the bar and the director of the NAACP Legal Defense and Educational Fund in Jackson, Mississippi, describe the emergency conditions existing in the Delta to a US Senate Subcommittee on Poverty, Senators Robert F. Kennedy and Joseph Clark embarked on a tour of the Delta. National press attention followed and all were astounded by what they witnessed there. The Senate Subcommittee on Poverty immediately sent doctors and psychologists to the region.

What Hamer had been saying for years now made national news: the social, political, and economic structures that maintained racial segregation also perpetuated poverty. A predominantly agricultural state, Mississippi had not kept pace with national trends toward diversifying its industries and retraining its workforce. White supremacy relied on economic oppression. As a result, Mississippi consistently ranked the poorest state—with the Delta as its poorest region—in the country. The dire need in Mississippi made the state a prime target for Johnson's War on Poverty initiatives, which included Medicaid and Medicare, food stamps, the Job Corps, and Head Start.

In fact, back in 1965, when the federal Department of Health and Human Services initiated the Head Start program, the newly formed Child Development Group of Mississippi (CDGM) was the first organization in the country to receive federal funding. Their charge was ambitious. The CDGM was granted $1.4 million dollars from the federal government to set up eighty-four Head Start Centers that would serve 6,000 children across the state. As a War on Poverty program, the Department of Health and Human Services stipulated that these programs should not only serve children affected by poverty, but that the programs should also involve the children's parents—they emphasized "maximum feasible participation by the poor." To accomplish this feat, the CDGM tapped into existing networks among Mississippi's impoverished citizens, many of whom had been woven together earlier in the decade by the Council of Federated Organizations' civil rights work.

The Child Development Group of Mississippi's outreach was successful. In that first summer of 1965, they created over 2,500 new jobs in the State of Mississippi—accounting for 10 percent of the state's overall job growth rate and constituting the largest industry in the state, outside of agriculture. Impoverished communities across Mississippi banded together. With federal financial support, they restored dilapidated buildings, acquired school buses, trained drivers, learned about early childhood education, supplied food to the schools, and more. The impact of these collaborations was not lost on Hamer. Speaking to the women gathered at that 1967 National Council of Negro Women's Workshop in Oxford, Hamer said, "We have in Sunflower County 1,400 children that we were able to get out of the country and most of these children had never seen a commode in their lives. Some of these children had never had their faces washed in a face bowl. But you see, I care. We got these children and brought them in the little town and began to work with them." Doctors and dentists visited the centers, hot meals were provided each day, and the children were engaged with age-appropriate curriculum.

Teachers reported that children in Head Start centers across Mississippi began to see themselves in a new light and that the program cast their parents with a new glow, too, as their mothers led classes, their fathers built classrooms, distributed food to centers, and drove buses. The jobs that Head Start created for parents of impoverished children carried with them not only pride of purpose, but also fair compensation. A domestic worker, sharecropper or day-laborer employed in 1965 Mississippi would earn approximately ten to fifteen dollars a week—if one could find this work at all by mid-decade. Head Start wages were set by the federal government, not by the whims of white supremacists. As a result, the pay—fifty to seventy dollars a week—was a substantial increase for most workers. Earning a fair wage and engaging in rewarding work boosted the self-esteem of Head Start employees and provided a new-found independence from Mississippi's white supremacists. No longer reliant upon the local white power structure for jobs, housing, and food, Head Start employees were free to act—and to vote—in ways that benefited their interests.

The new-found independence experienced by Head Start employees, who were predominantly black during the program's first phase, threatened the segregationist structure that had organized race relations in Mississippi since Reconstruction. White supremacists responded to this threat with violence, intimidation, and formal investigations. Head Start organizers had reached out to impoverished white families, and some initially joined the programs, only to withdraw after suffering violent harassment for participating in what was branded by white supremacists as "civil rights work." Head Start centers were vandalized, bombed, burned down, and riddled by buckshot blasts. Head Start workers were harassed and beaten. Furthermore, the Mississippi governor, Paul Johnson, attempted to block federal War on Poverty money from coming into the state. The five US congressmen from Mississippi also opposed the poverty program. James O. Eastland, the US senator from Sunflower County, went so far as to deny the existence of poverty in his home county. And just eight days into the initial run of the Head Start program, John C. Stennis (the other US senator sent from Mississippi) launched a federal investigation into the CDGM. Stennis was the chair of the Senate's Committee on Standards and Conduct. Under his leadership, this committee launched a series of attacks against the Child Development Group of Mississippi, accusing the organization of being a front for civil rights work, charging the group with fiscal mismanagement, and contending that the poverty money flowing into the state could be better spent on national security—to fund the war in Vietnam.

The investigation that Stennis launched into the CDGM turned up evidence that a few Head Start employees, who were detained after a civil rights protest, had been bailed out of prison with Head Start money earmarked as "salary advances." With this revelation, the Mississippi establishment's critiques of the Child Development Group of Mississippi gained traction. Although the investigation determined that less than .5 percent of the CDGM's initial expenditures were questionable, future funding for Head Start programs in Mississippi now required severing ties between Head Start and civil rights organizations. Over the next several years, the battles over Head Start funding in the state grew increasingly fierce. With the education, medical care, and—in some cases—the very *lives* of children hanging in the balance, politicians from Jackson, Mississippi, to Washington, D.C. debated how the poverty funds should be allocated. The compromise they struck flew in the face of Head Start's guiding mission to encourage maximum participation by the poor. The Child Development Group of Mississippi was led primarily by people experiencing poverty, but that organization was no longer funded. Instead, money went to newly established rival organizations, such as the Mississippi Action for Progress (MAP), which were established and run by middle and upper class black and white people.

Once hopeful about the Great Society programs she saw at work in Sunflower County, Hamer later characterized the War on Poverty as a "war against poor people" and claimed the Head Start program was aptly named because the people now running it had a head start over the poor and disenfranchised. She was disgusted by the way established leaders took over programs specifically aimed toward the empowerment of the poor. Instead of empowering poor people, insisted Hamer, these leaders marginalized them. Leaders claimed that people living in poverty were not qualified to run the programs, while usurping the very opportunities impoverished people had to become qualified. Hamer was also disappointed in the black people experiencing poverty who had internalized negative perceptions about their potential. She watched as those black voters routinely elected middle class black and white people over other black people experiencing poverty. This painful dynamic played out in the elections of Head Start board members and public officials alike.

Fannie Lou Hamer rose early on the morning of May 2, 1967. She dressed quietly so she would not wake Dorothy's babies, both sleeping soundly in the main room of their old white house on 626 Lafayette Street. The Hamers were eager to move into their new—slightly larger—home, but the elderly woman they had bought the place from was ill. What's worse, the old woman had taken out a second mortgage on her home to do some repairs, without fully understanding—or being made aware of—the loan's terms. The bank had eventually foreclosed on the elderly woman's mortgage, which was how the Hamers were able to afford her house. But when the Hamers learned that on top of her financial woes the woman was in poor health, Fannie Lou didn't have the heart to boot her from her home. So, they waited as their three-room house on Lafayette Street grew increasingly cramped.

Lenora Aretha was now almost twenty-months-old. She spent her days toddling through the grass patch in front of the Hamer home and doting on her baby sister. Jacqueline Denise, whom Perry Hamer took to calling

"Cookie," was born in September of 1966. Dorothy Jean was running herself ragged caring for an infant and a toddler.

Fannie Lou noticed Vergie stir. She'd be waking soon and heading into the previously all-white high school. It pained the Hamers to send her there, knowing that she daily braved insults from white students, low expectations from her teachers, and near-constant suspicion from the school's administration. To add to this heartache, Fannie Lou knew that Vergie hadn't been sleeping well—she worried about her sister and was woken throughout the night by Lenora and Jacqueline. Fannie Lou sighed deeply, as Perry Hamer urged her along. He planned to drive Fannie Lou to the small town of Sunflower before he ran his Head Start bus route.

When the Hamers arrived in Sunflower, they found the town hall building roped off. Fannie Lou, neither a voter in this particular race nor a certified election official, was barred from entry. She joined the growing crowd of civil rights supporters, local and national press gathered across the street on the post office lawn. Hamer exuded hopefulness about the prospect of political change. As she approached the crowd, an American flag rose up the post office's pole.

"Yes, that's the country's flag," she said to the crowd. "And this is the first day it's been ours, too. Remember the song we used to sing?"

> If you don't find me in the cotton fields,
> And you can't find me nowhere
> Come on over to the City Hall,
> I'll be voting right there!

Hamer smiled. "Well, this day is what that song was all about." The press widely circulated Hamer's optimistic words.

The confidence she felt on that dewy May morning was well-founded. The National Committee for Free Elections in Sunflower County, Mississippi, the political organization Hamer front-lined, had been working tirelessly to raise funds and to increase the number of registered black voters in the small towns of Sunflower and Moorhead. In March of 1966, the US Court of Appeals ordered reelections in these two Delta towns, siding with the plaintiffs in *Hamer v. Campbell*. Federal Judge Claude Clayton ruled that municipal elections should have been postponed so black voters could have had the opportunity to benefit from the equality in voter registration practices, ordered by the 1963 *US v. Campbell* verdict. The historic *Hamer v. Campbell* ruling marked the first time a federal judge had thrown out the results of an election because black voters did not have an equal opportunity to participate and this ruling momentarily drew the nation's attention back to the issue of voting rights in Mississippi.

The National Committee for Free Elections, run by Sandra Nystrom and Eleanor Holmes Norton, was headquartered in Manhattan. Hamer traveled there in March of 1967, two months prior to the May elections, and embarked on a ten-day tour throughout the Northeast. Her tour included stops in New York, Connecticut, and Massachusetts, where she attended house party fundraisers and gave press conferences, as well as radio and television interviews. At each stop, Hamer worked to incite empathy among her audience by stressing the convergence of their interests. "Nobody's free until everybody's free" was Hamer's core refrain.

She explained that donations to the National Committee for Free Elections would go toward voter registration work in Mississippi, paying for cars and gas so registration workers could reach potential voters, who were spread across the Delta's vast agricultural expanse. Funds raised also supported lobbying efforts in D.C., where the Committee's allies had been pleading with the Justice Department to deploy federal registrars to the Mississippi Delta. In her fundraising efforts, Hamer also responded to the most frequent question she received from national onlookers.

"Why, a year and a half after the Voting Rights Act passed, is black voter registration still so difficult in the Delta?" Hamer was often asked by well-meaning northerners.

"It's not being enforced," was Hamer's matter-of-fact reply.

She would go on to explain that just as US Senator Stennis used his political influence to redirect War on Poverty funds away from the Head Start programs spearheaded by poor black people, so too did US Senator Eastland block federal registration workers from entering his home county. Hamer was not alone in her accusations. Thirteen US congressional representatives banded together in support of the National Committee for Free Elections and brought an official request to attorney general Nicholas Katzenbach. The congressional coalition specifically asked for federal registrars to be dispatched to Sunflower County. The congressional representatives cited the county's alarmingly disparate voting registration figures: only 24 percent of eligible black people were registered to vote, whereas approximately 85 percent of the eligible white voting population was registered. Nevertheless, Katzenbach refused to send registrars, reasoning that no official complaint had been filed against the state registrars. Drew Pearson, a columnist for the *Washington Post*, reported a telling exchange between Katzenbach and Congressman Charles Diggs of Detroit.

"Is the reason Sunflower County has no federal registrars because Senator Eastland lives there?" Congressman Diggs asked.

"Oh, is that his home county?" Katzenbach reportedly "deadpanned" in response.

If the US senators from Mississippi could redirect federally funded programs like Head Start and determine the application of the 1965 Voting Rights Act, argued Hamer, then this was not just Mississippi's problem; their abuses of power threatened *all* Americans. Hamer told audiences throughout her Northeast tour that the funds they donated helped not only to "free me in Mississippi, but also to help free yourselves." She put it plainly to one audience: "Until I'm free in Mississippi, let's not kid ourselves, you're not free in Connecticut." Hamer raised over $7,000 on her ten-day tour, equivalent to $50,000 in today's currency, before returning to Mississippi for the last big voter registration push before the May reelections.

By May of 1967, Hamer had been actively involved in voter registration work across the Delta for nearly five years. Based on this experience, she held a clear view of the obstacles that inhibited black civic participation in that region of the country. The first obstacle Hamer identified was inconvenience. Registration in Sunflower County was conducted in just one location, the Indianola Courthouse. The courthouse was far away for many voters, some of whom had to find transportation for a fifty-mile round trip just to register. The courthouse was also only open during weekday working hours, making it difficult for many day-laborers to reach the county seat in time to register. The second obstacle was fear. Hamer recognized the widespread fear that still surrounded black civic assertion. In a report she shared with the US congressional delegation advocating for federal intervention in Sunflower County, Hamer described merely mentioning the word "register" to black Deltans and watching them all walk away. "The word register frightened them," she explained, but if "federal registrars could come to where the people are, many more people would vote. They would then feel that the federal government is behind them, and that the Voting Rights Act is not just a paper law."

Unfortunately, no federal registrars were sent to the Delta towns of Sunflower and Moorhead in advance of the historic May 2, 1967, reelection. Despite Hamer's consciousness-raising efforts, despite the support of US congressional allies, and despite the funds raised by the National Committee for Free Elections, the candidates backed by the Committee lost across the board. White mayors and aldermen were elected to lead both small Delta towns. Several scholars have studied the results of these elections and provide a variety of explanations. Some suggest the black candidates in Sunflower and Moorhead lost because of voter intimidation at the polling places. Historian J. Todd Moye noted that the white police chief greeted each black voter at the door of the Sunflower Town Hall, while another white man took each black voter's picture. Other scholars suspect that fraud contributed to the election of an all-white slate of candidates. Mississippi Freedom Democratic Party volunteers were barred from helping illiterate black voters, who were provided assistance by white poll workers instead.

In addition to fraud and intimidation, limited access to registration contributed to low registration figures among black people across the Delta. In the nearly two years since the passage of the Voting Rights Act, voter registration among black Deltans rose only 11 percent—from 13 percent in 1965 to 24 percent in 1967. Black voters, however, did constitute a majority in the small town of Sunflower, and, for the first time, white candidates actually pandered to their black constituents. Promising to pave roads in black neighborhoods, for instance, and spreading rumors about the inexperience and radical communist ties held by their black opponents. So it is possible, as Hamer biographer Kay Mills argued, that some black voters willfully cast their ballots for white candidates. In this regard, the reelections in Sunflower and Moorhead presaged the larger trend Hamer found so devastating. As Mills explained it, "black voters did not reward civil rights activism at the polls and sometimes found black candidates' backgrounds wanting in comparison to those of whites." Hamer believed that the brave black people who had put their lives on the line for the civil rights gains now enjoyed by the masses of black Mississippians should not be pushed out by the very white power structure they rose up against. Therefore, this particular voting trend affected her deeply.

Hamer's disappointment with the results of the reelections in Sunflower and Moorhead folded into the composite of worry, sympathy, and exhaustion she experienced as Dorothy's health continued to deteriorate. "Dorothy had been ill all her life—she was a sick baby. She always have been sickly," remembered her younger sister, Vergie. Dorothy suffered from aplastic anemia, which meant her body did not produce enough new blood cells. Side effects of this disorder include nosebleeds, which Dorothy had long suffered from. This condition worsened considerably after two pregnancies in two years drained Dorothy's body of blood and vital nutrients needed to produce new cells. "Her nose used to bleed all the time," Vergie recalled, "but this particular time her nose started bleeding and we couldn't get it to stop."

Hamer knew better than to take Dorothy to the nearby North Sunflower County Hospital, where Hamer herself had been sterilized without her consent in 1961, and where the McDonald family had been harassed while seeking emergency treatment for their bullet-ridden granddaughters in 1962. Instead, Perry and Fannie Lou Hamer took Dorothy to a doctor they trusted in a small town twenty minutes away from Ruleville called Minter City. Dr. Creek was able to stop Dorothy's bleeding on Saturday April 29, but the young mother remained weak. Vergie remembered that after the Minter City doctor's visit, they "brought Dorothy back home" and "mama laid her down."

But by that evening, Dorothy's bleeding had started again. The Hamers then brought Dorothy to the Tufts-Delta Community Health Center in the all-black town of Mound Bayou, where two Tufts University physicians received OEO funds to create the first federally qualified community health center in the United States. So serious was Dorothy's condition, that she was immediately admitted and treated for three weeks. Treatment for aplastic anemia during the late 1960s included medication and blood transfusions, as bone marrow transplants were still years away from widespread use.

Hamer probably felt a small measure of relief that her daughter was receiving professional care in Mound Bayou, and it was likely this relief, coupled with her enduring sense of commitment to the cause of civil rights, that enabled her to show up in the small town of Sunflower on May 2, 1967. In the weeks that followed, moreover, Hamer split her time between monitoring Dorothy's progress and caring for Dorothy's daughters, Lenora and Jacqueline. Each time Hamer visited Dorothy in Mound Bayou, she became more concerned. Hamer noticed that Dorothy's abdomen, which had never returned to its pre-pregnancy tautness, was now completely engorged—appearing as if she was fully pregnant once more. The pain and the abdominal swelling were caused by a growing uterine fibroid tumor, for which black women are at especially high risk. These ailments combined—the aplastic anemia and the rapidly expanding fibroid tumor—worried Hamer. She and Pap made the decision to transfer Dorothy to John Gasden Hospital in Memphis, Tennessee.

On the morning of May 23, 1967, Vergie was humming to herself as she finished breakfast. It was the last day of her school year, and she couldn't wait to be done with that place for a while. Her mother was bustling around the house, gathering Dorothy's belongings. Her parents had decided to take Dorothy to a bigger hospital in Memphis, and they planned to make the two-hour drive today. The thought of her sister traveling so far away brought a lump to Vergie's throat.

"Mama, can you bring her by school so I can say goodbye?" Vergie asked, her young voice quivering.

Hamer saw the crease in Vergie's forehead, the tears welling in her eyes. "We can do that, baby. We'll come by the schoolyard on our way out," she said.

Out the window of her classroom, Vergie watched for her family all morning. When she finally saw their old car roll into the side of the schoolyard, Vergie bounded toward them. Dorothy rolled down the window and called out weakly, "Girl, Mama said she was going to take me up there to Memphis and leave me!" Her smile revealed her playful nature and her bloodied gums.

Vergie's own smile did not reach her worried brown eyes. That now-familiar lump rose in her throat. With their mother's help, Dorothy got out of the car to hug Vergie, who froze at the sight of her sister's body. Vergie had expected the bloody gums, the cracked lips, and the dark circles that so often ringed her sister's kind eyes, but why did she look like she was about to have another baby? Dorothy sensed her sister's fear and, even in her weakened state, Dorothy eased Vergie's worry with laughter.

"You see that there," Dorothy said, pointing to an eighteen-wheeler that was driving by the schoolyard on Highway 8. The truck had a large cartoon camel emblazoned on its side. "See how that camel has a hump on his back? I ain't got no hump in my back, I got a hump in my stomach!"

"Girl, please!" Vergie said, laughing.

Perry and Fannie Lou Hamer exchanged nervous glances and the girls sensed it was time to say goodbye. As her family drove away, Vergie couldn't shake what she had just seen. She returned to class and, as the teacher droned on about the cursive sentences they were supposed to copy from the board, Vergie's mind returned to the image of her sister. On a piece of notebook paper, later preserved in her mother's archival collection, Vergie drew that disturbing image. In Vergie's pencil drawing, Dorothy stands smiling, with enlarged breasts, her hands clasped over her rotund belly, a hospital bed sketched behind her on one side and on the other side the Highway 8 sign. Below this drawing, Vergie wrote: "She's still pregnant. Dorothy and her Baby! She's going to the hospital bed! Look at the baby!"

Perhaps to Vergie's thirteen-year-old mind this was a hopeful way to cope with what must have been both frightening and confusing. She had seen the toll pregnancy took on her sister, but Dorothy had rebounded both times. If this was another pregnancy, Vergie knew what to expect. She would be back to joking with her beloved sister once the baby came.

But there was no baby this time. Just as the Hamers completed the 120-mile drive to Memphis, Dorothy suffered a massive cerebral hemorrhage. The Hamers had to carry an unconscious Dorothy into the hospital, where they soon learned their daughter's grim prognosis. Perhaps if they had brought Dorothy there earlier, the doctors explained, there was more they could have done. But after her cerebral hemorrhage—likely caused by the advanced size of the uterine fibroid tumor compressing the iliac vein and causing a paradoxical embolism—Dorothy wasn't expected to survive the night.

As the hospital staff worked to make Dorothy comfortable, Fannie Lou Hamer fell to her knees and prayed. Years later, Vergie insisted that her mother's prayers temporarily brought Dorothy back to life. Dorothy might have been stirred back to consciousness upon hearing the desperate and soulful prayers Hamer issued throughout the night of May 23. But on May 24, 1967, the twenty-two-year-old mother of two, the Hamers' eldest child, was pro-nounced dead.

For a split-second, Vergie was happy to see her Mom and Dad come through the door. But where was Dorothy? If she was in Memphis, at the hospital, why weren't they there, too, right by her bedside? Vergie looked up from the floor, where she sat playing with her nieces. She could tell by the way her father refused to look her in the eyes that something was terribly wrong. Vergie watched, heart racing, as her mother set her belongings down on the table and limped over to a chair near the girls. She placed her hand on Vergie's shoulder and started to explain.

More than forty years later, Vergie insisted that she would never forget what her mother told her that day. In shock and exhausted, Fannie Lou likely searched hard for the right words to explain what had happened. "Mama said they told her that growth was a *molecular moles*," remembered Vergie. "It's growing and it was eating up her blood." Through this image, Hamer did her best to describe Dorothy's uterine fibroid tumor—also called a *molecular myoma*—to thirteen-year-old Vergie, who had hoped they would return with her sister and Dorothy's third child.

Grief consumed the Hamer's home. Vergie lost her fun-loving sister, Lenora and Jacqueline lost their mother, and the Hamers lost their eldest child. Describing the scope of her mother's grief, Vergie compared Dorothy's death to the most harrowing experiences of Fannie Lou Hamer's entire life—her beating in the Winona jail cell and the 1961 death of her own mother, Lou Ella Townsend. Dorothy's death, of all her mother's suffering, was the most devastating. It "took tolls on Mama's little heart. Mama didn't even go that way, you know, she didn't go like that when Grandmama died—and that was her *Mama*," Vergie said.

Vergie and Fannie Lou grieved together, "Forgive me," Hamer would say to her young daughter, "I just can't get over it."

"It took a long time for me to get over that too," Vergie said. "Because we was close, very close."

White supremacy has no regard for black grief. No more than five days after Perry Hamer watched Dorothy die, he was harassed by the Chief of Police, Curtis Floyd, from the neighboring City of Drew. On May 29, 1967, Floyd pulled Mr. Hamer over to check his license. The next day, Floyd pulled Mr. Hamer over again. This time, Pap had a car filled with white students from Georgetown University, who were in Mississippi helping with voter registra-tion. Floyd arrested Mr. Hamer for speeding. An infraction that should have resulted in a ticket landed Mr. Hamer in jail for the night. On the morning of

May 31, the mayor of Drew, W. O. Williford, who also served as the small town's judge, presided over Perry Hamer's arraignment. Williford added to the speeding charge, alleging that Mr. Hamer needed a commercial license to transport the number of registration workers he had in his car at the time of his arrest. The Hamers recognized this harassment for what it was: an attempt to punish civically engaged black Mississippians and to curtail the registration of black voters.

Citing the federal protections now guaranteed by the Voting Rights Act, the Hamers sued. According to Kay Mills, the lawsuit *Hamer v. Floyd* became "the first lawsuit under the federal Voting Rights Act brought by private parties to try to block a state court prosecution." On June 7, 1967, the case was tried in the Federal District Court in Oxford. The Hamers sought a restraining order against Mayor Williford so they could continue their voter registration work unimpeded. Their request was denied by Judge Clayton, and the Hamers did not appeal the decision.

The proximity of this court case to Dorothy's death demonstrates that the Hamers had neither the luxury of time nor space to fully grieve the loss of their daughter. Perhaps the movement to register black voters in Mississippi encroached upon the Hamer family's mourning. Perhaps the Hamers were so committed to the struggle that they refused to step back. Perhaps the pain of Dorothy's death filled them both with even more resolve to dismantle the white supremacist structures that contributed to their family's suffering. The latter explanation seems plausible considering that, in the month following Dorothy's death, Fannie Lou Hamer played a pivotal role organizing a conference that brought together Sunflower County officials, local women, and the National Council of Negro Women representatives to discuss poverty politics. Further still, Hamer soon set her sights on running for the Mississippi State Senate in the November 1967 election, and she filled her platform with relevant issues, including access to health care and adequate nutrition staples for all Mississippians.

Unwilling to let the national support they incited for the reelections in Sunflower and Moorhead dissipate, Hamer and a team of political allies, including Martin Luther King, Jr., Jackie Robinson, and Howard Zinn, transformed the National Committee for Free Elections in Sunflower County into the National Committee for Free Elections in Mississippi. Run by the same Eleanor Holmes Norton-Sandra Nystrom partnership out of New York, this committee served as an intermediary between the Mississippi Freedom Democratic Party's grassroots organizing in the state and liberal allies across the nation. The Committee continued to lobby the Justice Department to send federal registration workers into Mississippi. To support their plea, they cited widespread harassment, including the arrest of registration workers on trumped up charges (like those Perry Hamer had endured) and death threats hurled at registration workers, which Fannie Lou Hamer frequently received.

In spite of the harassment, black voter registration was on the rise in the state. In a final fundraising push before the November 1967 midterm election, Hamer wrote to supporters of the National Committee for Free Elections in Mississippi. In this letter dated October 23, she boasted that over "225,000 black registered voters have put up their own slate of 70 black Mississippians who are running for offices ranging from a Justice of the Peace to State Senator as independents or under the banner of the Mississippi Freedom Democratic Party." She assured potential donors, "Your money is crucial and will go very far. It will give election workers something to live on while they organize voters, lead citizenship workshops, bring Mississippi people together and tell it 'like it is.'" What's more, Hamer reminded readers that their freedom was bound to the freedom of black people in Mississippi when she wrote, "The North also has a definite stake in this challenge to the Eastlands and Stennises, who are dedicated to making the nation as backward as they have kept Mississippi."

As US senators Stennis and Eastland worked at the national level to slow the pace of civil rights progress, their counterparts in the Mississippi legislature passed thirty laws undermining the 1965 Voting Rights Act. One such law stipulated that voting in a party's primary disqualified one from running as an Independent in the general election. This stipulation kept Hamer's name and the names of nineteen other black candidates from appearing on the November 1967 ballot. Nevertheless, Hamer campaigned heartily for the slate of seventy MFDP-backed candidates, whose names would appear on the fall ballot. There were good reasons to believe that this slate of candidates would fair well in the election. Not only was black voter registration up significantly across the state, but black people now constituted a majority in four counties. And yet, just six of the seventy black candidates Hamer and the National Committee for Free Elections supported won their contests, and no black candidates were elected in Sunflower County. Of those six victories, Hamer took great pride in the election of one Robert Clark.

When Clark, a schoolteacher from Holmes County, was sworn into the Mississippi State House of Representatives on January 2, 1968, he became the first black legislator elected to serve since Reconstruction. Clark had Hamer to thank, in part, for his seat. Although poll records indicated that Clark had beaten his opponent, James P. Love, by 116 votes, the election results were contested. Hamer saw through this ruse and threatened to expose it to the nation, calling the Mississippi Secretary of State and announcing that if Clark was not seated she would alert the national press and lead a major march to the State Capitol in Jackson. She did not have to make good on those threats, however, as the challenge to Clark's congressional seat was soon dropped. Clark understood that Hamer's status as a national figure was pivotal to this swift resolution, a point she did not let him forget. Once he was sworn in, Hamer wasted no time calling Clark to inform him that if he didn't "do right" in his new post, she would launch a similar challenge against him. Thankfully, Hamer was never pressed to make good on her threat to Clark either.

Although she was spared from trying, it is doubtful that the national press would have descended upon Mississippi in the winter months of 1967–1968. The escalating war in Vietnam, civil unrest in northern cities, and organizations like the newly formed Black Panther Party divided the media's attention. By the summer of 1967, deadly uprisings in urban cities across the North overshadowed stories about nonviolent struggles for civil rights in the South. In what became known as the "long hot summer of 1967," rebellions erupted in 159 northern cities, where substandard living conditions, lack of economic opportunities, poor education, and police brutality incited widespread civil unrest. By the end of the decade, there would be over 300 uprisings in urban centers across the North, taking the lives of 250 people, leaving thousands of people seriously injured, and costing millions in property damage. The widespread frustration felt by those suffering from the effects of poverty and racism in the US was only exacerbated as the country intensified its military presence in Vietnam. By the end of 1967, half a million Americans were drafted to fight overseas, including Dorothy Jean's widowed husband, Sylvester Hall. While the civil rights movement had engendered tangible gains, what Martin Luther King, Jr. identified as the triple evils of militarism, capitalism, and racism continued to oppress people of color. Hamer added sexism to King's analysis of interlocking oppressions, and she took her radical solutions to the problems posed by this oppression with her to the 1968 Democratic National Convention (DNC).

It was, in Hamer's words, "the funeral of the Democratic Party."

In late August 1968, she approached the International Amphitheatre on a bus filled with Loyalist delegates. A coalition of progressive groups, who formed the Loyal Democrats of Mississippi, commonly known as the "Loyalists," brought the 1968 credentials committee challenge to the all-white delegation sent from their state. Hamer reluctantly joined this coalition. On the way to the DNC, she rolled her eyes as Loyalist Party leaders, Dr. Aaron Henry and Charles Evers, instructed her about this year's challenge and the planks of their party's platform.

"Who are *you* to be telling *me* something?" She asked the men. "Perry Hamer is the only one who breathes on my face at night, and he's the only one who can tell me something." She had the bus full of Loyalists in stitches following that remark, remembered the newly inaugurated Mississippi legislator, Robert Clark.

Out of the bus windows, the Loyalists noticed large billboard-sized pictures of birds chirping and flowers blooming that were plastered along the Chicago city streets. As they got closer to the convention hall, they observed redwood fences blocking the view and masking the stench of surrounding stockyards. And when they reached the hall, they were greeted by a large sign, written in all caps: "HELLO DEMOCRATS! WELCOME TO CHICAGO."

Mayor Richard J. Daley's attempts to create a calm and welcoming convention atmosphere were offset by his efforts to control the impending chaos. This was, after all, August of 1968, and it seemed to many Americans that the nation was coming apart at the seams. Northern cities smoldered from civil unrest. The series of surprise Viet Cong attacks against American forces, known as the Tet Offensive, dashed any hope that the war in Vietnam would find swift and peaceful resolution. Many in the nation mourned the recent deaths of Martin Luther King, Jr. and Robert F. Kennedy, both slain by assassins' bullets in the spring of 1968. Amidst this national and international chaos, President Lyndon B. Johnson shocked the country by announcing he would not seek a second term. The Republican Party advanced Richard M. Nixon, whom they touted as an experienced "law and order" candidate. The Democratic Party was tasked with deciding between Hubert Humphrey, Senator Eugene McCarthy, and Senator George S. McGovern. Democrats were deeply divided over these candidates, as well as solutions to the war in Vietnam and to the domestic battles waging in urban centers across the nation. Democrats were united, however, in their passionate calls for change. This passion manifested itself in shouting matches between and among delegations, convention walk-outs, credentials committee challenges, and—most abhorrently—by the tear gas, mace, and brute force that 23,000 National Guardsmen used against 10,000 antiwar protestors. By the end of the 1968 DNC, over 500 protestors were injured, 152 police officers were wounded, and nearly 100 bystanders had been affected by the violent clashes.

Fearing the large crowds of protestors and possible assassination attempts against the presidential candidates, Mayor Daley called in the guardsmen, bulletproofed the doors to the International Amphitheatre, and lined the convention hall with steel fencing, topped with barbed wire. In addition, the Chicago police force was armed and helmeted, security guards roamed the convention, and gray-suited men from the Secret Service trailed the most controversial delegates. Hamer remembered a sad-faced, blue-eyed man following her every move. She reported feeling "fenced in" by Daley's security measures and "watched like a criminal" by the man she presumed was an FBI agent. To make matters worse, Hamer had strong reservations about the Loyalist delegation to which she grudgingly belonged at the 1968 DNC.

The National Democratic Party had responded to the MFDP's 1964 credentials committee challenge by promising never again to seat a segregated delegation. The previously segregated delegation from Mississippi, in turn, responded by ignoring this pledge. The "Regular Party" brought another all-white delegation to Chicago in 1968. The Loyalists, meanwhile, created a multiracial coalition, consisting of Mississippi branches of the NAACP, the American Federation of Labor-Congress of Industrial Organizations (AFL-CIO), the Young Democrats, the Black Prince Hall Masons, and the Black Mississippi Teachers Association. Feeling displaced by the more moderate, more securely middle-class leaders of this Loyalist Party, the Mississippi Freedom Democratic Party resisted joining until the fall of 1967. At that point, Freedom Democrat Lawrence Guyot negotiated a merger with the Loyalists' leadership. Guyot explained the difficulty of this alliance: "For political purposes, we needed to create a coalition with some people who had opposed our very existence and fought to destroy us. And I'm very proud of the fact that I was able to hammer out that agreement." Guyot persisted in the negotiations because "somebody was going to be seated other than the Regulars," and he wanted the MFDP "to be a part of that."

Hamer shared Guyot's ambivalence. Hamer attributed offensive motives to the largely middle-class membership of the Loyalist delegation, claiming that if the MFDP would have been seated at the 1968 DNC, "it would be too much recognition for a bunch of n—rs. So, why not step on the bandwagon and take it over?" Her hostility toward the Loyalists was bound to the bitter disputes still raging throughout the state over control of poverty programs. Initially led by the poor themselves, many Head Start programs were now controlled by middle-class black and white people. And many of these same people now controlled the Loyalist coalition. Loyalist member, Hodding Carter, III, for instance, was a white journalist from the Carter family, who owned and operated the *Delta Democrat-Times*. Carter was also hand-picked to chair the Mississippi Action for Progress, a Head Start agency that now served 10,000 children in the state. The agency Carter led effectively diverted funding away from the initial Child Development Group of Mississippi, which was run by impoverished black Mississippians, some of whom had ties to the early civil rights movement work in the state. Hamer often characterized these Johnny-come-latelies as "sell outs." Right before the 1968 Convention, Hamer explained her position to an interviewer who asked what she thought about this year's challenge: "I really don't know because [there are] some folks going up there that I know would sell whoever is for sale." At the same time, Hamer felt strongly "that we should have a challenge, so I'm going on with the challenge. But I definitely think that we as FDP people should keep our identity, to let the world know we are still FDP," Hamer said.

Hamer made several attempts to let the world know what the Mississippi Freedom Democratic Party stood for. On August 26, 1968, the second day of the DNC proceedings, Hamer provided official credentials committee testimony on behalf of the integrated delegation from Alabama. In her brief testimony, Hamer spoke in the third person, acknowledging her significance within the Democratic Party: "In 1964, Fannie Lou Hamer was on the outside trying to get in." She also railed against the war in Vietnam and chastised the party for its tokenism, all before calling the party to "stop pretending that we are, but act in the manner that we are." To Hamer, the Democratic Party could live up to its values by seating the integrated delegation from Alabama, a coalition "that represent all the people, not just a few—representing not only the whites, but the blacks as well."

The following day, Hamer spoke out about what she perceived as the lackluster slate of presidential candidates. She had favored the candidacy of Robert F. Kennedy, whom she had met on his 1967 poverty tour of the Delta. When Kennedy was assassinated shortly after winning the California presidential primary, many of his supporters began favoring Senator McGovern. Hamer, however, told several Loyalists that she was going to the conference podium to nominate Kennedy's brother, Ted, to become the Democratic Party's 1968 presidential candidate.

Both Lawrence Guyot and Hodding Carter, III claim to have accompanied Hamer to the podium to make this bold announcement. Both men also mentioned their reservations about doing so. Guyot was in favor of McCarthy's antiwar stance, and Carter was primarily concerned that the delegation from Mississippi would "catch holy hell" if Hamer threw such a wrench into the carefully orchestrated proceedings. Guyot remembered that John Lewis, who was a member of the Georgia delegation, stopped Hamer just as she ascended the platform stairs. Carter recalled encouraging Hamer to call Ted Kennedy first. According to Carter, the pair could not reach Kennedy himself, but they did reach his brother-in-law, Steve Smith, who advised Hamer in no uncertain terms: "For God's sake, don't do that." However she was ultimately dissuaded, either by Lewis or by Smith, the power that Hamer held to once again turn the tide of a major party's political convention was not lost on Carter or Guyot.

Hamer harnessed that power into pushing the Loyalist delegation to set forth a more radical platform than many of the moderates within the party were comfortable advancing. The Saturday before the convention began, Hamer and Guyot shared the Freedom Democrats' ideas for social, political, and economic change. These ideas included both national and international policies such as a guaranteed annual income, free medical care for all, free higher education, land grants, and low interest federal loans for food cooperative programs. To support these initiatives, the Freedom Democrats advocated an immediate end to the war in Vietnam and to the shipment of arms to the Middle East and South Africa. The Freedom Democrats also proposed resuming diplomatic relations with Cuba and China.

Further still, Hamer took it upon herself to call out the male dominance within the 1968 Loyalist coalition. Not one woman held a leadership post within the delegation. Wes Watkins, a lawyer for the Loyalists, said his "most vivid impression of Mrs. Hamer was and will always be that she was the first person who ever read me the riot act about women's rights, and she did it to the whole delegation in private caucus through one of her impassioned, incredibly cogent, right-to-the-point, tough, righteous" speeches. In fact, Hamer's speech about gender equality within the coalition so moved the Loyalists that they committed to increasing opportunities for women within the 1972 delegation—a promise that was faithfully kept.

Unfortunately, Hamer's incisive speech before the 1968 credentials committee on behalf of the Alabama delegation was not as successful. The committee did not vote to seat the Alabama delegation, but they did vote to seat half of Georgia's integrated delegation, and they voted overwhelmingly to seat the Loyalist delegation from Mississippi as the official party sent from their state. When Hamer took her hard-won seat as a badge-wearing delegate on the Democratic National Convention floor, she received a standing ovation from the party.

While this tribute and the multiple acknowledgments of her influence throughout the 1968 convention were doubtlessly gratifying to Hamer, her resolve could not be tempered by flattery. She was seeking fundamental change, not fame. In fact, the principled positions she took during this middle phase of her activist career often eroded her secure base of power. When SNCC narrowly voted to expel white people from their organization, for instance, Hamer could have remained silent, ridden the wave of their ideological transformation, and remained connected to the organization. Instead, she advocated for her deeply held values and upheld the organization's foundational principles. As a result, Hamer was deemed "no longer relevant." When the powers-that-be in Mississippi undermined efforts by impoverished people to control their own poverty programs, Hamer could have parlayed her notoriety into a position on one of the newly formed Head Start boards—seated alongside those middle-class teachers and "chicken-eating preachers" she chastised. Instead, Hamer called these Johnny-come-latelies to task and demanded that the Office of Economic Opportunity uphold its own mission to encourage the "maximum feasible participation by the poor." And when the Loyalist

Figure 5.1 Fannie Lou Hamer received a standing ovation at the 1968 Democratic National Convention in Chicago. Getty Images, photo credit: Bettman.

coalition from Mississippi secured its place as *the* delegation sent from her state, Hamer could have compromised with their platform and supported their all-male leadership team. Instead she spoke out and, in so doing, was branded as extreme by the party's leadership.

By the turn of the decade, Hamer could no longer find an organization that advocated for the economic, political, and social empowerment of impoverished people and was also led by a multiracial cross-class coalition of women and men. So, in her indomitable way, Hamer took what she had learned from her near-decade of activism and created her own. She called it the Freedom Farm Cooperative.

· 6 ·

The Fight for Human Rights

I don't want to hear any more talk about "equal rights." I don't want to be equal to people who raped my ancestors, sold my ancestors and treated the Indians like they did. I don't want to be equal to that. I want "human rights."

—Fannie Lou Hamer, Speech at Duke University, 1969

*W*hen President John F. Kennedy reintroduced the Depression-era food stamp program in the early 1960s, the federal government began replacing its surplus food commodities program in the Mississippi Delta with a food stamp initiative. Instead of receiving free food from the government, poor people now had to purchase stamps to then buy food at a lower cost from area grocers. This replacement in federal policy occurred alongside the Delta's shifting economy. Between 1959 and 1966, the Delta region lost nearly 63,000 cotton-picking jobs alone. Just as the majority of black workers were replaced by farm machinery, chemical weed killers, and federal subsidies that paid landowners not to flood the marketplace with their produce, the US government replaced the food commodities program with a food relief initiative that required the now out-of-work black Deltans to purchase food stamps. The absurdity of this shift in policy was underscored at a meeting Fannie Lou Hamer helped organize in June of 1967. Held at the Travelodge Motel in Indianola, Mississippi, the meeting brought together state and federal officials, National Council of Negro Women representatives, and local women from across the Delta. An official from the US Department of Agriculture (USDA) addressed the audience, proudly announcing that the federal government would now charge people at the lowest income levels just fifty cents (down from two dollars) for twelve dollars worth of food.

"What do you do if you have no income?" a sixty-two year old black woman asked the USDA official.

"That could be a problem," he admitted, but then added, "You may not have cash but you must have *some* income."

141

"I wonder where mine is hid," the woman reportedly deadpanned. "I can't find none."

And she certainly was not the only Deltan who lacked the income required to benefit from this desperately needed federal poverty program. According to the 1960 Census, 68 percent of Sunflower County residents lived on less than one thousand dollars a year—a little over eight thousand dollars in today's currency. The US congressman who represented this region, Jamie Whitten, chaired the agricultural appropriations subcommittee. This powerful committee provided $23.5 million in farm subsidies for the .3 percent of Sunflower County residents who owned large plantations, and just four million dollars in food relief aid for the majority of Sunflower County residents who were living in abject poverty. Moreover, one of Sunflower County's most well-known residents, US Senator James O. Eastland, received $170,000 in 1967 for *not* planting cotton on his plantation—while the seventy-eight black families still living as sharecroppers on his land struggled to stave off starvation. Fannie Lou Hamer often referred to Senator Eastland, without a trace of hyperbole, as "the biggest welfare recipient in the state of Mississippi."

In US Congressman Whitten's role as the chair of the agricultural appropriations subcommittee he not only lined the pockets of the Delta's landowning class, he also used his position to block investigations into the region's shifting economy and to block programs that could retrain its workforce. When campaigning against Whitten in 1964, Hamer told audiences about a federal job training program that would have benefited thousands of Delta sharecroppers, but was blocked by Whitten because the program would have been racially integrated. Further still, reporter Nick Kotz wrote that by "opposing all studies exploring the effects of a changing agriculture upon people, Whitten helped insure that Agriculture Department farm policy would never seriously include consideration of the effects of its programs on sharecroppers or farm workers." To be sure, poverty in the Mississippi Delta grew out of the region's history of slavery, white supremacy, and the exploitative sharecropping system. But the roots of this poverty were also firmly planted in discriminatory federal policies.

Finding solutions to an intergenerational, government-sanctioned epidemic must have seemed overwhelming to Hamer. And by the end of the 1960s—after losing her eldest daughter to complications related to malnutrition, after the harassment she and Perry Hamer endured in their struggle for voting rights, and after being excluded from meaningful leadership roles within area Head Start programs, nobody would have blamed the Hamers for leaving the Delta. In fact, between 1960 and 1970 there was a 25 percent dip in the region's population—part of what became known as the second wave of the Great Migration. During this time, black Deltans left the rural South in search of manufacturing work in northern cities. Hamer recognized that many white Mississippians encouraged this black exodus. Local officials, she told northern audiences, "don't want poor people to have anything to eat, so that they will go away, up North, maybe, to the ghettos and slums of Detroit and Chicago and Newark and New York City." Now that 90 percent of the farm labor involved in cotton production was done by chemical weed killers and mechanical pickers, Hamer reasoned, "we have become a surplus."

Even the mayor of Ruleville, Charles M. Durrough, responded to Hamer's frequent protests by saying, "Fannie Lou, if you're really tired of what's going on in Mississippi, you ought to leave."

To which she responded, "If you're sick of looking at me in Ruleville, you pack your bags and you leave!"

Hamer believed she had every right to stay in the land of her birth, land cleared by her ancestors, tilled by her grandparents, and farmed by her parents, siblings, and herself—an entire region's economy built upon the backs of black Deltans unremunerated labor. What's more, Hamer felt an obligation to stay in the rural South to help others. During the Great Migration's first wave, when many of her siblings moved North in search of economic opportunities and political rights, Hamer felt a strong tug of duty and stayed behind to care for her aging parents. Now, as then, Hamer insisted on staying in the Delta and caring for her impoverished community.

By the turn of the decade, Hamer's care took many forms. She helped reporter Nick Kotz with a Public Broadcasting Service documentary entitled *Hunger—American Style*. She appeared in the documentary, boldly condemning both Senator Eastland and the war in Vietnam. Hamer also functioned as a valuable local contact for the film's production. She connected Kotz with people to interview who were experiencing poverty across one of the nation's most destitute regions, especially people living on US Senator Eastland's plantation. From her work on voting rights earlier in the decade, Hamer had learned that national exposure to problems in the Delta could help bring about local change. Hamer was also buoyed by her more recent experience with Senator Robert F. Kennedy. After traveling to the Delta in 1967, and witnessing the region's poverty epidemic firsthand, Kennedy became a fierce supporter of the Southern Christian Leadership Conference's (SCLC) Poor People's Campaign and he demanded an increase to federal poverty programs throughout the state. Hamer was confident that if she could communicate the gravity of her region's poverty epidemic to northern audiences, shining a light on the unparalleled rates of malnutrition, type 2 diabetes, hypertension, and infant mortality rates among the region's black population, she could help bring some immediate relief to her community. In the process of spreading this urgent message to audiences across the country, moreover, Hamer also precipitated long-lasting change.

Fannie Lou Hamer worked quietly in the kitchen as Jaqueline and Lenora rested. Pap would be home from his Head Start bus route soon and Vergie was now headed back from school. Hamer needed to prepare something for the family to eat that night. As she searched their cupboards, she heard a whimper. Heading back to the bedroom to check on the girls, Hamer came face to face with their neighbor. The woman's eyes were bloodshot, tears rolled down her cheeks, and she clenched a handkerchief in her fist. Hamer embraced the woman. Hamer understood the depth of her neighbor's grief and encouraged her to let it out, gently patting her back. Just two days before, this woman's eighteen-year-old son had died from malnutrition. His body was so weak that he had never walked a day in his life. "The boy never had bones strong enough to walk on," Hamer would later tell northern audiences.

As Hamer knew all too well, hunger in the Mississippi Delta was a matter of life and death. Beginning in 1967, she focused the lion's share of her energy on disseminating that knowledge to a network of northern supporters whom she had met during her years of voting rights activism. She penned letters to civil rights allies, enlisting their help in the fight against hunger. These letters included her neighbor's story as well as her family's struggle with malnutrition. "My own daughter is sixteen-years-old," Hamer wrote. "She was in the hospital a few years ago. They fed her glucose because she was suffering from malnutrition." Hamer chose to share Vergie's experience with malnutrition rather than the far more tragic story of her older daughter, Dorothy. Hamer rarely discussed Dorothy's death publicly, in fact, even when the circumstances surrounding the loss of her eldest child—poverty, malnutrition, and lack of access to quality health care—related directly to the issues Hamer was engaging. The pain of Dorothy's loss was often too difficult for Hamer to invoke. Instead, Hamer used the platform and networks built by her civil rights activism to broadcast her neighbors' stories and—in the recollections of one northern supporter—"open people's eyes to widespread suffering in the Mississippi Delta."

Initially, Hamer reached out to northern friends to help purchase food stamps for Deltans with little or no income. In 1968, activists from a group called Measure for Measure based in Madison, Wisconsin met with Hamer on a trip to the Delta. Formed in 1963 by John Colson, a librarian at the Wisconsin State Historical Society, Measure for Measure supported "self-help programs" connected to civil rights movement activism. Measure for Measure had supported the neighboring North Bolivar County Cooperative for several years when the Madison-area activists met Hamer. After she explained the dire situation in Sunflower County, the Measure for Measure organization raised $5,000 in donations to help residents purchase food stamps. But within several months' time the money was gone and black Deltans were again left hungry. Hamer recounted her community's desperation to an audience in Madison:

> I went up last Tuesday to the food stamp place and there was a young woman there—had seven children—and her baby hadn't had milk in two days. She told them she was going to set in the food stamp office until they would let her have some stamps. They had given her some stamps and after she left they called out to her and taken the stamps back from her because they said they heard she would start work tomorrow.

As this anecdote revealed, food was being used as a mechanism of control and a form of punishment for black advancement in the Delta. The years-long battles over localized administration of federal food commodities, not to mention the more recent war over Head Start funding, made it clear to Hamer that she would need to find another solution to the dire needs surrounding her. "If what the politicians have done to the poverty program hasn't taught us anything else," Hamer reasoned, "it has taught us that we are not going to get much help from the politicians." If Black Deltans were to survive, she declared. "We are going to have to do for ourselves."

In 1969, Hamer learned that a local bank was threatening to foreclose on the property of one of the few landowning black farmers in Ruleville. She knew this was her chance. Only seventy-one of Sunflower County's 31,000 black residents owned any land, and no white landowner would sell to Hamer. She wasted no time contacting northern supporters—Measure for Measure's treasurer, two teaching fellows she had met when speaking at Harvard University the previous year, and Harry Belafonte, with whom she had toured Guinea five years earlier. As luck would have it, two professors at the University of Wisconsin-Madison had recently inherited a large sum of money, which they donated to Measure for Measure and which Measure for Measure, in turn, offered to Hamer. The Harvard teaching fellows raised $1,300 from donors in Cambridge. And, through an ongoing fundraising letter campaign, Belafonte provided the remaining money Hamer needed to purchase the first forty acres of land for what would soon become Freedom Farm.

Around the same time, the National Council of Negro Women (NCNW) worked with Hamer to start a livestock share program she called the Pig Bank. The NCNW purchased fifty pigs (forty-five gilts and five boars); they also purchased feed for the pigs and all the supplies to create pig pens on Freedom Farm's newly acquired land. Heifer International also lent its expertise in care and maintenance of Freedom Farm's pigs in what was the first US-based project in the organization's twenty-five year history.

Once a gilt became impregnated by a boar, she was given to a hungry family, who agreed to return her and two of her offspring to the bank after she birthed the litter. Sows typically birth between eighteen and twenty piglets, so the pig agreement also stipulated that the family would pass on several pigs from the sow's litter to other hungry families in the area. Hamer referred to the Pig Bank as a "beautiful program"—one that provided a free source of protein to people across the Delta who could not otherwise afford to eat meat. The initial forty pigs Hamer purchased with NCNW funds multiplied to nearly 3,000 by 1972. "At one one time it looked like pigs was coming out of our pockets!" Hamer joked about their newfound plenty. To an observer from the NCNW, Hamer boasted that "there's nothing no better than getting up in the morning and having a huge slice of ham and a couple of biscuits and some butter." Recipients of the pork enjoyed it fresh and also froze it to eat during the Delta's winter months. Hamer realized, however, that "man cannot live on pork alone." And she set out to provide nutrient-rich produce for her malnourished community.

"Give us food and it will be gone tomorrow," Hamer said. "Give us land and the tools to work it and we'll feed ourselves forever." Hamer's take on this well-known proverb was complex. She was inspired by the turn to both economic justice and community empowerment that characterized this era of the movement for black freedom. Hamer was an initial signatory of James Forman's 1969 "Black Manifesto," which agitated for reparations from churches and synagogues for their role in the slave trade and the perpetuation of black exploitation. Forman envisioned the reparations money funding a range of black-led and black-operated initiatives, such as food cooperatives. Hamer was also inspired by the particular model of communal farming she saw in the nearby North Bolivar County Cooperative (NBCC). The NBCC also connected their efforts to employ and feed the community to the larger push for black political empowerment. "When black people have a steady job," a NBCC pamphlet stored in Hamer's papers explained, "we don't need to worry about what the white folks are thinking. We can vote for whom we want without having to fear anybody." To be free from hunger and the threat of economic reprisal would mean that black Deltans could more freely and more fully participate in political life.

The NBCC lent Hamer's Freedom Farm tools and equipment, and they even donated the seeds for the farm's first growing season, during which the fledgling organization cultivated cucumbers, corn, peas, beans, squash, okra, and collard greens. In the Delta's rich soil, Freedom Farmers also planted cash crops like soybeans and cotton, which they sold to pay taxes on the land and to provide salaries for their administrative staff. The organization also established a board and drew up bylaws, which set the co-op membership fee at one dollar per month. Only thirty families in the area could afford this fee, so the remainder of Freedom Farm's 1,500 members joined without paying the membership fee. But membership was not required to receive produce from the farm. In exchange for a few hours' work, a hungry person could take home a bushel of produce, canned food, or cured pork. By 1970, Hamer estimated that Freedom Farm had fed approximately 5,000 people from the organization's first forty acres, noting that these recipients "didn't get *everything*, but that many people was allowed to get *something*." Still, Hamer wanted to provide even more for her community.

Owing to her near-decade of outspoken and tireless activism, she now had mechanisms to ensure relative economic security, which Hamer considered essential for full citizenship, for black Deltans. Fannie Lou Hamer was a widely sought after speaker on college campuses by the turn of the decade. As the voluminous records from this period of her activist career indicate, between 1968 and 1972, Hamer spoke in every region of the country during community celebrations and at colleges and universities such as Harvard, Northwestern, Duke, Shaw, Florida State, Carleton, Goucher, the University of Wisconsin-Madison, Seattle University, and the University of California-Berkeley. During this latter period of her activist career, Hamer also appeared in several documentaries and on a variety of television shows including *The David Frost Show*, the *Gil Noble Show* (New York City), *Kup's Show* (Chicago), and *Tony Brown's Journal*. Through these public appearances, Hamer raised national awareness and money from northern audiences, whom she brazenly asked to "search their hearts *and* their pocketbooks." Audiences listened. After hearing Hamer speak, college students organized "Walks for Development" and "Hunger Hikes" across Midwestern cities like Madison, Chicago, and Milwaukee. These walks raised over $200,000 for her Freedom Farm organization—that's over a million dollars in today's currency. In direct response to Hamer's national television appearances and public talks, donations also poured into the NCNW's Freedom Farm Fund. Over one thousand donation envelopes from places as far reaching as Anchorage, Alaska; Sugarland, Texas; and Issaquah, Washington, fill boxes in the archived collection of Hamer's papers. With these funds, Freedom Farm made a down payment on an additional 640 acres of land between Drew and Ruleville, Mississippi.

By 1971, the organization's combined farmland grew to nearly seven hundred acres, and Hamer remarked that "for the first time in our lives, we will have a chance to control some of our destiny." Freedom Farm used the land and the influx of funds to expand existing operations and to start new endeavors. The board issued college scholarships to area youth and supported

Figure 6.1 Fannie Lou Hamer organized Freedom Farm, an interracial food and housing cooperative, to combat widespread malnutrition, homelessness, and joblessness in her home community. Magnum, photo credit: Bruce Davidson.

a garment factory, which became the second largest employer in Sunflower County—Head Start was the first and Freedom Farm the third. The women working at the garment factory needed low-cost childcare, so Freedom Farm created the Fannie Lou Hamer Daycare Center, which remained active in Ruleville for decades after Hamer's death. Hamer also poured the honoraria and donations she received from her national travels back into Freedom Farm's operations. As a result, she was able to support the construction of two hundred houses for people whose living structures were so shoddy they were, in Hamer's words, "living almost outdoors."

Employees on Freedom Farm's growing payroll helped families in need of quality homes secure low-interest loans from the Federal Housing Authority (FHA). For those who could not secure an FHA loan, Freedom Farm would purchase their home and sell it back to them at a low monthly payment, or, if the family could not afford that, they could live temporarily in a home provided by Freedom Farm. What's more, the construction of these homes provided additional jobs for out-of-work farmers across the region. Hamer's own family benefited from the housing component of the Freedom Farm Cooperative; they were finally able to move the modest yellow-brick bungalow they'd purchased years earlier onto a lot on James Street, which was later re-named Fannie Lou Hamer Drive.

Although black Deltans represented the majority of Freedom Farm's membership and the initial board was all black, Hamer insisted that "the cry of hunger is the cry of hunger whether it come from blacks, whites, brown or red." Several white families benefited from the farm's produce and at least one white family moved onto Freedom Farm's land in 1971. As she recounted before northern audiences, a white father came to her in distress. "I've got five children and I got nowhere to live," he said. "I don't have food. I don't have anything. And my children, some of them is sick." Freedom Farm provided his family with a home, food, and medical care for the sick children.

As an interracial endeavor, Freedom Farm distinguished itself from other cooperatives in the area and other contemporaneous programs for economic sovereignty. Dr. L. C. Dorsey, a founding member of the North Bolivar County Cooperative, noted that Hamer "was one of the first people who really started reaching out to poor *white* people." Dorsey recalled that Hamer wanted white people to envision Freedom Farm as an "opportunity to put aside the difference in our colors." In fact, Hamer encouraged impoverished white people to recognize that "if you can't feed your children, if you can't protect your family, if you can't earn a living, then there's something wrong with that picture." Hamer urged impoverished white people to "cast your lot with us and try to make it right."

Freedom Farm—Hamer's multifaceted poverty program—was led by those experiencing poverty themselves and was supported by activists across the nation. What's more, Freedom Farm's board included women not only in supporting roles, but in meaningful leadership and decision-making positions. Freedom Farm linked citizenship to food security. The program reached out to impoverished Deltans—black and white alike—to share the message that full citizenship is only made possible by securing one's basic needs for food, shelter, and health care.

As a multiracial program, led by black women, created for impoverished people by impoverished people, Freedom Farm was revolutionary in its context and well beyond. After a speech Hamer delivered at the University of Wisconsin-Madison in 1971, for example, the student newspaper ran an article praising Hamer and the visionary organization she led. "The dignity of the people, reinforced by the Sunflower Farm Co-op [Freedom Farm] is the strongest basis yet for viable political struggle," the students wrote, touting Freedom Farm as "an example from which student radicals likely have a lot to learn."

More than forty years later, John T. Edge, the director of the Southern Foodways Program, penned an op-ed for the *New York Times* entitled, "The Hidden Radicalism of Southern Food." In this piece, Edge described the multiple facets of the Freedom Farm Cooperative that Hamer created, before declaring: "The work of Fannie Lou Hamer makes it clear that the South has served the nation as more than a place to situate (and eat) good food." By taking a closer look at Hamer's Freedom Farm, Edge learned that "in the South, America has identified food-system problems and developed solutions." He continued, "As Americans agitate for food sovereignty in our contemporary context the bold agricultural ideas conceived in the late 1960s by Fannie Lou Hamer and other radical Southerners suggest paths for us to follow out of our food deserts."

Freedom Farm's success in the late 1960s and early 1970s was emblematic of advances earned across the Delta by persistent and assertive black-led activism. Just thirty minutes west of Ruleville in the 2,500-person town of Shaw, for instance, black residents filed a class action lawsuit claiming that their rights under the equal protection clause of the Fourteenth Amendment had been violated by the unequal distribution of municipal services. The 1970 case, *Hawkins v. Town of Shaw*, reached the United States Court of Appeals and demonstrated along the way that access to, and the quality of, municipal services such as street paving, street lights, sewers, and storm water drainage were starkly differentiated by race. In 1972, the court ultimately intervened in what had traditionally been considered a legislative matter, ordering the town to submit a "program of improvements that will, within a reasonable time, remove the disparities that bear so heavily on the black citizens of Shaw."

Around this same time, Hamer served as the lead plaintiff in another significant court case coming out of the Mississippi Delta. In May of 1970, Hamer joined 104 other plaintiffs in filing the class action lawsuit, *Hamer v. Sunflower County*. Similar to the *Hawkins'* suit, these plaintiffs alleged that their constitutional right to equal protection under the law had been violated. In the *Hamer* case, however, the issue was public school segregation. More than fifteen years after the *Brown v. Board of Education* decision, and several years after the Justice Department had filed lawsuits across Mississippi to enforce the historic desegregation ruling, Sunflower County schools remained racially segregated. Equally troubling, the threat of public school closures loomed large in towns like Ruleville, where white students fled to private segregated academies to avoid the threat of desegregation. Hamer worried that public school closures would result in black teachers and principals losing their jobs. Judge William Keady of the US District Court heard the case and ordered the formation of a biracial committee of Sunflower County residents charged with creating an effective desegregation plan. Hamer chaired this committee, which redrew district lines to create more integrated schools and to maximize the use of existing buildings. Since public school funding is allocated per pupil, white flight to segregated academies strained the public schools' resources. Therefore, the committee also developed a nondiscriminatory plan to ensure that black principals, teachers, and aides would not be targeted because of their race and unduly affected by inevitable reductions in staff.

As was so often the case in the staunchly segregated Delta, however, black activism and advancement were met with vitriolic and lethal assertions of white supremacy. For the lead plaintiffs in the *Hawkins* suit, demanding their right to basic municipal services cost them everything. In 1972, Mary Lou Hawkins was shot and killed by a police officer in Shaw. The Hawkins home was also set on fire, twice; the second fire killed Mary Lou and Andrew Hawkins' son, as well as their two granddaughters. In January of 1971, a firebomb was left on the front porch of the Hamers' home; the house and the family inside were spared when it failed to explode. And that spring, as an NAACP-led voter registration drive galvanized black voters for the upcoming statewide election, registration workers' tires were slashed, a white grocery store owner killed a black customer in northeast Mississippi, and a white policeman killed a black man in Sumner.

On the evening of May 25, 1971, Jo Etha Collier walked home from Drew High School's graduation ceremony. The eighteen-year-old graduate was beaming. She had just been recognized as the track team's most valuable member and had also received a school-wide award for her "good conduct and attitude." Integrating the previously all-white school in her small rural town was challenging, but Collier persevered and now held in her hands a diploma and two awards—testaments to her strength, determination, and success. She paid no mind to the car full of drunken white teenaged-boys heckling her as she crossed in front of their small town's grocery store. She'd learned to tune out this type of harassment at school, focusing instead on where she was headed. Collier marched forward until a bullet hit the back side of her neck—forcing her to the ground. She lay face down, blood pooling around her, the sound of tires screeching as the car full of white teenagers fled the murder scene.

Jo Etha Collier's death shook the small rural town of Drew, Mississippi, and the aftershocks of this senseless, racist killing reverberated nationally. Demonstrations erupted in Drew and in Hamer's neighboring town of Ruleville, where thirty-one people were arrested. The mayors of both towns enlisted Hamer to help quell the uprisings. She refused. "She didn't promise anything except more demonstrations," the mayor of Drew, W. O. Williford, told the press.

Hamer wasn't looking to keep the peace; she was outraged. "How much longer are things like this going to be allowed to happen?" she asked the reporters, who swarmed her and Collier's grief-stricken mother, Gussie Mae Love.

Reverend Ralph Abernathy, who led the Southern Christian Leadership Conference after Martin Luther King, Jr.'s assassination, delivered the eulogy at Collier's funeral. Hundreds of mourners gathered in the same high school auditorium where Collier had graduated just days before. Abernathy implored those present to "get in the movement and make life better for ourselves and for our children."

Mrs. Hamer was also invited by the family to speak. Her remarks at Collier's funeral convey a deep sense of frustration and despair. "Jo Etha Collier was smart and she was black. That was too much for the whites," Hamer said, before bursting into tears.

Having lost her own daughter four years before, Hamer forged a close relationship with Jo Etha Collier's mother—both of whom could trace their family's tragedy to injustices rooted in white supremacy. In the months that followed, Hamer helped raise money for Jo Etha Collier's family to buy their first home. She also brought Collier's mother along with her on her frequent travels. Perhaps most notably, Gussie Mae Love accompanied Hamer to the founding meeting of the National Women's Political Caucus (NWPC) in Washington, D.C.

Suspicious of the white organizers' intentions and concerned she'd be used as a token representative, some women of color warned Hamer not to attend the historic NWPC meeting. She registered their concerns, but Hamer was under no illusions about the role she would play when she entered Washington, D.C.'s Statler Hilton Hotel on July 10, 1971. Hamer and Love sat among an audience of nearly three hundred women, gathered from across twenty-six states. They listened as rising stars in the nascent Women's Liberation Movement (WLM) addressed the crowd. Betty Friedan, author of *The Feminine Mystique*—the watershed book that compelled many suburban white women to recognize the insidious nature of gender-based oppression—was a key organizer. Gloria Steinem, widely heralded as the spokesperson for the WLM and the soon-to-be co-founder of *Ms. Magazine*, also took part in this inaugural meeting. So, too, did Bella Abzug, the newly elected US congresswoman, who represented Manhattan's west side.

As the meeting unfolded, Hamer listened to Abzug, nicknamed "Battling Bella," pointedly ask the attendees what priorities "a Congress with adequate representation of women and other groups" might set. Abzug asked the attendees if they believed that a more representative Congress would address the infant mortality crisis in the US and the lack of affordable high-quality child care. She insisted that women in political office would vote to fund schools instead of missiles, decent housing and health centers instead of weapons. Abzug also insisted that a more representative Congress would have brought an end to the war in Vietnam long ago. Hamer nodded in agreement to much of Abzug's speech. Her own Freedom Farm was a valiant effort to stem the tide of infant mortality that disproportionately affected the black population in the Mississippi Delta. Despite her political qualms with the program's administrators, Hamer also continued to support Head Start Centers, and she had recently organized an independent childcare facility for the children of local garment factory workers.

Like most of the feminists gathered at the inaugural NWPC meeting, moreover, Hamer virulently opposed the war in Vietnam. In fact, she had publicly spoke out against the war since the summer of 1965. Her resistance was based on the fact that young men were fighting and dying in Vietnam for rights and liberties that were not guaranteed in the United States. All the while, vast resources were being poured into the war that could be spent on poverty programs so desperately needed across the country. Further still, Hamer opposed the imperialist nature of the war and the needless destruction it wrought upon Vietnamese men, women, and children. By 1971, Hamer's opposition to Vietnam had also grown deeply personal. Her late daughter Dorothy's husband, Sylvester Hall, had been drafted mere months after Dorothy's death. Hall's parents, who lived just around the corner from the Hamers, helped Perry and Fannie Lou care for Dorothy and Sylvester's young children. When Hall returned from the war with injuries so severe that he required kidney dialysis for the remainder of his life, Hall's parents became overwhelmed by caregiving duties. His parents offered to adopt one of Dorothy's children, Lenora, the older daughter who was healthier than the younger Jacqueline, but they could no longer raise both girls and provide care for their injured son. Fannie Lou knew Dorothy would not have wanted to split up her children, so she and Perry enlisted the services of a local lawyer and—with Hall's consent—the Hamers officially adopted Jaqueline and Lenora in 1969.

As a working mother of young children, who fought against the triple forces of racism, sexism, and poverty every day of her life, Hamer both related to and critically questioned the more privileged NWPC speakers' messages. When it was Hamer's turn to speak, University of Wisconsin-Madison professor, Kay Clarenbach, introduced Hamer as a founder of the Mississippi Freedom Democratic Party, the founder of the Freedom Farm Cooperative, and "one of the great civil rights leaders of our time." Hamer approached the dais in what attendees recall as "obvious physical discomfort." Her limp had worsened, she sweated profusely, and she now grimaced as she moved. Nevertheless, Hamer thanked the audience for their applause and told them it was a pleasure to be there. Then Hamer took a deep breath and spoke her mind.

"Listening to different speakers," Hamer gestured to the white feminists who had held the floor that morning, "I've thought about if they've had problems, then they should be black and in Mississippi for a spell."

The women of color in attendance burst into applause at this opening line. Women such as Myrlie Evers, a California legislator and widow of the slain Mississippi civil rights activist, Medgar Evers; Beulah Sanders, the National Welfare Rights Organization vice president; Dorothy Height, president of the National Council of Negro Women; LaDonna Harris, Native American rights leader, and Shirley Chisholm, the first black woman elected to the US Congress—were all gratified to hear Hamer address the intersectional nature of their lived experience.

To give presence to the gravity of interlocking oppressions, Hamer gestured toward another woman of color in the audience, Gussie Mae Love. For several years, as invitations for Hamer to speak poured in and her health steadily deteriorated, she insisted on bringing a traveling companion. Each trip Hamer took, therefore, provided not only an honorarium that she then donated back to the fledgling Freedom Farm, but also an opportunity for a member of her community to experience life outside their small rural town. Just six weeks after Love's young daughter was murdered on her graduation day, Hamer shared Love's story at the founding meeting of the NWPC. In her devastation, which Hamer acknowledged was wrought by "racism and hate," Love joined legions of black mothers like Mamie Till-Mobley, whose fourteen-year-old son Emmett was lynched in Mississippi, and Fannie Lee Chaney, whose twenty-one-year-old son was killed during Freedom Summer. Hamer contended that Love's experience as a grieving black mother was common to many women of color in attendance. Whether these women had lost their children to a murderer's bullet or to malnutrition and inadequate access to health care, as had Hamer, the lethal effects of racism dominated the lives of black women.

Hamer also recognized that women of color share the pain of loss with some white women in the audience—women who might have lost their sons to the war in Vietnam or their daughters during deadly protests at places like Kent State. "A white mother is no different from a black mother," Hamer reasoned. "The only thing is they haven't had as many problems. But we cry the same tears. And under the skin it's the same kind of red blood."

Hamer's involvement in the NWPC inaugural meeting and, to a large extent, her interactions with the Women's Liberation Movement of the 1970s, were marked by ambivalence. On the one hand, Hamer supported "bridging the gap," which she explained as the coming together of women from all walks of life. She challenged the NWPC attendees to stop thinking about different groups of women as "minorities." The word "minority," Hamer argued, might lead people to assume the group was too small to have any power. Instead, Hamer urged the women gathered in D.C. to join forces with other groups of oppressed people, who shared their concerns. "If you think about hooking up with all these women of all different colors and all the minority hooking on with the majority of women of voting strength in this country we would become one *hell* of a majority!" Hamer exclaimed.

On the other hand, however, Fannie Lou Hamer opposed core aspects of second wave feminism and she warned white feminists against using the banner of sisterhood to erase significant differences among women's lived experiences. Part of the Women's Liberation Movement agenda included establishing reproductive autonomy. Hamer—having been sterilized without her consent in 1961—held a different perspective about this core issue. She often spoke out about forced sterilization, a procedure that was so common in her state that it was colloquially referred to as a "Mississippi Appendectomy." By the late 1960s and early 1970s, even as the Women's Liberation Movement pushed for reproductive rights, the Mississippi legislature was debating two bills that proposed sterilization for "anybody convicted of a third felony" and for "any parent of a second illegitimate child." Hamer understood these measures as the "new repression" and she viewed this legislation in race-based civil rights terms, recalled her friend and fellow activist, Reverend Edwin King.

Hamer objected not only to forced sterilization, but also to all forms of reproductive control. She voiced this opposition in several speeches delivered during 1971 and in an interview with *Essence* magazine. Before an audience at Tougaloo College, for instance, Hamer said, "The methods used to take human lives, such as abortion, the pill, the ring, et cetera amounts to genocide. I believe that legal abortion is legal murder and the use of pills and rings to prevent God's will is a great sin." At the University of Wisconsin-Madison, Hamer suggested that if birth control pills had been available in her mother's day, then Hamer probably wouldn't be standing there today. Having made what she described as a "narrow escape to be here," Hamer took it upon herself to "fight for other kids too, to give them a chance." As Hamer explained, her opposition to reproductive control was rooted in her religious convictions, her love of children, and in a well-founded fear of state control over the bodies of its most vulnerable citizens.

Hamer was not alone in her opposition to second wave feminists' push for legalized abortion. "Black feminists assailed white women's failure to acknowledge class and racial aspects of the abortion issue," sociologist Benita Roth explained. Roth cited ways in which black feminists expanded the conversation about reproductive justice beyond "abortion on demand," to include "concerns that were tied to class power: involuntary sterilization; life circumstances that compel poor women to abort; and the possibility that women on welfare would be forced by the state to have abortions." Rather than characterize Hamer as a "Black Feminist," who expanded the conversation about reproductive justice in ways that address a range of life circumstances, however, Hamer's contemporaries as well as her biographers contend that she was decidedly "not a feminist." Her friend and fellow activist, Lawrence Guyot, explained that while "Hamer supported women's empowerment, she was not a feminist." Instead, Guyot characterized Hamer as a "humanist," reasoning that she "had a broader vision."

Unlike some white feminists' insistence on seeking liberation from men, for instance, Hamer's broader vision included empowering black men. In 1965, Daniel Patrick Moynihan released his report, *The Negro Family: The Case for National Action*, in which the Assistant Secretary of Labor argued that the matriarchal structure of the black nuclear family was the primary impediment to black men's ability to function as leaders in their communities. Hamer found Moynihan's report ridiculous even as she recognized its broad cultural influence. To counter this influence, the defense of black women and the promotion of black men became prominent features of her public discourse. She dismissed Moynihan's thesis outright in her 1971 interview in *Essence* magazine. She said, "You know that Moynihan who wrote about black matriarchal society knows as much about a black family as a horse knows about New Year's day." In Hamer's estimation, it was not the matriarchal composition of black families that disempowered black men, rather it was welfare policies that withheld support to families if men of working age were living in the home, a criminal justice system that targeted black men, and centuries of white supremacist exploitation of black men's labor that resulted in fewer black men excelling in the arenas of politics and economics. In no uncertain terms, Hamer announced to the NWPC gathering:

> I'm not fighting to liberate myself from the black man in the South because, so help me, God, he's had as many and more severer problems than I've had. Because not only has he been stripped of the right to be a politician, but he has been stripped of the dignity and heritage and all the things that any citizen of a country needs.

Just two months before Hamer delivered this NWPC address, moreover, she spoke at the NAACP's Legal Defense Fund's conference on the plight of black women. In this speech, Hamer told the audience, with pride: "I got a black husband, six foot three, two hundred and forty pounds, with a fourteen shoe, that I don't *want* to be liberated from."

In truth, Perry Hamer was one of the most empowering forces in Fannie Lou Hamer's life. In a 1969 article titled "Rights Matriarch Pleads for Action Now," a reporter for the *Wisconsin State Journal* focused, in large part, on Hamer's family life. "When she's away from home, traveling around the country, speaking on college campuses," Gay Leslie wrote, "she worries about her family." As Hamer often did, she connected her public work to her role as a mother. "I worry about the kids," she said, "but to make things better for them in the years to come somebody has got to do something now." Leslie noted that Hamer "says her husband is 'fantastic.'" And she quoted Hamer as saying both "without a husband like that I couldn't be around doing what I do" and also emphasizing that Perry Hamer is "a man. He's not just a shadow of me."

Citing the public activism with which she was engaged as well as her familial arrangements that enabled this work, biographer Chana Kai Lee referred to Hamer not as a feminist or an anti-feminist, but rather a "non feminist." Lee claimed that while Hamer disagreed with aspects of the feminist movement, her "life and powerful presence had undeniably feminist consequences." However, the way in which Brittney Cooper has more recently defined Black Feminism in her essay, "Capital B, Capital F"—citing its historical forebears Maria Stewart, Sojourner Truth, Anna Julia Cooper, Ida B. Wells, and the women of the Combahee River Collective while connecting Black Feminism to a profound love of black women as well as a deliberate centering of their experiences and their communities' needs—suggests that "Black Feminist" is, indeed, the most fitting label to describe Fannie Lou Hamer's activism. Hamer's previous biographers and contemporaries alike seem to be operating under a narrow understanding of feminism as, in Cooper's words, "white women's shit" when they refuse to associate Hamer with this label. If second wave feminism is conceived of strictly as the liberation of women from patriarchal relationships and a movement to secure reproductive rights, then no, Fannie Lou Hamer was not a feminist per se. If one privileges Cooper's understanding of feminism's capaciousness—variously as a movement to end gender inequality, to center the needs and experiences of women, and to better understand the interconnected nature of multiple oppressions—then Hamer was not only a feminist in her time, but she should continue to stand as a powerful feminist exemplar in ours.

As a Black Feminist, Hamer's presence, her broad-ranging advocacy, and the consequences of her activism certainly inspired many women within the 1970s liberation movement to battle what bell hooks has dubbed the "imperialist white supremacist capitalist patriarchy." To be clear, the WLM not only grew out of an awakening spurred by manifestoes like *The Feminine Mystique*, it was also spurred by women's struggles with the pervasive sexism of the civil rights, antiwar, and New Left movements. According to Congresswoman Shirley Chisholm, who would soon become the first black female candidate for US president, second wave feminists knew "that if they expected to start a women's organization, they should have Fannie Lou Hamer and Shirley Chisholm there." Chisholm insisted, "We were both known to be fearless." Hamer's fearlessness manifested during her bold address to the NWPC and it resounded throughout the inaugural meeting. Over the course of proceedings, Hamer allied herself with Chisholm, Evers, Height, and Beulah Sanders. Together, they formed a Black Caucus within the NCNW and wove a bold antiracist commitment into the fabric of the organization's mission.

The expressed goals of the NWPC were two-fold: to secure more positions of power for women in elected and appointed political offices and to make the existing system of power more responsive to the concerns of women. At the outset of the Women's Liberation Movement, very few women held formal political power and influence within the US. There were only twelve US congresswomen, one female senator, and no women on the US Supreme Court. Nevertheless, the NWPC's Black Caucus insisted that there should be clear guidelines, enforced by a policy council, to determine which female candidates the organization would support. They believed it was not enough to elect *any* woman to office; the women the NWPC supported should align with the organization's values. Prominent members of the fledgling organization agreed. As Abzug reminded the gathering, "Women, like men, have stoned black children going to integrated schools. Women have been and are prejudiced, narrow-minded, reactionary, even violent. *Some* women. They, of course, have a right to vote and a right to run for office. I will defend that right, but I will not support or vote for them."

The Black Caucus within the NWPC was instrumental not only in raising the issue of selective value-based support, they were also integral in developing the very criteria by which candidates would receive NCNW backing. The guidelines stipulated that NCNW-backed candidates must fight for "the elimination of sexism, racism, violence and poverty," as well as an end to the war in Vietnam. Further still, members of the NWPC's Black Caucus threatened to walk out of the inaugural proceedings unless the organization passed a firm anti-racism resolution, committing publicly and unequivocally that members of the organization "will have no part of racism in any of its forms." They were not pressed to make good on this threat because the antiracism resolution passed during the inaugural meeting of the NWPC.

As Chisholm remembered, Hamer was outspoken throughout the proceedings. She repeatedly warned such high profile participants as Steinem, Abzug, and Friedan that "black women would never join their organization unless they understood the particular depth of our concerns." Chisholm admitted Hamer was "kind of harsh" and that she "told them off." Hamer's harsh

Figure 6.2 Fannie Lou Hamer was a founding member of the National Women's Political Caucus. She is pictured here in Washington, D.C., seated next to Betty Smith, former vice chairman of the GOP in Wisconsin; Dorothy Haener, International Representative Women's Department United Automobile Workers Union; and Gloria Steinem, member of the Democratic National Policy Council, July 10, 1971. Getty Images, photo credit: Bettman.

critiques likely surprised many white women in attendance, who had imagined the meeting as a generative experience, one of coming together under the banner of sisterhood. But Hamer came to the meeting with markedly different objectives. Just as she had understood her involvement in civil rights activism as a prophetic fulfilling of God's will, she cast her participation at the NWPC in biblical terms. She concluded her formal address to the three hundred women gathered from twenty-six states with an allusion to the Book of Esther. "So I'm saying to you today," Hamer intoned. "Who knows but that I have cometh to the kingdom for such a time as this?"

By likening herself as an outsider—the Jewish queen married to a Persian king, someone who came to the seat of power and risked her life to save her people—Hamer echoed Chisholm's admonition. "Black women want to be part of the women's movement," Chisholm insisted, "but we are also part of another movement—the liberation of our own people." Far from being used by the white second wave feminists, Hamer, Chisholm, and other members of what became the NCNW's Black Caucus leveraged their participation to engender support from the NWPC for issues related to black empowerment. And it worked.

Hamer received a standing ovation from the NWPC participants when she formally announced her intention to run as an Independent in the upcoming Mississippi State Senate race. As the local election day drew near, moreover, members of the NCNW demonstrated their commitment to electing female candidates who embodied the organization's values by traveling to Mississippi and campaigning on Hamer's behalf.

In between East Coast speaking tours in New York and Washington, D.C., Hamer spent the summer of 1971 campaigning across Mississippi's eleventh district. Stretching from Sunflower to Bolivar County, across the vast agricultural expanse located in the northwestern region of the state, the eleventh district was a sizable area to canvass. But Hamer felt strongly that the more face-to-face interactions she had with voters, the better her chances would be to defeat the incumbent, Robert Crook. With support from the Voter Education Project and the Concerned Citizens of Sunflower County to Elect Black Officials, Hamer developed a compelling platform that included reforming Mississippi law in five key areas: welfare, voter registration, education, law enforcement, and taxation policy.

On the stump, Hamer advocated hiring more black people to welfare policymaking positions, increasing welfare provisions, creating state-run medical centers, and providing low-income housing for the sick and elderly. She also included longstanding critiques of voter and candidate suppression as part of her platform, advocating for mobile voter registration, lowering the voting age from twenty-one to eighteen, and doing away with laws that unnecessarily restricted candidates from running—such as the Mississippi statute that disqualified candidates from running as Independents if they had previously voted in a party's primary. Hamer promoted laws requiring that Black History be taught in public schools and proposed that public school teachers be provided tenure after three years of service, which would protect them from the economic retaliation that often accompanied their civil rights activism. Finally, Hamer campaigned on promises of free lunch programs for impoverished students, an end to discriminatory law enforcement practices, and uniform tax rates—so that wealthy landowners would be required to pay a more reasonable share of state taxes.

By the early 1970s, many of Hamer's civil rights allies had abandoned establishment politics. Some joined Black Separatist and New Left organizations, each of which urged their own form of revolutionary social and political change. Hamer, though highly critical of establishment politics, continued to work both within and outside of the system to bring about the radical changes she sought. Her 1971 run for office suggested both a deep-seated faith in the democratic process and a recognition that holding political office could help expand the radical programs for economic justice she had created. Many of the issues she campaigned on, in fact, mirrored the problems her independent Freedom Farm was tackling. Her run for public office, therefore, demonstrated her remarkable ability to advocate for fundamental changes on multiple fronts simultaneously. Thankfully, she was not alone in this work. Over three hundred black candidates ran for public office in the fall of 1971, including Charles Evers, who campaigned to become the state's first black governor—and the first black governor in the US since Reconstruction.

Although the 1971 Mississippi election did not garner the level of national attention paid to previous contests, the elections were, indeed, historic. The Justice Department finally sent election observers—if only to thirty-six of the eighty-two counties across the state. Many observers were local federal employees, however, who reportedly refused to intervene in voter fraud as it occurred. Instead, they took note of voter suppression, intimidation, and fraud, filing reports which could be investigated further—if suits were filed. Perhaps more immediately effective were the scores of poll watchers who came to Mississippi at the bequest of the Voter Education Project (VEP). These high school, college, and graduate students from Wisconsin, New York, New Jersey, Boston, California, and Washington State strengthened the resolve of fearful black voters and demonstrated to white supremacists that the nation was literally watching. What's more, John Lewis, the newly appointed executive director of the VEP, worked throughout the summer of 1971 to increase black voter registration and to support black candidates in Mississippi. In the weeks leading up to the election, Lewis, the former chair of SNCC, was joined by fellow SNCC activist Julian Bond, who was now serving as a congressmen in the Georgia State Legislature. Lewis and Bond were also reunited in their efforts with D.C.-insiders like Joseph Rauh, who had represented the MFDP at the 1964 Democratic National Convention.

Hamer relished working alongside her old civil rights movement compatriots, even as she called upon her new feminist friends. She wrote a letter to the NWPC asking for campaign support and poll-watching assistance. Betty Friedan was the first to respond. One week before the election, Friedan expressed confidence in Hamer's political career. "It's no joke now that a woman could be elected president in 1976," Friedan told the crowd gathered in the small town of Moorhead, Mississippi. "Fannie Lou Hamer could be elected and would make a better president that the man in there now." The crowd roared with applause.

Hamer's campaign for state senate was part of the NWPC's long-term strategy. The organization viewed state senate campaigns as the first step to ultimately electing more women to the US Congress. Friedan, perhaps more acutely than most, understood what Hamer had been professing since she had spoken alongside Malcolm X in 1964. Ever since that Harlem address, Hamer had been telling national audiences that what happened in Mississippi was not just Mississippi's problem, reasoning that unfair elections in her home state affected national and international politics as well. While campaigning for Hamer in Mississippi, Friedan gave voice to her own understanding of this fundamental truth. No more than fifteen miles from US Senator James O. Eastland's home, Friedan recounted an exchange she'd had in Washington with Eastland, in his role as a member of the Senate Judiciary Committee. In 1970, Friedan had testified in opposition to President Nixon's Supreme Court nominee G. Harold Carswell. Friedan explained her opposition to the committee, noting that Carswell's nomination should be blocked based on his history of race and sex-based discrimination. To which Senator Eastland responded, "I've never heard of anyone opposing a Supreme Court nomination simply on the basis of discrimination against women." Surely, sending Hamer to the US Senate would engender more conscientious decision-making.

As Hamer had declared at the inaugural meeting of the NWPC, she planned to parlay a successful Mississippi State Senate campaign in 1971 into a 1972 US Senate campaign against Eastland. Just days before the November 1971 election, Hamer reached out to another feminist friend, Liz Carpenter, to help ensure her initial success. Carpenter, who served as Lady Bird Johnson's Chief of Staff, came right away—bringing with her a graduate student from Harvard University, Xandra Kayden. Soon after Carpenter and Kayden arrived in Mississippi, they borrowed a Winnebago and drove with Hamer across the Delta countryside. Up Highway 49 and across Highway 8, Hamer, Carpenter, and Kayden belted out traditional hymns. Soulful renditions of "Amazing Grace" and "His Eye Is on the Sparrow" connected these women, who seemed, on the surface, so different from one another.

The Washington insider, the Harvard graduate student, and the candidate for Mississippi State Senate stopped to meet with voters across the district and to broadcast Hamer's message. For their trek across the eleventh district, Hamer brought two thousand dollars in cash wrapped unassumingly in an old handkerchief. Hamer used these campaign funds to purchase air time on Delta radio stations. Purchasing power, however, did not immediately translate into access. For that, Hamer leaned on Carpenter, a well-connected political powerhouse whom radio stations were eager to interview. During those interviews, Carpenter not only endorsed Hamer's candidacy, she also persuaded reluctant small town stations to sell airtime to Hamer. If need be, Carpenter would invoke the nondiscrimination clause in Federal Communications Commission law, insisting the station acknowledge Hamer's right to equal airtime access.

Despite the support of Hamer's new feminist friends, old movement allies, and national organizations and in spite of her ramped up campaign efforts, crisscrossing the northwest section of the Delta, organizing high profile speakers, and spreading her message of change across the airwaves, Hamer lost to Robert Crook—11,770 to 7,201. It is unlikely, however, that these official results accurately reflect the will of Mississippi's district eleven voters. Volunteer poll watchers returned to every corner of the United States with an arsenal of incriminating stories to tell. Articles citing white supremacist voter suppression ran in major periodicals such as the *Wisconsin State Journal* and the *New York Times*, as well as in student newspapers. Northern onlookers alleged that some black votes were bought outright with whiskey and cash. Others were deemed "damaged" and thrown out at polling places. Still more votes were wrongfully cast; claims that white volunteers willfully mis-recorded the votes of blind and illiterate citizens abounded. Egregious instances of black Mississippi voters being fined, arrested, and beaten alongside their northern poll-watching allies also made national news.

Despite rampant black voter suppression, fifty of the 309 black candidates running in the largest black challenge to white rule in United States' history did win their bids for public office. These victories brought the total number of black elected officials to 145—earning Mississippi the honorable distinction as the state with the most black elected officials in the nation. Still, Charles Evers lost his election for the governorship and not one of the thirteen candidates running on the slate to which Hamer belonged, the Concerned Citizens of Sunflower County to Elect Black Officials, won a race. These losses in a section of the state where eligible black voters outnumbered eligible white voters by considerable margins enraged Hamer. She told a reporter she was "hopping mad" about the outcome of the 1971 elections. What's worse, the disappointing election results poured in just days after the white teenager charged with shooting Jo Etha Collier received a lenient manslaughter charge and not a murder conviction. This verdict, paired with the election results, left Hamer both angry and deeply depressed.

As the fall of 1971 turned into the winter of 1972, Hamer withdrew. She had long-suffered from the effects of the Winona beating, which left her with permanent kidney damage, backaches and headaches, and severely compromised eyesight, but the pain and exhaustion she experienced over these winter months suggested there was something else ailing her. Her unbearable physical pain combined with psychological worry—rooted in a lifetime of trauma—kept Hamer up at night and in bed most of the day. Jacqueline was now a kindergartener and Lenora a first grader. One cold January afternoon in 1972, the girls found their mother lying in bed when they returned from school. The curtains were drawn, but the winter sun snuck through the fabric's edges and glinted off the plaques hanging along the wall.

With help from Lenora, Jacqueline read the words aloud, filling the shadowy room with Hamer's many accolades. "Fannie Lou Hamer, First Lady of Civil Rights, presented by the League of Black Women Voters," read Jacqueline.

Lenora continued, "Fannie Lou Hamer, recipient of the Mary Church Terrell Award."

"Fannie Lou Hamer, 'Noble Example of Black Womanhood.'" The young girls read in tandem.

Then a frantic knock came from the front door.

As the girls ran to see who was there, Fannie Lou slowly sat up, wrapped herself in a striped housecoat, and limped toward the front porch. Once there, she found yet another devastated parent with tear-stained cheeks in need of help. Through sobs, the distressed black mother told Hamer that a local white storeowner—a relative of J. W. Milam, one of Emmett Till's killers—had just physically assaulted her black daughter. Like her mother before her, who carried a loaded gun into the fields to protect her children and who fought back when a white man raised a hand to her child, Hamer would not stand for white violence against black children. She and the girl's mother came up with a plan to initiate a boycott of the store, which would be reinforced by a round-the-clock picket line, until the storeowner issued an apology to the aggrieved family and pledged to treat black customers with respect. For two weeks, Hamer supported black Rulevillians who boycotted and demonstrated, even as she grew weaker, dizzier with each day spent on the picket line.

Then came the afternoon in late January when cold sweat trickled from Hamer's forehead as she squinted against the winter sun's glare. The picket line chants faded into the background and her legs became numb. She fell to the pavement slowly, it seemed, fellow demonstrators rushing to her side. Tattered handkerchiefs mopped her soggy brow. Concerned faces crowded her vision. Perry Hamer soon arrived and carried his wife to the car. Her heart was pounding. Her ears were ringing. She couldn't catch her breath. Over the course of the thirty-minute car ride to the Tufts-Delta Community Health Center in Mound Bayou, Hamer's heart rate slowed down a bit, and she was finally able to take deeper breaths. Perry Hamer wheeled her inside and a doctor examined her. In the midst of their panic, Fannie Lou and Perry Hamer tried to focus as the doctor explained to the shaken couple the symptoms of nervous exhaustion.

· 7 ·

"The Last Mile of the Way"

$\mathcal{F}$annie Lou Hamer was admitted to the Tufts-Delta Community Health Center in Mound Bayou, Mississippi, after collapsing on the picket line on that late January afternoon in 1972. What doctors first described as nervous exhaustion or a "nervous breakdown," was in fact a mental health emergency closely linked to a range of physical ailments. The medical professionals in Mound Bayou ran tests and listened carefully as Hamer described her fatigue, blurred vision, aches, pains, and feelings of frustration, hopelessness, and despair. The stress of running Freedom Farm and a campaign for State Senate, while traveling nationally and caring for Jacqueline and Lenora—then just five and six-years-old—had taken a mental, emotional, and a physical toll on Hamer. Her aches, pains, and blurred vision were not only lingering effects from the beating she endured in that Winona jail cell back in 1963. These ailments were symptomatic of untreated hypertension and type 2 diabetes—both of which contributed to her heart disease. The doctors in Mound Bayou began treating Hamer's conditions. Then she was moved to Meharry Medical Center in Nashville, Tennessee, one of the nation's oldest and largest historically black teaching hospitals.

The doctors in Mound Bayou were well-equipped to treat Hamer's ailments. But they were overwhelmed by the tide of visitors flooding into the hospital to wish her well. Along with their well wishes, visitors brought Hamer updates. Some of their news was good. Visitors reported that the white Ruleville grocer who had kicked a black teenage girl—the incident that brought Hamer to the picket line on that fateful January afternoon—did eventually apologize, and, in a desperate attempt to win back black customers, the grocer and his wife vowed to be more respectful to their black patrons. But most of the news Hamer received while lying in the Mound Bayou hospital bed was distressing. She was missing speaking engagements across the country, and the funds she would have raised during these events were essential to Freedom

Farm's operations. Not only was Freedom Farm falling behind on its loan payments to area banks, but Hamer, ever the compassionate listener and innovative problem-solver, was not there to manage the community's day-to-day struggles. So people brought those struggles directly to her, only intensifying the feelings of frustration, hopelessness, and despair that already threatened to engulf an ailing Hamer. The move to Meharry, a five-hour drive north from the Mississippi Delta, provided Hamer with both specialized care and the rest she so desperately needed.

By early March of 1972, Hamer was back home in Ruleville and in better spirits. She left Meharry with prescriptions to help manage her chronic conditions and a grateful heart. "I wish to express my warmest appreciation to you and the members of your medical staff, who worked so closely with me during my stay in the hospital," Hamer wrote to Dr. Matthew Walker on the third of March. She compared the staff at Meharry to the three wise men in the story of Jesus's birth. She drew the comparison, explained Hamer, "because the young Doctors would always be in a team of threes . . . the youngest with black hair, the second with light graying hair, and the oldest with complete white hair. This to me spelled wisdom and understanding as well as a deep devotion to healing." During the spring of 1972, Hamer, too, seemed devoted to her own care and healing. In an uncharacteristic move, she canceled six months' worth of planned speaking tours.

Hamer did, however, agree to an interview with Dr. Neil R. McMillen, a professor of history at the University of Southern Mississippi. On April 14, 1972, McMillen traveled three and a half hours to Hamer's home to conduct the interview for the Mississippi Oral History Program. Hamer and McMillen sat on the front porch of the Hamer home, talking for a half hour before McMillen suggested, "Let's rest a minute." In the audio recording of this short interview, Hamer reflected on her childhood through her early years working for civil rights. The recording also offers a rare glimpse into Hamer's life and the state of her health in the spring of 1972. Her voice is hoarser, deeper, and quieter than in previous recordings. She speaks more slowly, with less enthusiasm and more audible strain than ever before. In the background, the phone rings intermittently and the Hamers' young girls can be heard playing—sweet voices squealing and light feet padding around the floors of their new home on James Street. Before McMillen offered Hamer a rest, her speech began to slur slightly. She was unable to resume the interview on that April day.

By most accounts, Hamer's health was not much better by the summer of 1972. Yet, she summoned the strength to attend both the Mississippi Loyalist Democratic Party meetings in Jackson, Mississippi, and the 1972 Democratic National Convention (DNC) in Miami Beach, Florida. At the Loyalist meeting where Mississippi Democrats elected their committee chairs and delegates to the national convention, Hamer was immediately thrust back into the spotlight.

In the eight years since the Mississippi Freedom Democratic Party (MFDP) challenged Mississippi's all-white delegation at the 1964 DNC, the more radical MFDP had been replaced by the more moderate Loyalist Party. In an attempt to represent the concerns of their radical grassroots coalition at the 1972 DNC, the MFDP members who remained involved with the Loyalist Party nominated Hamer to serve alongside Dr. Aaron Henry as the party's committee co-chairwoman. Henry, a black pharmacist from Clarksdale, whom Hamer had threatened to physically assault if he went against the MFDP's "no compromise" vote in 1964, was now the committee co-chairman of the Loyalist Party. Representation was a watchword for the Loyalists in 1972. After Hamer and others criticized the 1968 Loyalist delegation for its failure to include women within its leadership ranks, the party pledged balanced representation in terms of both race and gender. For many Loyalist members, therefore, it was necessary to elect a white woman to represent the state alongside Henry, a black man. Those who pushed for Hamer's candidacy, however, disagreed. They did not think the integrated party had to be absolutely racially balanced at all levels, and they objected to the candidacy of Patricia "Patt" Derian, a white woman and a more moderate establishment politician.

The contest between Derian and Hamer quickly turned from a philosophical dispute about the value of balanced representation to pragmatic questions about Hamer's health and finances. Rumors swirled that Hamer would not be well enough to attend the July convention. Others suggested her health would not permit her to travel to the meetings in Washington, D.C, a job requirement for the committee chairwoman. Further still, Derian supporters spread word that Hamer could not afford the travel costs and insisted the party could not afford to pay her way. While these rumors likely affected Hamer's candidacy, other Derian supporters viewed their *de facto* opposition to Hamer's candidacy as a humane act. Loyalist delegate, Wes Watkins, viewed the MFDP's promotion of Hamer as "inhumane." Watkins insisted that Hamer should have been in a hospital. He said, "They propped her up there and she was an icon. I felt very sorry for her and very angry." As Charles Evers recalled, Hamer "didn't want to run at first, but they [the remaining MFDP members] convinced her," preying upon what many recognized as Hamer's inability to say "no" to the people she cared about. In the end, Hamer lost the election for committee co-chairwoman to Derian, but Hamer won a seat to the DNC as a delegate. She was also invited by the Loyalist Party to deliver a speech at the statewide convention, which attendees remember as "passionate" even as they recall Hamer mentioning that her health might, in fact, bar her from attending the 1972 DNC. And perhaps it should have.

Mine eyes have seen the glory of the flame of women's rage
Kept smoldering for centuries, now burning in this age
We no longer will be prisoners in that same old gilded cage
That's why we're marching on.

Feminists gathered at the 1972 Democratic National Convention sang this anthem to the tune of the "Battle Hymn of the Republic," as they marched on, spoke out, and refused to have their voices silenced by the patriarchal political machinery. While Hamer was convalescing in the early winter and spring months of 1972, the political landscape was rapidly shifting. In January, Barbara Jordan became the first southern black woman elected to the House of Representatives. By June, Black Panther Party (BPP) member Bobby Seale's candidacy to become the mayor of Oakland resulted in a run-off election. Fellow BPP member, Elaine Brown, ran for a city council seat on the same ticket as Seale. Although neither Brown nor Seale were victorious in 1972, their campaigns paved the way for Lionel Wilson to be elected as Oakland's first black mayor in 1976. Meanwhile, the National Women's Political Caucus (NWPC), which Hamer helped found the previous summer, had been lobbying Congress to pass the Equal Rights Amendment. The NWPC had also been pushing for reproductive justice and supporting US congressional representative Shirley Chisholm in her quest to become both the first female and the first black president of the United States. The NWPC brought their lobbying efforts to Miami Beach. In spite of her compromised health, Hamer could not resist joining this historic push for women's rights.

Chisholm was realistic about her odds of ultimately winning the presidential nomination from a party that also supported the candidacy of George Wallace, the notorious white supremacist governor from Alabama. Chisholm didn't necessarily run to win the nomination. She ran because she hoped her campaign could garner enough support to persuade the eventual nominee to take seriously the rights of people whose identities and interests were woefully underrepresented within the Democratic Party. Congresswoman Chisholm ran a competitive campaign. She carried 152 delegate votes into the July DNC, which put her in fourth place, ahead of both Hubert Humphrey and Edmund Muskie. But she still lagged behind Senator George McGovern, Senator Henry Jackson, and Wallace—who was shot five times during a failed assassination attempt several months prior. Once it became clear that McGovern had the votes of over 1,700 delegates, Chisholm's supporters urged her to consider the vice presidency. She refused, but her supporters did not give up. Betty Friedan, author of *The Feminine Mystique*, who had recently campaigned for Hamer's 1971 Mississippi State Senate bid, US Representative Bella Abzug, and Gloria Steinem convened an emergency meeting. They plotted their next steps in a women's bathroom at the convention hall to avoid being overheard by the mostly male press corps.

On July 13, 1972, Yvonne Braithwaite Burke, the DNC convention chair, called the session to order and solicited nominations for the vice presidency. Gloria Steinem—NWPC leader and co-founder (with Dorothy Pitman Hughes) of *Ms.* magazine—approached the podium. The nomination she set forth quickly quieted the raucous convention crowd.

"Sissy Farenthold meets all the standards apparently being used in this 1972 vice presidential search," Steinem said. "She is from Texas; she is an experienced and very successful campaigner; she is a Catholic and she is a fighter for the issues that have brought George McGovern to victory at this convention."

Steinem continued to inform the convention's delegates about Frances Tarlton "Sissy" Farenthold's merits, noting Farenthold's opposition to the war in Vietnam as well as the way her campaign for governnor of Texas had created a powerful coalition of racially diverse working class men and women. While she addressed the convention, Steinem's eyes remained fixed upon Hamer, who was making her way to the podium. This was the plan designed in that women's restroom: first Steinem nominates, then Hamer seconds, then Allard K. Lowenstein, former US congressional representative from New York and Mississippi Freedom Vote volunteer, provides the third endorsement for Farenthold's candidacy. But Hamer began to doubt her physical ability to play her part. Her legs ached. Her chest was pounding. Her head throbbed. She could not see clearly or catch her breath. As she passed Texas delegate David Lopez, Hamer leaned on his shoulder, whispered in his ear, and handed him her prepared remarks. He headed straight for the podium.

"A great American wanted to precede me to the microphone tonight," Lopez said. "Though her heart is strong, her body has temporarily given her a little trouble. I refer to that courageous Democrat from the State of Mississippi, Fannie Lou Hamer." The convention hall filled with applause, as Hamer made her way slowly toward the platform, drenched in perspiration. Lopez unfurled the note Hamer passed to him and began to speak her prepared remarks.

"This has been a good week for all Americans," Hamer had written. "This week the people, the people of our country, have been represented here by their own kind, other people just like them. Many of us have worked many years for this week. Now I ask you to make it all very real. Help to be born tonight a new America. It is struggling to be born. Help it. Vote for my fellow southerner and a fine human being, Sissy Farenthold of Texas."

Lopez looked up from the speech to see that Hamer was getting close. He stalled, adding his own endorsement for Farenthold's candidacy as convention officials helped Hamer ascend the stairs to the podium. Onlookers recall that it looked like she was "fixing to have a heart attack." Hamer spoke breathlessly into the microphone.

"Madame Chairman, fellow Democrats and *sister* Democrats, I am not here to make a speech, but just giving support and seconding the nomination of Sissy Farenthold for Vice President." Hamer paused to catch her breath. "If she was good enough for Shirley Chisholm, then she is good enough for Fannie Lou Hamer. Thank you." These few words in support of Farenthold were the last Hamer would speak before a party convention.

Many feminists had promoted Chisholm and Farenthold as the dream team. *Ms.* magazine soon featured them on their January 1973 cover, right below the headline, "Chisholm/Farenthold: The Ticket that Might Have Been." And Hamer's final words carried power. Hamer was now an icon within the party, and her endorsement helped Farenthold garner 407 delegate votes. In the end, Farenthold came in second out of seven candidates for vice president, losing to Senator Tom Eagleton of Missouri, the candidate McGovern had tapped to be his running mate long before the DNC ever took nominations from the floor.

By the fall of 1972, McGovern had replaced Eagleton as his running mate with Sargent Shriver, the former Office of Economic Opportunity Director who had implemented many of Johnson's War on Poverty programs. The McGovern-Shriver challengers lost to the Republican incumbents, President Richard M. Nixon and Vice President Spiro Agnew, by one of the widest margins on record. The first Republican ticket to ever sweep the South, the Nixon-Agnew team carried forty-nine states and over 60 percent of the popular vote. As the Democratic Party slowly diversified its leadership, Nixon's "law and order" message, his promises to quell political uprisings in urban centers, and to appoint conservative justices drew former southern white Democrats to the Republican Party in droves.

Hamer continued to pay close attention to national political trends, which she referenced when writing fundraising letters, delivering speeches, and giving interviews—as her health permitted. Throughout the early 1970s, Hamer criticized Nixon's anti-poverty measures, citing the 1969 conference on hunger she attended in Washington, D.C. At this conference, Hamer told Nixon she would never return to D.C. to learn about hunger because folks in Washington "don't even know what they're talking about." She had harsh words for the Democratic Party, too. Hamer chastised the Democrats for the small strides they had made in diversifying their ranks. She told an audience in Madison, Wisconsin, that the "nation is sick" to celebrate "just some selected few, a few people out of millions with jobs while people throughout this country are suffering from hunger and malnutrition."

On the other hand, Hamer was proud of the progress she saw in Mississippi. She told one northern audience that she would prefer to live in the South than to live any place in the North because "we have made some real strides in the State of Mississippi. In fact, what they're going through in Boston, we done it ten years ago." Hamer was referring to the Boston desegregation busing crisis. She frequently compared the violent white supremacist resistance there to her own positive experience interacting with white families at her daughters' school. "Look at what's happening in Boston," she told a reporter from the *Delta Democrat-Times*. By contrast, "our little kids go to school together right around the corner from here every day. You go to a PTA meeting, and there's black and white together—and I would be shocked if somebody threw a rock." Hamer was admittedly surprised that these drastic changes in race relations had come to Ruleville. "I really didn't think it would come about in my lifetime," Hamer said. "I didn't believe I'd live to see it."

Hamer celebrated the progress to which she contributed. To supporters of the Voter Education Project (VEP) in the spring of 1976, for instance, Hamer wrote, "In 1962, only about 23,000 blacks were registered out of Mississippi voting age population of over 450,000 black people." Fourteen years later, she continued, "almost 300,000 black voters have registered and we have made some changes in Mississippi. We now have 226 black elected officials—one of the largest numbers of any state in the country." Hamer reasoned that voter registration had given black people in Mississippi a sense of pride and self-respect—those feelings, in turn, engendered changes throughout the state. "Some white folks a few years ago would drive past your house in a pickup truck with guns hanging up in the back and give you hate stares," Hamer wrote to VEP supporters. "These same people now call me *Mrs.* Hamer, because they respect people that respect themselves." Citing the astounding increase in voter registration, as well as the increase in interracial cooperation and respect among people in the South, Hamer would surprise her northern audiences by contending that the South could now lead the country along the path toward racial reconciliation.

On January 25, 1973, Professor Neil McMillen returned to Hamer's home to complete the oral history interview they began nine months before.

"How about your health," McMillen asked Mrs. Hamer. "Are you in good health now? You look better than when I saw you last."

"I'm not in really good health, though," she replied.

"Is it serious?" McMillen pressed.

"Yes, I think it is," Hamer admitted. "Yes, I'm thankful that I made it this far. I don't know how many more steps I'll have to make, but I'll keep going."

"Maybe you ought to slow down," McMillen suggested.

"OK, well I'm not going as much as I've been, but wherever I can go—you know, folks keep calling me. . . . If I felt up to it, I suspect I'd be out there more," Hamer replied.

Hamer had a strong desire to advocate for social, political, and economic change. She enjoyed the work and saw it as her calling. This desire coupled with a generous disposition made it difficult for Hamer to say "no" to the frequent requests she received, even when she badly needed rest. Over the years, her husband Perry "Pap" Hamer supported her in fulfilling these requests, as Hamer told McMillen.

"Sometimes I would be really tired and wouldn't want to go out," Hamer remembered. "And I think it's been part of my strength that Pap would say, 'Now look, this is your job and this is what you have to do. You have to go to the people and not disappoint people.'"

When she was able to travel, she never disappointed, even when the demands on her time and energy were exorbitant. Hamer gave a talk at Fisk University on her fifty-fifth birthday, for example, and after the talk, the question and answer period, and the reception, two female employees from Fisk followed Hamer back to her hotel where they conducted a forty-five minute interview with Hamer—beginning at 10:45 pm. Similarly, when Hamer traveled to Madison, Wisconsin, in January of 1976, she spoke in at least three locations in two days, gave scores of media interviews, and was the guest of honor at a Measure for Measure potluck reception. While Hamer sincerely enjoyed interacting with people all over the country, these trips took a toll on her. "I have been just totally exhausted from speaking," she told McMillen. "People wouldn't have no idea how tired I would be."

And yet, whenever she was able, Hamer responded to calls from universities that invited her to headline their lecture series, sororities that wanted to honor her during their founders' day celebrations, and black-owned banks and cooperatives that praised her work toward economic independence. All the while, Hamer engaged in human rights work closer to home. She chaired the board of the daycare center that bore her name, and she took an active role in Jacqueline and Lenora's elementary school, volunteering for the parent-teacher organization. Hamer also served on a local citizens committee with whom she toured Mississippi's notorious Parchman Penitentiary to observe the prisoners' living conditions and to advocate for reform. In March of 1973, she testified as a witness in a federal trial court on behalf or two women fired from their jobs with the Drew School District for bearing children out of wedlock. In May of 1973, Hamer traveled to New York to appear on the "Black Leaders '73" episode of Tony Brown's *Black Journal*. Hamer sat right next to Angela Davis and Stokely Carmichael, sharing her perspective on intraracial class dynamics and the Vietnam War.

Hamer's intermittent travels were at once too much for her to bear and yet not enough to save the Freedom Farm Cooperative (FFC). Hamer's poor health precluded her from regularly tending to relationships with northern donors, who had previously helped fundraise for Freedom Farm's operations. Hamer's declining health also coincided with the 1973–1975 economic recession. Past donors started to raise questions about FFC's fiscal management at a time when it was increasingly difficult to solicit new donors. By 1973, the FFC consisted of over 600 acres, fed at least 300 families, provided seventy houses, and employed over thirty-five people in both full and part-time roles. The FFC also helped families buy food stamps, awarded scholarships to area graduates, and supported a daycare for garment factory workers. To survive, the FFC board realized they needed to reorganize and consolidate their efforts. First, they separated social service projects from the farm operations, indicating that the social service projects would now need to be self-sustaining. Many of these projects were, thereafter, discontinued. Then, the FFC board consolidated their debts, estimating that they owed approximately $150,000 ($850,000 in today's currency) in land and equipment payments to area banks. The FFC board approached the US Department of Agriculture and other federal organizations that invest in local poverty programs. They also reached out to charitable groups like the Delta Foundation to seek help with repayment. Further, Harry Belafonte launched another fundraising letter campaign on the FFC's behalf.

The FFC's widespread outreach did not yield enough assistance to compensate for their major donor losses. In a last-ditch effort to become financially solvent, the FFC decided to plant less produce for their members to consume and more cash crops such as cotton and soybeans to sell. The timing was bad: the cash crops were first drowned out by heavy rains, then scorched by a growing season marked by severe drought, and then washed away again by flooding that devastated the entire region. The inclement weather, at this pivotal moment of reorganization, devastated the Freedom Farm Cooperative. By 1974, the FFC lost all its land and equipment to creditors—save a few machines donated directly by Measure for Measure and the first forty acres Hamer had purchased outright.

The Hamers' family finances fared no better. Their monthly expenses were modest—totaling no more than $300 (approximately $1,700 in 2019 dollars). While Perry Hamer continued to work for Head Start as a bus driver until 1975, Fannie Lou was removed from the payroll of the National Council of Negro Women as a result of her partisan activity, namely, her failed 1971 State

Senate campaign. And her medical bills continued to mount. Between hospital stays and the cost of her blood pressure and diabetes medication, the Hamers regularly needed an additional $100 a month. So Perry Hamer, who was now in his sixties, began working twelve-hour days to make ends meet. When he wasn't driving the Head Start bus, he would pick cotton on area plantations for $1.50 an hour.

When members from Measure for Measure came down from Madison to Ruleville to visit Hamer and check in on the FFC in the summer of 1973, they found the FFC in a state of disrepair and the Hamers' own cupboards bare. Fannie Lou was heavily medicated for pain, remembered Measure for Measure treasurer, Jeff Goldstein. She was unable to care for her children or to keep up with basic household tasks. Vergie had moved to Memphis in search of a better life and the Hamers' niece had moved into their home to help with Jacqueline and Lenora. Before the Measure for Measure members left Ruleville, they stocked the Hamers' cupboards and their freezer with hundreds of dollars worth of food. When they returned to Madison, Goldstein started the "Friends of Fannie Lou Hamer" fund, which gathered enough funds to send the struggling Hamers $100 a month (equivalent to nearly $550 in 2019).

In spite of her niece's help with the girls, the generosity of her friends and supporters, and Perry Hamer's near-constant efforts, by January of 1974, Hamer was back in the hospital again suffering from what doctors continued to describe as nervous exhaustion. While there, she applied for disability income to help offset the medical bills she was incurring. Her application was first denied, but, upon review by Dr. Robert Smith, who recognized her name from his previous movement work, Hamer was granted supplemental disability income in 1974. In July of that year, the Hamers' friends threw them a thirtieth wedding anniversary party to raise both their spirits and enough funds to cover their unmet expenses. Measure for Measure contributed a $1,500 cashier's check to the fundraising effort. Though Fannie Lou was not feeling well, she and Perry Hamer enjoyed the celebration, where they recited their wedding vows and reunited with friends and family. Conspicuously absent from the festivities was Joe Harris, FFC's farm manager whom Hamer loved like a son. Harris had been hospitalized after suffering a heart attack earlier that month. On August 5, 1974, Harris died from complications related to the earlier cardiac event. He was just thirty years-old.

> *If I walk in the pathway of duty*
> *If I work 'til the close of the day, Lord*
> *I shall see the great King in all his beauty*
> *When I've gone the last mile of the way, Lord, yes sir*
> *When I've gone the last mile of the way*

Figure 7.1 Fannie Lou Hamer stands in front of her home on James Street with Ronald Thornton of the North Bolivar County Cooperative and two of her daughters, Jacqueline and Lenora, in the summer of 1973. Photo courtesy of Jean Sweet (in author's possession).

During the last several years of her life, friends recall hearing Hamer sing the lyrics of "The Last Mile of the Way," an old gospel song, made popular by her fellow Mississippi Deltan, Sam Cooke. Perhaps it was Joe Harris's untimely death, her own frequent hospital visits, or the cancerous lump she discovered in her left breast, but by her late fifties Hamer sensed the end was near. She took great pains to pay down the family's debts; she gave instructions regarding her last rites and assured those who visited her that she had made her peace with God. Nevertheless, Hamer continued to "walk in the pathway of duty" whenever she was called on to do so. She served on the Board of Trustees for the Martin Luther King, Jr. Center for Nonviolent Social Change. She worked with John Lewis on the Voter Education Project all the way up to 1976, penning fundraising letters and traveling across fifteen counties to encourage registration. She campaigned (unsuccessfully) on behalf of Henry Kirksey, who sought to become Mississippi's first black governor. She also hosted visitors from developing nations, who traveled to the Delta from the International Women's Year meeting held in Mexico City. And in the fall of 1976, she traveled to Jackson to join the three-hundred person protest against Mississippi's new co-pay requirement for individuals receiving prescriptions through Medicaid. At the rally outside Mississippi's capitol building, Hamer summoned the strength to lead the protestors in stirring renditions of "We Shall Overcome" and her signature anthem, "This Little Light of Mine."

Alongside continued human rights advocacy work, Hamer's final years were punctuated by small moments of joy wrought by recognition and expressions of gratitude, set against a backdrop of overwhelming hardship. In the fall of 1976, for example, Hamer was honored by a Fannie Lou Hamer Day Celebration in Ruleville. During this local celebration, a representative from the Alpha Phi Alpha Fraternity presented Hamer with the Paul Robeson Award for Humanitarian Service. Loyalist Democrats Charles Evers and Amzie Moore also spoke at the event, praising Hamer's many contributions to her community and encouraging attendees to contribute to a fund for her medical expenses. They raised $2,100 for the Hamers that October day. The previous month, Hamer traveled to Washington, D.C., to receive a national honor from the Congressional Black Caucus (CBC), which recognized her decade and a half of human rights activism with their George W. Collins Memorial Award for Community Service. That year's gala featured performances by comedian Dick Gregory and singer Ella Fitzgerald. US Representative Barbara Jordan was the evening's keynote speaker.

Jordan's ascendancy through the ranks of the Democratic Party likely brought Hamer well-deserved pride. In many ways, Hamer had blazed the path Jordan followed. Nevertheless, Hamer probably watched the televised version of Jordan's keynote address to the 1976 DNC—delivered two months before the CBC gala—with a mixture of both pride and longing. Hamer wasn't able to attend the 1976 DNC because she was recovering from a mastectomy. Her battle with breast cancer had precluded her from participating in this convention, the first she had missed in more than a decade, which also meant that Hamer wasn't present for the first keynote address delivered to the DNC by a black delegate.

While some expressions of gratitude for Hamer's remarkable contributions to human rights were grand, others were much more intimate. When she traveled to Washington, D.C., for the CBC gala, Hamer visited her long-time friend and fellow activist, Eleanor Holmes Norton. Hamer confided in Norton about her recent mastectomy, admitting that she'd felt a lump in her breast for some time before seeking treatment. Hamer had hoped it would go away on its own. Hamer also shared with Norton that she'd been stuffing what she called "a rag" in her left bra cup to balance out her frame. Hamer complained that it felt like a "great weight" when the rag became soaked with perspiration. Norton was reportedly "horrified" to learn about all of this and immediately bought her friend a proper prosthesis.

With similar compassion, June Johnson—the young woman who was jailed and beaten with Hamer in Winona—frequently stopped by to visit Hamer toward the end of her life. Johnson sometimes found her old friend in tears and other times in a confused mental state. One time, Johnson remembered, Hamer was quite agitated. Hamer had sent for a neighbor to come help her comb her hair and hours had gone by—no one had returned to help her. Johnson comforted Hamer by gently combing and setting her friend's now-sparse strands of hair.

Hamer was admitted to the Tufts-Delta Community Health Center in Mound Bayou for the last time in the early winter months of 1977. This time, she was being treated for complications related to heart disease, diabetes, and breast cancer. The Hamers no longer had to worry about a steady stream of visitors interrupting Fannie Lou's rest; that stream had largely dried up over the last several years as Hamer's condition steadily worsened. These days, Perry Hamer lamented, the only way he could get people to come visit his ailing wife was if he paid them. And he had even less money to do so by 1977, having lost his steady job with Head Start two years before, when the federal operation downsized its Delta outreach.

Thankfully, a few friends and family members stayed by Hamer's side until the very end. Her sister, Laura Ratliff, remembered Hamer's final days. "I had never seen anybody in that much pain before," Ratliff recalled. "She cried, oh, how she cried. She was just ready to go to the Lord."

Charles McLaurin, Hamer's campaign manager, also remembered his last visit to see her in Mound Bayou.

"Mac, I don't want to be buried on a plantation," Hamer insisted from her hospital bed. Likely recalling the unmarked graves that contained her mother's and father's remains, the thought of resting in the very land that enslaved her grandparents greatly distressed Hamer.

McLaurin fell silent. He was in denial about how close to death she was. Hamer was legend in McLaurin's mind. He recalled, "I thought she would live forever!"

But Hamer knew better. "I want you to promise me that I will not be buried on a plantation," she said, staring intently into McLaurin's eyes.

"Okay, I promise," McLaurin reassured her, not knowing he'd be pressed to make good on his words in just a few days' time.

Both June Johnson and Measure for Measure leader, Martha Smith, knew Hamer would not live much longer. In a letter she wrote to Hamer's "friends, brothers, and sisters," Johnson sounded the alarm that Hamer was "seriously ill with cancer." Johnson pleaded, "Brothers and sisters, it is very important that many of us come to her bedside, or send cards, letters and donations for all the medical expenses" and the support of her children.

Similarly, after Smith visited Hamer in Mound Bayou in early March of

1977, she returned to Madison and penned an emergency memorandum to Measure for Measure supporters. *"Fannie Lou Hamer is dying of cancer,"* the header announced. Within the memo, Smith appealed for funds to "help with medical expenses and to try to make the family secure." She explained that "Fannie Lou must have someone with her in the Mound Bayou hospital around the clock which is costing Pap about $75/day for nursing services alone." Smith shared how "very hard" it was for her to "see such a strong, generous, and idealistic woman lying helpless, hopeless, broken and broke." During their March visit, Hamer had shared her worries with Smith, who then conveyed them to the Madison activists. "She worries about her 65-year-old husband and her two little granddaughters, Nookie who is eleven and Cookie who is only ten," wrote Smith. "If you feel you can help out with this crying and urgent need please send a check to Measure for Measure—earmarked the Fannie Lou Hamer Fund."

But before Smith's urgent plea for help ever reached the mailboxes of Measure for Measure supporters, Fannie Lou Hamer died. Her heart failed on March 14, 1977, at 5:15 pm. She was fifty-nine years old.

News of Hamer's death quickly spread across the nation and the world. Obituaries ran in papers from coast to coast, and friends living as far away as Africa learned that the storied human rights activist would soon be laid to rest. Telegrammed condolences flooded the Hamer home. In one telegram from the Congressional Black Caucus, Representative Walter E. Fauntory wrote, "Fannie Lou Hamer will live as a symbol of courage and dedication to the principles of human rights for all people." Gloster Current and Roy Wilkins of the NAACP praised Hamer as a "great freedom fighter" and a "vigorous defender of the rights of all people." Telegrams from Representative John Conyers and the Reverend Jesse Jackson, Sr., respectively, cast Hamer as a "dedicated fighter in the struggle for equality" and as a "soldier in the army who would not accept excuses but pursued excellence while she sought a just entitlement for all its citizens." Further still, the "Democratic National Committee Family" praised Hamer as a "model champion for the causes of political reform, human and civil rights, and humanitarian ideals." Other telegrams suggested that Hamer "plowed furrows in the conscience of the nation," that she "paved the way for the New South," and that she "changed history." Telegrams from those who knew her best, like Diane Nash, praised Hamer as a "warm and for real person," noting her "compassion for others," her "love and generosity," and her remarkable ability to teach audiences about love's "healing power." Even as Hamer's family sought comfort in these condolences, they worked with Hamer's movement friends to raise the requisite funds for her funeral. In just six days' time, Hamer's friends and family organized the largest memorial celebration the small town of Ruleville had ever seen.

On March 20, 1977, Andrew Young chartered a government plane from Washington, D.C. to the Indianola Municipal Airport. His plane touched down just three short miles from the Indianola Courthouse, where Hamer had tried to register fifteen years before. With a police escort, Young headed toward Ruleville's Williams Chapel Baptist Church, where Hamer had first learned about her right to vote. During the half-hour drive to the church, Young put the finishing touches on the eulogy he would soon deliver. Looking out at the expansive plantations lining US Highway 49, Young likely reflected on just how much had changed since he secured Hamer's release from the Winona jail cell in 1963. Surely, he couldn't help but think about how much Hamer had done to bring about those changes. Young would soon encourage the hundreds of mourners crammed inside the modest chapel to be grateful, as he was, for having known Mrs. Hamer—a woman who, in his words, "not only refused to be turned around herself, but a woman who literally helped turn this nation around." Young pointed to the Democratic presidential candidate Jimmy Carter's narrow victory over Gerald Ford, which was so close that it hinged on results in just two states—Hawaii and Mississippi. Young, whom Carter appointed as Ambassador to the United Nations, had waited up until three o'clock in the morning to learn that the State of Mississippi had indeed voted to elect the Democratic candidate. "The hands that had been picking cotton had finally picked a president!" Young would soon proclaim at Hamer's funeral.

Ambassador Young tucked his speaking notes inside his coat pocket as his police escort rolled into Ruleville. He had expected to find a large crowd, but *this* was unlike anything he'd ever seen in a small southern town. The state highway patrolman escorting Young informed him that the day's crowd was expected to double Ruleville's 2,500-person population. An hour before the service was set to start, the chapel was already filled to capacity. Hamer's family and friends lined the walls and aisles of the church as an organist played her favorite hymns. Hundreds more mourners poured out of the chapel onto the church lawn. Some held banners reading, "I Question America," others ran after small children, and still more greeted one another with outstretched arms. Loudspeakers fastened to the sides of the old building broadcast the service. Signs directed the remaining traffic toward an additional memorial being held at Ruleville Central High School.

On this crisp and sunny afternoon, Young spotted many old friends among the crowd. VEP Director John Lewis, Georgia State Senator Julian Bond, Michigan Congressman Charles Diggs, Assistant Secretary of State Hodding Carter, Mississippi Representative Robert Clark, and NAACP Chairman

Aaron Henry all sat near the front of the church. Unita Blackwell, the first black woman elected as mayor in Mississippi, stood talking with Dorothy Height, the president of the NCNW, and Hamer's mentors, Ella Baker, L. C. Dorsey, and Annie Devine. In the back corner of the chapel, Young spotted Jamil Abdullah Al-Amin and Kwame Ture or, as he once knew the former SNCC activists, H. Rap Brown and Stokely Carmichael. Young let out a deep sigh. There was Perry Hamer, seated in the center of the first pew in a dark suit with a white tie, his gaze fixed on his wife's pale blue coffin.

It was an open casket funeral, and Fannie Lou Hamer looked nothing short of regal. She was dressed in a white gown, her black hair carefully combed and resting against the casket's white satin pillow. Yellow roses and white carnations tied with blue ribbon filled the stuffed chapel with their soft fragrance. Both the Jackson State University Community Choir and the Tougaloo College Choir led the parishioners in mournful versions of "Precious Lord," "Lift Every Voice," and "We Shall Overcome" that were carried over the loudspeakers.

Before Young's eulogy, Ella Baker delivered what funeral organizer Owen Brooks recalled was "the best" address that day. "Many from whom we expected support—civil rights leaders, churchmen," remembered Baker of the 1964 DNC, "condemned us and told us we were asking too much. But Mrs. Hamer could not betray those under the heel of oppression back home." Baker praised Hamer's integrity and reminded the audience of her refusal to compromise. "She knew you must do what is right no matter what others think," Baker said, warning the audience that Hamer would now be watching over all the individuals gathered there to ensure they carried on where she left off.

Dorothy Height praised Hamer's abiding faith, sharing her trademark refrain, "You can't love God and have hate in your heart." Reverend Edwin King recalled, similarly, that Hamer "always said there could be no freedom for whites until there was freedom for blacks." Hodding Carter, III, a leading member of the Loyalist Party in Mississippi with whom Hamer had clashed in recent years, spoke during her service as well. Like Hamer, Carter held Mississippi up as a model of racial reconciliation. The Assistant Secretary of State shared that he was filled with "excitement" on his trip from Washington, D.C., to Mississippi that day. "As a Mississippian," Carter explained, "I was coming back to a state that I could be far prouder to live in because of the life of Mrs. Fannie Lou Hamer." Carter shared Hamer's faith that Mississippi could become great and that, with regard to the high number of black elected officials and the high level of contact between the races, the state was ahead of the rest of the country. Carter contended that Hamer had much to do with the seismic shifts in their home state. "Mrs. Hamer did a lot of freeing in her lifetime," he said with a quiver in his voice. "I think that history will say that among those who were freed more totally and earlier by her were white Mississippians—if they had the will to be free—from themselves, from their history, from their racism, from their past." Carter looked down and gripped the lectern. He said, "I know there's no way for us, who have been free, to adequately thank those who freed us, except to try to also continue the work that Mrs. Hamer and so many of you began, are continuing, and will continue in the future."

Young concluded the three-hour service by thanking Mrs. Hamer and those in attendance for the work they had done, while also providing "marching orders" for the work that remained. "Everything I learned about preaching, politics, life and death, I learned in your midst," the US Congressional Representative-turned-UN Ambassador announced. "When I see people gathered in this room, knowing where you are now, I know that none of us would be where we are now, had we not been here then." He cited his own trajectory from civil rights worker to ambassador, before drawing several more lines of influence from the Delta to the national political stage. Young reminded his audience of the elected officials who got their start as voter registration workers and of those now working on federal poverty programs and human rights initiatives who had cut their teeth in the Delta. White men and women, inspired by the spirit of black Deltans with whom they stayed during Freedom Summer, returned to their own communities and "started teach-ins on Vietnam" and "put in place a movement to bring about the liberation of the women of this nation." Young insisted it was the spirit of one woman who had inspired all of these people, programs, and protests. Fannie Lou Hamer showed the world just "how far we can come simply on the power and faith of the human spirit." For this reason, Young insisted:

> We are not here to mourn, but we are here to gather strength from each other. Get our marching orders, go back to our various places of calling and in the differing ways to which we've been called, say to Mrs. Hamer: Thank you for the inspiration. Thank you for the example. Thank you for so strengthening our lives that we might live so God can use us. Anytime. Anywhere.

He sang the first verse as a clarion call.

> *This little light of mine, I'm gonna let it shine*

Then Hamer's family, friends, and fellow activists responded, rising to their feet and clapping in time. The song Fannie Lou Hamer had loved since those childhood Sundays spent listening to her father preach reverberated through Williams Chapel, over the loudspeakers, and into the world beyond:

> *This little light of mine, I'm gonna let it shine*
> *Let it shine, let it shine, let it shine.*

Afterword

"It's in Your Hands"

The modern Black freedom struggle remains one of the most important examples of the power of ordinary people to change the course of the nation. But the popular stories we get impoverish our ability to see how change happens. A more expansive history transforms how we imagine what a movement looks like, sounds like, and pushes for, and understand how it is received and often reviled. It shows us that leadership, vision, steadfastness, and courage came in many forms, as did the opposition to it. Giving us necessary tools for understanding the past, it suggests lessons for long-distance runners in the struggle for racial and social justice today.

—Jeanne Theoharis, *A More Beautiful and Terrible History*, 2018

𝓕annie Lou Hamer's life story holds transformative power, contributing to a more expansive history that challenges what Jeanne Theoharis dubbed the "national fable of the civil rights movement." Belying the whitewashed popular narrative about who contributed to the movement, how social, political, and economic changes were effected, and where the struggles for black freedom were waged, Hamer's biography complicates and enriches our understanding in empowering ways. Readers of *Fannie Lou Hamer: America's Freedom Fighting Woman*, for instance, learn by Hamer's example the importance of "discerning the signs of the times." James Bevel's 1962 sermon at the mass meeting in Williams Chapel Baptist Church primed Hamer to recognize the "fulfilling of God's word" in the Council of Federated Organizations' members who began traveling across the state, encouraging the masses of black people to register to vote. It is my hope that contemporary readers of Hamer's story might be inspired by her example to recognize—in the creative protests taking place on our streets, at our sporting events, and across our webs of social media—that our time, too, is ripe for radical change.

Hamer's life story teaches contemporary readers that in order to bring about radical change, one has to be ready and willing to join the struggle for freedom. In the fall of 1962, as *America's Freedom Fighting Woman* recounts, Hamer had fled to Cascilla, narrowly escaping white supremacist night-rider's bullets. When McLaurin asked her to leave the relative safety of her niece's remote cabin and join him at a Student Nonviolent Coordinating Committee meeting in Nashville, Tennessee, she accepted his invitation on the spot. Through this example, and countless other stories included in the pages of *America's Freedom Fighting Woman*, Hamer's life story encourages readers to ask: Am I running from the struggle or am I, like Hamer, ready to fight for freedom?

Moreover, *America's Freedom Fighting Woman* underscores Hamer's resourcefulness—a trait she learned from her mother, who would cut the tops of greens to feed her twenty hungry children and would tie bags around their bare feet so they could walk to school during Mississippi's coldest winter months. As those who engage her life story learn, Hamer transformed traditional spirituals that she learned in her father's church into powerful black freedom movement anthems, she encouraged voter registration by gathering food and clothing donations from northern supporters, and she parlayed the skill of tilling the Delta soil into an interracial food cooperative she called Freedom Farm. These examples culled from Hamer's biography encourage contemporary readers to consider the creative ways they might use their own resources—however modest—to contribute to the ongoing struggle for freedom.

Hamer's ability to recognize the potential for change within and around her, Hamer's willingness to join the black freedom struggle in the face of white supremacist retaliation, and her inventive resourcefulness are just some of the lessons for contemporary audiences that her biography teaches. As I note in the introduction to *America's Freedom Fighting Woman*, Hamer's biography also holds contemporary relevance because the very struggles she waged—against white supremacy, police brutality, sexual assault, voter disenfranchisement, segregated education, food insecurity, health care access, and governmental control over reproductive health—are strikingly similar to the challenges facing many Americans today. In Hamer's example, therefore, readers have wells of wisdom upon which to draw. Drawing upon Hamer's wisdom in the face of similar challenges, I hope, will both inform and inspire contemporary movements for social, political, and economic change. *America's Freedom Fighting Woman* recounts not only the knowledge that informed her activism, but also the activism by which Hamer challenged a variety of exclusions. The principled stances Hamer took, her propensity to "speak truth to power," and her embodied disruptions of systemic exclusion encourage contemporary readers to develop a healthy disrespect for respectability politics.

In light of all that Hamer's life story has to offer contemporary readers, the core question that continues to animate my research is: How can I keep Hamer's memory alive and inspiring for generations to come? To answer this driving question, I sought lessons from how Hamer's legacy has been crafted in the forty years since her death. Through the study of local and national efforts to memorialize Hamer, I came to recognize the similarities between freedom fighting and movement memorialization work. Like the constant struggle for freedom, efforts to keep alive the robust, multifaceted, and inspirational memory of freedom fighters takes creativity, requires resources, and invites controversy. The struggle to carry forth the complexity of freedom fighting forebears' stories, like the struggle for freedom itself, attracts people from all walks of life. Collective decision-making among diverse groups of culture carriers, just like action-planning among diverse groups of freedom fighters, presents opportunities for dynamic, collaborative, and far-reaching work; and it also requires patience, time, grace, and forgiveness. "Freedom is a constant struggle," Hamer would often say. Memorialization, too, is a constant struggle, I have learned from the work of Hamer torch-bearers.

Fannie Lou Hamer's memorial services, held at both Williams Chapel and Ruleville Central High School, ran so late into the evening of March 20, 1977, that there was little daylight left to lay her to rest. The following day, a smaller crowd gathered in a large open field between Center and Byron Streets in Ruleville, Mississippi. This was the site of Freedom Farm's first and last forty acres, land that Hamer purchased outright with funds raised from northern donors. And this was the site that Charles McLaurin had spent the last week struggling to secure for Hamer's burial, fulfilling the deathbed promise he made to his beloved friend: Fannie Lou Hamer would *not* be buried on a plantation. Fulfilling this promise was no easy task, however. In a state of shock over her passing, McLaurin contemplated gravesites. "I thought about Mount Galilee, but that's on a plantation. Then I thought about out here east of Ruleville, it's on a plantation. See, she knew something I didn't know," he explained. "She knew the only places *to be* buried were on a plantation!"

Having run out of conventional options, McLaurin thought of Freedom Farm's land. But he encountered resistance both from the remaining members of the Freedom Farm Board and from the City of Ruleville, which held a zoning stipulation that bodies of the dead could not be buried on private property within the city's limits. McLaurin sought the counsel of Cleve McDowell, a civil rights attorney and the second black person to enroll in the University of Mississippi (following James Meredith). McDowell suggested granting the land over to the city, thereby making it public property and thus enabling Hamer's burial. In a few short days, McLaurin and McDowell successfully lobbied the Freedom Farm Board and Ruleville's Board of Alders, securing agreement regarding their land-granting and rezoning plan. Ruleville's Board of Alders attached just one condition to the agreement, stipulating that a monument must be erected on the property within three years or Hamer's grave would need to be moved to a more conventional burial site. McLaurin agreed to this condition, and Hamer's plot was secured—replete with a bronze plaque and a headstone bearing her famous quotation: "I'm sick and tired of being sick and tired."

Those three years came and went and no monument was erected. What's worse, in that time, the bronze plaque and tombstone were stolen and the site itself was vandalized. When Linda Jones Malonson, a self-described Hamer protégé from Houston, Texas, came upon Hamer's final resting place in May of 1979, all that remained was a trampled picket fence surrounding the concrete casing that covered her role model's grave. Malonson was dismayed at the site's neglect. Nevertheless, she explained the community's lack of care for the site in graceful terms. "A lot of people didn't want to remember what happened because of Fannie Lou Hamer," Malonson reasoned. "They don't want to remember the pain."

For her part, Malonson got right to work. She enlisted the help of contacts at Howard University, an historically black college in Washington, D.C., which had awarded Hamer an honorary doctorate during her lifetime. As a result of Malonson's urging, Howard's School of Architecture and Planning ran a contest encouraging its students to design a Fannie Lou Hamer monument to be built at the Ruleville site. Concomitantly, Malonson began raising funds to construct the winning design, which she estimated would cost anywhere from $100,000-$125,000 to create and install.

Meanwhile, Charles McLaurin submitted his own monument design proposal to the city and received approval for a Greco-Roman-inspired white marble structure honoring his fallen hero. Perry Hamer, however, strongly objected to McLaurin's design. Mr. Hamer, in fact, favored the winning monument proposal from the Howard University contest. Malonson lobbied the City of Ruleville to reconsider implementing McLaurin's design, citing Perry Hamer's objection. The Ruleville Board of Alders agreed, rejecting McLaurin's proposal and approving the winning Howard memorial design, which would be constructed entirely from native Mississippi materials and would feature "four 15-foot hands reaching to the sky. In the center, a collar around an abstract bust of Mrs. Hamer will collect rainwater and dew and bleed it through her heart back into the state of Mississippi."

Unfortunately, Malonson could not raise enough funds to bring this visionary monument to Ruleville. Fortunately, Ruleville's Mayor, Carrol Land, insisted that the city had no plans to disturb Hamer's gravesite—even in the absence of the agreed upon monument. Though Hamer's stolen tombstone was eventually replaced, Hamer's gravesite was untended throughout the 1980s. Visitors report wading through overgrown grass, braving the sting of fire ants, and standing in the blazing sun to pay homage to Fannie Lou Hamer.

It might appear from her untended gravesite and from Malonson's inability to raise enough money to construct a proper memorial for Hamer that the once-beloved freedom fighter was nearly lost to history, just years after her death. But there is much more to the story of how culture carriers have worked at both the local and the national levels to keep her memory alive and inspiring. While Hamer's friends, family members, and fellow activists were not consistently tending her gravesite and while few donated to the statue fund in the 1980s, many were living out what Dr. L. C. Dorsey described as an "action memorial." Dorsey urged those who loved Hamer to devote their lives and their livelihoods to the *causes* Hamer cared most about. And many of Hamer's friends were doing just that. Measure for Measure Activists, Jean and Charlie Sweet, for instance, became involved in the movement for prison reform and prisoners' rights that Hamer championed after her tour of Mississippi's egregious Parchman Penitentiary. As a thank-you letter from Jacqueline and Lenora Hamer suggests, the Sweets also continued to send financial support to Perry Hamer and the girls years after Fannie Lou Hamer's death. Not long after Hamer passed, furthermore, Eleanor Holmes Norton was appointed by President Jimmy Carter to chair the Equal Employment Opportunity Commission. In this post, Norton carried forth the legacy of her friend and confidante by promoting race and gender-based equity, even as Norton continued to advocate for universal human and civil rights. Lawrence Guyot, Hamer's Mississippi Freedom Democratic Party compatriot, also began working in Washington, D.C., in the late 1970s. Guyot honored Hamer's memory in his work for the Department of Health and Human Services and in the leadership training workshops he offered to empower local people. June Johnson, who was jailed with Hamer in Winona and who continued to care for her throughout the remainder of Hamer's life, kept Hamer's spirit alive in the legal battles she waged against the unjust treatment of black people in Greenwood and Leflore County, Mississippi. Still others were contributing to public memory about Hamer by writing about her. Throughout the late 1970s and 1980s, Hamer's legacy was artfully crafted by poems, essays, newspaper articles, and even a one-woman show.

In fact, action memorials and artful renderings kept Hamer's memory alive and inspiring well into the 1990s, when Perry Hamer succumbed to high blood pressure and was laid to rest next to his beloved wife. In July of 1992, just two months after Mr. Hamer's death, both presidential candidate Bill Clinton and vice presidential candidate Al Gore paid tribute to Fannie Lou Hamer in their acceptance speeches at the 1992 Democratic National Convention. A year after Perry Hamer died, Kay Mills published her groundbreaking biography *This Little Light of Mine: The Life of Fannie Lou Hamer* and the National Women's Hall of Fame honored Fannie Lou Hamer with a posthumous induction. By the late 1990s, Dr. Leslie McLemore had co-founded the Fannie Lou Hamer National Institute on Citizenship and Democracy to "nurture a generation of young people engaged in and committed to discourse" about "civil rights, social justice, and citizenship." The Hamer Institute, housed at Mississippi's historically black Jackson State University for twenty years (1997–2017), infused public memory of Hamer with particular emphases on the local and continual struggle for social justice. Chana Kai Lee's 1999 biography, *For Freedom's Sake: The Life of Fannie Lou Hamer*, also emphasized Hamer's perseverance in the face of constant pain and struggle, providing a more complex and robust portrait of the ostensibly indefatigable activist.

In 2004, poet Maya Angelou and actors and activists Ossie Davis and Ruby Dee, were joined by members of the original Mississippi Freedom Democratic Party (MFDP) on the main stage of the Democratic National Convention. During this forty-year anniversary tribute to the MFDP's credentials committee challenge, Angelou read the conclusion of Hamer's heart-wrenching testimony and declared: "It is important that we know the words that came from the mouth of an African-American Woman. It is imperative that we know that those words came from the heart of an American." Just two years later, the United States Congress named the reauthorization of the 1965 Voting Rights Act after Rosa Parks, Coretta Scott King, and Fannie Lou Hamer. In 2009, the United States Postal Service featured an image of Hamer and of fellow Mississippi activist, Medgar Evers, on a postage stamp commemorating the 100th Anniversary of the National Association for the Advancement of Colored People (NAACP). In 2014, Paulene Angelicia Simmons quit her job as a lawyer and founded the Fannie Lou Hamer Institute of Advocacy & Social Action to "empower, equip, and uplift Black women and girls through culturally contextualized settings." This North Carolina-based institute seeks to honor Fannie Lou Hamer's civil rights work by creating "a world where Black women and girls thrive!" In the summer of 2018, furthermore, Tami Sawyer—nicknamed "Tamie Lou Hamer"—took her oath as a Shelby County Commissioner on a biography of Hamer and a collection of her galvanizing speeches. Sawyer is presently running to become Memphis, Tennessee's first black female mayor, and she frequently mentions Hamer's inspirational example in her campaign speeches and promotional materials.

Even as national tributes such as these bring Hamer's inspiring life story to ever-broader audiences, culture carriers in Hamer's local community continue to protect and carry forth her legacy. For instance, Patricia Thompson, founder of the nonprofit organization Repaying Our Ancestors Respectfully (ROAR), united Dr. Dorsey's action memorial concept with a renewed dedication to constructing a physical memorial for Fannie Lou Hamer. In 1999, Thompson began working with Hattie Jordan, the former Freedom Farm Board Member-turned-City of Ruleville Alderwoman. Together, Thompson and Jordan raised funds to create a Fannie Lou Hamer Memorial Garden; they

Figure 8.1 Tami Sawyer chose to be sworn into office as a Commissioner in Shelby County, Tennessee, on the collection of Fannie Lou Hamer's speeches that I compiled (with Davis W. Houck), citing Hamer's inspirational example. Photo courtesy of Commissioner Tami Sawyer.

set up a regular lawn care service to tend the Hamers' gravesite; and they convinced Ruleville's mayor to install signs reading "Home of Fannie Lou Hamer" at the city's entrances. ROAR also began hosting an annual memorial celebration for Fannie Lou Hamer, on or around her October 6 birthday.

By the time I connected with ROAR in the summer of 2007, a bright red gazebo etched with the names of courageous movement elders like Herman and Hattie Sisson, Joe and Rebecca McDonald, Robert and Mary Tucker had been erected next to the Hamers' gravesite. A wrought-iron gate with the words "Fannie Lou Hamer Memorial Garden" arched above the entrance and welcomed visitors. Brick pillars and floodlights combined to protect the gravesite from theft and vandalism, while fountains, professional landscaping, and a message board invited visitors to pause and reflect on Hamer's legacy. In the back corner of the memorial site, a space had been cleared for a Fannie Lou Hamer statue.

When Thompson invited me to join the Fannie Lou Hamer National Statue Committee in the fall of 2009, the group had enlisted the leadership of Charles McLaurin as the project director and Dr. Patricia Reid-Merritt, a professor at Stockton College in New Jersey, as the committee's chair. Over the next two and a half years, I worked as part of a team of scholars, politicians, and benefactors drawn from across the country, local leaders (including June Johnson's son, Hakim), and Fannie Lou Hamer's family members (including her daughter, Vergie). As a group, we deliberated about how to best raise funds, who to hire as a sculptor, which design to choose, which Hamer quotations and photographs to feature around the statue's base, and how to best unveil the tribute. At times, long-standing tensions between local activists and national committee members cropped up in our deliberations. I'll never forget one phone conference that devolved into a shouting match when it appeared that the recommendation of a national committee member would override the preferences of a local activist. With grace, understanding, and a shared sense of purpose, our committee was able to resolve disagreements and finally, thirty-five years after Hamer's passing, secure a proper monument for her.

The Fannie Lou Hamer statue erected in her hometown of Ruleville increased the nationwide total of outdoor sculptures honoring black women to just over two dozen. According to the Smithsonian registry of outdoor sculptures, an official inventory that includes over 5,500 monuments spread across the country, fewer than 200 outdoor statues depict women and just a little over 10 percent of those women depicted are black. As the recent push to take down Confederate monuments makes clear, statues matter. Monuments provide nodal points through which Americans view their shared past and understand our society's values; they're built to pay homage to people and events we collectively respect and their continued presence ought to provide inspiration, suggesting an admirable example to emulate. In short, statues signal who and what is worthy of our attention, praise, and remembrance. Because the Hamer statue brought a long-awaited memorial for her to her home community, because it increased the representation of black women in the American statuary, and because it offered a tangible counterpoint to the scores of monuments across the South valorizing the Confederacy, our statue fund committee planned a big unveiling celebration—scheduled for October 5, 2012.

We invited local and national politicians, media personalities, scholars, activists and family members, and we also invited public school teachers throughout the Delta, hoping they would attend and bring students to this truly monumental celebration. The teachers' responses to our outreach, however, surprised me. I know that Fannie Lou Hamer is not a household name. Her biography troubles the "national fable of the civil rights movement," and she is not often included among the whitewashed versions of convenient heroes that fill popular textbooks. But I also know that Mississippi was one of the first states in the nation to *require* that the civil rights movement be taught in public schools, and I was aware that their state standards explicitly mention Fannie Lou Hamer by name. So, when teachers in the Delta told us that they would try to make it to the unveiling, but that they had no materials to teach about Hamer and that their students had only a vague idea of who she was or why she was significant. I was, indeed, surprised. Back in 2012, I responded to the Delta-area teachers by providing CDs of Hamer's songs and speeches, copies of campaign posters, and newspaper articles. I gathered anything I could think of from my Hamer research that might get Delta students interested in learning about this phenomenal woman from their home county. I hoped it would be enough to inspire them to attend the unveiling celebration and to appreciate the event's significance.

On October 5, 2012, the day before what would have been Hamer's ninety-fifth birthday, I was heartened to see local school-aged children arrive at the Fannie Lou Hamer Memorial Garden by the busloads. They waved "I'm Sick and Tired of Being Unhealthy" signs and donned Fannie Lou Hamer t-shirts. Members of the extended Hamer and Townsend families were there as well. Vergie Hamer Faulkner offered a tribute on their behalf, singing a stirring rendition of "I'm on My Way" in a voice that so closely resembled her mother's it brought tears to my eyes. Hamer's fellow activists were there, too. I had the pleasure of thanking Charles McLaurin, Leslie McLemore, Hattie Jordan, and Patricia Thompson for their mentorship. I also enjoyed listening to tributes by Ruleville Mayor Shirley Edwards, State Senator Willie Simmons, and US congressional representative Bennie Thompson, who all acknowledged the path Hamer blazed for their political careers. Dr. Molefi Kete Asante, pioneer in the fields of Communication and Afrocentric Studies, offered the day's libation and the Ruleville Central High School Band played "Lift Every Voice and Sing." Both tributes connected Hamer's life and legacy to the national and the global struggle for black empowerment. In all, nearly six-hundred people joined this jubilant day of reunion, gratitude, and celebration, which culminated in the unveiling of a nine-foot bronze statue of Fannie Lou Hamer, sculpted by Brian Hanlon.

Hanlon's statue renders Hamer in an active speaking pose, one arm raised toward the heavens, the other firmly clasping the receiver of a megaphone. The bronze sculpture sits atop a square marble base. The base is adorned with images chosen by our committee—one of Hamer picketing alongside marchers in her home state, another of her speaking at the 1964 DNC, and a third picture of Hamer standing next to her fellow 1965 congressional challengers, Victoria Gray Adams and Annie Devine. Hamer's famous quotations accompany these images. After much deliberation, our committee decided on these lines: "This little light of mine, I'm gonna let it shine," "If I fall, I'll fall five feet four inches forward for freedom," and "Nobody's free until everybody's free." Her most famous quotation, "I'm sick and tired of being sick and tired," is etched into her nearby gravestone. Throughout that warm October morning, attendees took turns posing in front of the hard-won monument.

The following morning, on Hamer's ninety-fifth birthday, I attended a much more modest community celebration held in the Fannie Lou Hamer Recreation Center. A crowd of fifty or so people gathered that day to celebrate the grand opening of the Fannie Lou Hamer Museum, housed within the recreation center and directed by Hattie Jordan. I joined the crowd in touring the museum, singing freedom songs, recognizing local Fannie Lou Hamer scholarship recipients, and enjoying Hamer's birthday cake, which glowed brightly with all ninety-five candles set ablaze.

Before leaving Ruleville on that overcast October day, I wanted to catch one more glimpse of the statue. As I walked across the dewy grass toward the memorial garden adjacent to the recreation center, I breathed a deep sigh of relief. The work was over, I momentarily thought to myself. Then, I came upon this scene.

As I witnessed this young girl gazing up at Mrs. Hamer with reverence and awe, I felt conflicted—equal parts proud and concerned. On the one hand, I felt profoundly grateful to have been a part of an historic effort to keep Hamer's memory alive and inspiring for generations to come. This statue, I knew, was hard-won—thirty-five years in the making and an important contribution to the shamefully small number of outdoor sculptures depicting black women in the American statuary. On the other hand, I couldn't help but wonder if the Statue Fund Committee had unwittingly created a larger-than-life hero out of an activist with whom we had hoped young people in Hamer's community would relate. After all, we had literally set Hamer on a pedestal! Had we set her accomplishments out of reach as well? Without providing the details of her life story, I worried, was this statue, like the national fable of the civil rights movement, potentially *disempowering* to Delta-area students? Perhaps the material from my Hamer research that I shared with public school teachers had provided some substance to this symbolic structure, I thought. Students and teachers did show up in droves to the celebration; their signs were on point and they seemed genuinely engaged in the previous morning's tributes. But I also knew how overburdened public school teachers in this region of the state are—a region the Department of Education has consistently classified as existing in a "state of emergency," given their districts' high poverty and high teacher turnover rates, as well as low student test scores. I also knew that many public school teachers in the Delta were working several jobs because teacher salaries in this region consistently rank among the nation's lowest. In light of this, I imagined that Delta-area teachers had little time to contextualize and craft meaningful lessons from the smattering of primary source materials I shared. I began to feel quite differently about the Hamer statue. Rather than

Figure 8.2 During the community celebration of Fannie Lou Hamer's 95th birthday, a young girl gazed up to the Fannie Lou Hamer statue in Ruleville, Mississippi, October 6, 2012. Photo by Maegan Parker Brooks.

viewing it as the successful completion of a project to memorialize Fannie Lou Hamer, I began hoping it would become the opening salvo to a much more meaningful public education project.

Over the next five years, I worked with Hamer's great grandniece, Ms. Monica Land, and a team of talented artists, activists, and scholars to raise funds for a K-12 Fannie Lou Hamer-centered curriculum, for the first full-length documentary to be told in Hamer's own words, and for a young filmmakers' workshop to provide Delta-area youth with filmmaking equipment and professional training to tell their own stories through the digital medium. By 2017, when I flew back to Mississippi to celebrate the centennial anniversary of Hamer's birth, our team had raised enough money to compensate Delta-area teachers for their involvement in our curriculum-design project and to sponsor Delta-area students to attend a summer-long filmmakers' workshop. We had also prepared a short centennial film tribute to play during the celebration.

When I arrived to the Fannie Lou Hamer Memorial Garden on the morning of October 6, 2017, I spotted Charles McLaurin right away. He welcomed me with a warm embrace and passed me a stack of programs to hand out. I stood at the garden's entrance greeting attendees and passing out programs as the crowd grew. There were far fewer people at this celebration than the six-hundred gathered for the statue unveiling. Nevertheless, former Freedom Summer activists came from all corners of the country to share their memories of Mrs. Hamer and to describe how the summer of 1964 had influenced the last fifty years of their lives. The New Jerusalem Choir sang and Dr. Alphonso Sanders, recently named Delta Blues Musician of the Year, played the saxophone. All three of the Hamers' daughters, Vergie Hamer Faulkner, Lenora Hamer Flakes, and Jacqueline Hamer Flakes, were there. This was the last time I would see them all together, as Vergie and Lenora both passed away within the next two years.

The Hamer tribute that I remember most clearly from her centennial celebration was the closing speech delivered by Hattie Jordan, who has also recently passed away. I remember Jordan's tribute, in part, because of how very tired she looked that day. She was noticeably thinner and her voice had become much more faint than when I saw her last. And yet, I vividly remember how Jordan spoke with conviction at the close of Hamer's centennial celebration. "If you claim to love Fannie Lou Hamer *so* much," she said as she looked out to the audience, "then you will contribute to the causes that carry forth her legacy. You will support the Fannie Lou Hamer Museum and you will support the Fannie Lou Hamer Foundation." It felt as if her piercing eyes were calling out particular people in the crowd. "Don't tell me that you love her," Jordan continued, trembling hand outstretched, eager to pass the torch, "if you're not willing to help!" Something about Mrs. Jordan's weariness, man-

Figure 8.3 Fannie Lou and Perry Hamer's three daughters (from left to right): Jacqueline Hamer Flakes, Lenora Hamer Flakes, and Vergie Hamer Faulkner pose with Maegan Parker Brooks at the Centennial Celebration of Fannie Lou Hamer's birth, Ruleville, Mississippi, October 6, 2017. Photo in author's possession.

ifest by the shakiness of her outstretched hand, combined with this celebration of Fannie Lou Hamer's 100th birthday in her hometown, surrounded by her family and friends, called to my mind an illuminating parable Hamer shared with an audience gathered at the NAACP headquarters in 1971. "I would like to tell you in closing a story of an old man," Hamer said.

> This old man was very wise and he could answer questions that was almost impossible for people to answer. So, some people went to him one day, two young people, and said, "We're going to trick this guy today. We're going to catch a bird, and we're going to carry it to this old man. And we're going to ask him, 'This, that we hold in our hands today, is it alive or is it dead?' If he says 'dead,' we're going to turn it loose and let it fly. But if he says, 'alive,' we're going to crush it." So they walked up to this old man, and they said, "This, that we hold in our hands today, is it alive or is it dead?"

He looked at the young people and he smiled. And he said, "It's in your hands."

It's in *our* hands now, I realized. More expansive and empowering histories that trouble the "national fable of the civil rights movement" and provide direction amidst the confusion of our contemporary context, require researchers, meaning-makers, and storytellers. The struggle for social, political, and economic change also requires torch-bearers to keep the flame of freedom burning brightly. Keeping Hamer's example alive and inspiring for generations to come, ensuring that the remarkable contributions she made during her lifetime will not be forgotten, whitewashed, papered over, or co-opted—that significant memorial work, which is itself a powerful form of activism, is in all of our hands.

Acknowledgments

I appreciate Davis W. Houck, John David Smith, and Jon Sisk's encouragement to write this book for Rowman & Littlefield's Library of African American Biography Series. I am also grateful to Willamette University for providing me with a generous research leave, travel, and writing support to complete the project. My Civic Communication and Media Department colleagues, Cindy Koenig Richards, Catalina de Onís, Vincent Pham, Robert Trapp, and Trina Morgan doubtlessly worked overtime so I could take a research leave—I appreciate their sacrifice, their friendship, and their ongoing support of my research and teaching. Sarah Sentilles read every chapter of this manuscript and pushed me all along the way to be bolder, clearer, and more incisive. I am so very grateful for her encouragement and insight.

I had the distinct pleasure of writing *Fannie Lou Hamer: America's Freedom Fighting Woman* while researching the documentary film, *Fannie Lou Hamer's America*, editing the *Find Your Voice* K-12 curriculum, and consulting on the Fannie Lou Hamer BrainPOP animation. While juggling these multiple projects proved quite difficult at times, the synergistic ways in which the projects mutually informed one another made it well worth the effort. I am grateful to Monica Land, Joy Davenport, Pablo Correa, Keith Beauchamp, Davis W. Houck, R.J. Fitzpatrick, Shelby McConville, and the generous *Fannie Lou Hamer's America* sponsors. I am also grateful to the teachers I worked with in Mississippi. Mrs. Valerie Fairley, Mrs. Alicia Ervin-Rawls, Mrs. Danielle Creel Martin, Mr. R.J. Morgan, Mrs. Brenda Kirkham, Mrs. Latasha Rodgers, Mrs. Grenell Bounds, Mrs. Mamie Washington, and Ms. Rosemary Collins have held me accountable and taught me better ways to share Fannie Lou Hamer's life story.

I was also fortunate to develop ideas for *America's Freedom Fighting Woman* while delivering talks at the University of Southern Mississippi, the University of Georgia, the Race and Pedagogy National Conference, the Northwest

Race, Rhetoric, and Media Symposium, and the Centennial Tribute to Fannie Lou Hamer in her hometown of Ruleville, Mississippi. I appreciate these invitations to share Fannie Lou Hamer's story with audiences across the country; Rebecca Tuuri, Sammi Riptoe, Luke Christie, Kundai Chirindo, and Charles McLaurin thank you for hosting me.

Both my scholarship and my life have been profoundly impacted by the incredible people whom I have met while researching Fannie Lou Hamer. I appreciate the wisdom shared with me by Hamer's friends, family members, and fellow activists, especially: Pam and Greg Bell, Owen Brooks, Rita Schwerner Bender, Charles Cobb, Dr. L. C. Dorsey, Martha Fager, Vergie Hamer Faulkner, Jeff and Sarah Goldstein, Lawrence Guyot, Reverend Jesse Jackson, Sr., Hattie Jordan, Reverend Edwin King, Dorie Ladner, Monica Land, Charles McLaurin, Dr. Leslie McLemore, Mary Moore, Jean and Charlie Sweet, Tracy Sugarman, and Ambassador Andrew Young.

Most importantly, I thank my family and friends. Over the last decade, my involvement in book clubs from Maple Valley, Washington to Denver, Colorado and now Wilsonville, Oregon, has brought me joy and provided pivotal lessons in writing effectively for broader audiences. I am grateful to my dear friends—especially Erin McNicholas, Sara Winegar Budge, Nadine Genece, Lindsay Hill, Kelli Payne, Carol Li, David Knierem, Louise W. Knight, Linda Ingalls, Shelby McConville, and Sally Novitsky—who variously offered support, listened to my complaints, and helped me work through challenging sections of the book. My incredible partner, David W. Brooks has supported me throughout the fifteen-year research and writing journey that has culminated in *Fannie Lou Hamer: America's Freedom Fighting Woman*. Sawyer and Evalyn, our brave and compassionate children, not only shared their mama with this project, but they inspired me to write it. *Fannie Lou Hamer: America's Freedom Fighting Woman* is dedicated to our children and to the next generation of young people whom I hope will learn to "Fight Like Fannie Lou!"

A Note on Sources

Fannie Lou Hamer: America's Freedom Fighting Woman was inspired, and fundamentally informed, by Hamer's own words. I located these words in Fannie Lou Hamer's autobiography, *To Praise Our Bridges* (recorded in 1965 and available online through the SNCC Digital Gateway), her album *Songs My Mother Taught Me* (recorded in 1963 and re-released by Smithsonian Folkways in 2015), as well as in the transcripts and recordings of speeches Hamer delivered across the United States—many of which are preserved within the pages of the edited collection Davis W. Houck and I compiled, *The Speeches of Fannie Lou Hamer: To Tell It Like It Is* (Jackson: University Press of Mississippi, 2011). I also consulted interviews conducted directly with Fannie Lou Hamer, including interviews she gave to: Jack Minnis (1964), J. H. O'Dell (1964), Colin Edwards (1965), Project South (1965), Anne Romaine (1966), Robert Wright (1968), Gil Noble (1971), and Neil R. McMillen (1972 and 1973). As a starting point for gathering Hamer's words and learning the arc of her life story, I engaged two excellent biographies, Kay Mills, *This Little Light of Mine: The Life of Fannie Lou Hamer* (New York: Penguin, 1993) and Chana Kai Lee, *For Freedom's Sake: The Life of Fannie Lou Hamer* (Urbana: University of Illinois Press, 1999).

Additional biographical works written about Hamer include: June Jordan, *Fannie Lou Hamer* (New York: Thomas Y. Crowell Company, 1972); Susan Kling, *Fannie Lou Hamer: A Biography* (Women for Racial and Economic Equality, 1979); David Rubel, *Fannie Lou Hamer: From Sharecropping to Politics* (Englewood Cliffs: Silver Burdett Press Inc., 1990); Laura Baskes Litwin, *Fannie Lou Hamer: Fighting for the Right to Vote* (Berkeley Heights: Enslow Publishers, 2002); Chris Myers Asch, *The Senator and the Sharecropper: The Freedom Struggles of James O. Eastland and Fannie Lou Hamer* (Chapel Hill: University of North Carolina Press, 2008); Earnest N. Bracey, *Fannie Lou Hamer: The Life of a Civil Rights Icon* (Jefferson: McFarland Press, 2011); Maegan Parker Brooks,

A Voice that Could Stir an Army: Fannie Lou Hamer and the Rhetoric of the Black Freedom Movement (Jackson: University Press of Mississippi, 2014); Carole Boston Weatherford, *Voice of Freedom: Fannie Lou Hamer* (Somerville: Candlewick, 2015); and Davis W. Houck, "Fannie Lou Hamer on Winona: Memory, Trauma, and Recovery," in *The Rhetorical History of the United States: Social Controversy and Public Address in the 1960s and Early 1970s* (East Lansing: Michigan State University Press, 2017).

Fannie Lou Hamer's papers are housed at the Amistad Research Center at Tulane University in New Orleans. In addition to drawing upon materials from this archival collection, *America's Freedom Fighting Woman* is informed by a broad range of primary sources, including personal letters, photographs, television and radio interviews, film footage, newspaper clippings, and campaign platforms. I gathered these primary sources from the following archival collections: the Moorland-Springarn Research Center's Oral History Collection at Howard University in Washington, D.C.; the Lyndon B. Johnson Presidential Library in Austin, Texas; the Student Nonviolent Coordinating Committee Papers within the Archives Department of the Martin Luther King Jr. Center for Nonviolent Social Change in Atlanta, Georgia; the Fannie Lou Hamer file within the Mary McLeod-Bethune Museum and Archives in Washington, D.C.; the Fannie Lou Hamer Vertical File and Collection, the Mississippi Sovereignty Commission, and the Tougaloo Zenobia Coleman Library Collections housed at the Mississippi Department of Archives and History in Jackson, Mississippi; the Citizens' Council Radio Forums within Mississippi State University's Archives and Special Collections in Starksville, Mississippi; the George Breitman Papers Collection within the Tamiment Library/Robert F. Wagner Labor Archives at New York University; the Moses Moon Collection housed within the National Museum of American History's Smithsonian Institution in Washington, D.C.; the Project South Papers in the Department of Special Collections at Stanford University; the Civil Rights and Race Collection within the University of Mississippi Archives and Special Collections in Oxford, Mississippi; Kay Mills' Papers within the National Women in Media Collection at the State Historical Society of Missouri; the Sue Sojourner Lorenzi Papers within the University of Southern Mississippi's McCain Library in Hattiesburg, Mississippi; the Vanderbilt Television News Archive in Nashville, Tennessee; the Civil Rights Collection, the Measure for Measure File, the Mississippi Freedom Democratic Party File, the Social Action Vertical File, and the Sweet Papers at the Wisconsin Historical Society in Madison, Wisconsin.

Oral history interviews that I conducted with Fannie Lou Hamer's friends, family members, and fellow activists yielded additional primary sources from their private collections including personal letters, photographs, speech and song recordings. The oral history interviews I conducted also provided further insight regarding Hamer's own reflections and about the primary sources I gathered through archival research. In particular, my interviews with: Greg and Pam Bell, Owen Brooks, Rita Schwerner Bender, Charles Cobb, L.C. Dorsey, Martha Fager, Vergie Hamer Faulkner, Jeff and Sarah Goldstein, Lawrence Guyot, Jesse Jackson, Sr., Hattie Jordan, Edwin King, Dorie Ladner, Monica Land, Charles McLaurin, Leslie McLemore, Mary Moore, Charlie and Jean Sweet, Tracy Sugarman, and Andrew Young offered contextual information about and provided nuance to Hamer's life story.

I also consulted interviews with Hamer's friends and fellow activists conducted by other scholars, including: interview with Bernice Johnson Reagon by Bill Moyers (1991); interview with Harry Belafonte by Kay Mills (1991); interview with Senator Walter Mondale by Morgan Ginther (2011); and interview with Euvester Simpson by John Dittmer (2013). I read these interviews alongside biographical and autobiographical accounts of Hamer's fellow activists and of her opponents, including: Eric Burner, *And Gently He Shall Lead Them: Robert Parris Moses and Civil Rights in Mississippi* (New York: New York University Press, 1994); Stokely Carmichael with Ekwueme Michael Thelwell, *Ready for Revolution: The Life and Struggles of Stokely Carmichael {Kwame Ture}* (New York: Scribner, 2003); Robert Dalek, *Flawed Giant: Lyndon Johnson and His Times: 1961–1973* (New York: Oxford University Press, 1998); James Forman, *The Making of Black Revolutionaries* (Seattle: Open Hand Publishing, 1985); J. Todd Moye, *Ella Baker: Community Organizer of the Civil Rights Movement* (Lanham: Rowman & Littlefield, 2013); Barbara Ransby, *Ella Baker and the Black Freedom Movement: A Radical Democratic Vision* (Chapel Hill: University of North Carolina Press, 2003); Tracy Sugarman, *Stranger at the Gates: A Summer in Mississippi* (New York: Hill and Wang, 1966); Tracy Sugarman, *We Had Sneakers, They Had Guns: The Kids Who Fought for Civil Rights in Mississippi* (Syracuse: Syracuse University Press, 2009); and *Malcolm X Speaks: Selected Speeches and Statements*, edited by George Breitman (New York: Grove Weidenfeld, 1965).

Organizational histories, histories of Mississippi, and historical accounts of events related to Hamer's activist career provided a further layer of context to the primary sources I analyzed and the biographies that I read. Secondary sources I found most helpful in this regard include: Clayborne Carson, *In Struggle: SNCC and the Black Awakening of the 1960s* (Cambridge: Harvard University Press, 1995); Emilye Crosby, *A Little Taste of Freedom: The Black Freedom Struggle in Claiborne County, Mississippi* (Chapel Hill: University of North Carolina Press, 2005); *Civil Rights History from the Ground Up: Local Struggles, A National Movement*, edited by Emilye Crosby (Athens: University of Georgia Press, 2011); John Dittmer, *Local People: The Struggle for Civil Rights in Missis-*

sippi (Urbana: University of Illinois Press, 1995); Aram Goudsouzian, *Down to the Crossroads: Civil Rights, Black Power and the Meredith March Against Fear* (New York: Farrar, Straus and Giroux, 2014); Wesley C. Hogan, *Many Minds, One Heart: SNCC's Dream for a New America* (Chapel Hill: University of North Carolina Press, 2007); Hasan Kwame Jeffries, *Bloody Lowndes: Civil Rights and Black Power in Alabama's Black Belt* (New York: New York University Press, 2009); J. Todd Moye, *Let the People Decide: Black Freedom and White Resistance Movements in Sunflower County, 1945–1986* (Chapel Hill: University of North Carolina Press, 2004); Charles M. Payne, *I've Got the Light of Freedom: The Organizing Tradition and the Mississippi Freedom Struggle* (Berkeley: University of California Press, 1995); Frank R. Parker, *Black Votes Count: Political Empowerment in Mississippi after 1965* (Chapel Hill: University of North Carolina Press, 1990); Crystal R. Sanders, *A Chance for Change: Head Start and Mississippi's Black Freedom Movement Struggle* (Chapel Hill: University of North Carolina Press, 2016); Jeanne Theoharis, *A More Beautiful and Terrible History: The Uses and Misuses of Civil Rights History* (Boston: Beacon Press, 2018); Stephanie Rolph, *Resisting Equality: The Citizen's Council, 1954–1989* (Baton Rouge: Louisiana State University Press, 2018); and Monica M. White, *Freedom Farmers: Agricultural Resistance and the Black Freedom Movement* (Chapel Hill: University of North Carolina Press, 2018).

To recreate the vivid historical scenes in which Hamer acted, I screened several documentaries, including *We'll Never Turn Back* (Harvey Richards, 1963); *Hunger, American Style* (CBS, 1968); *Freedom On My Mind* (California Newsreel, 1994); *America's War on Poverty* (Blackside, Inc., 1995); and *Freedom Summer* (PBS, 2014). Additional audio/visual materials I consulted include Sue Lorenzi Sojourner's *Mrs. Hamer Speaks* photography exhibit and *Voices of the Civil Rights Movement: Black American Freedom Songs, 1960–1966* (Washington, D.C.: Smithsonian Institution Folkways Recording, 1980). Guy and Candie Carawan's freedom song publications, *We Shall Overcome!: Songs of the Southern Freedom Movement* (New York: Oak Press, 1963) and *Freedom Is a Constant Struggle: Songs of the Freedom Movement* (New York: Oak Press, 1968) inspired me to incorporate movement music throughout the book.

News coverage contemporaneous to Hamer's life helped me to further reconstruct the historical scenes in which she acted. In particular, I referenced Robert Analavage, "Negroes Not Represented," *Southern Patriot*, May 1967; John Childs and Noel Workman, "More Choppers Join Farm Labor Strike," *Delta Democrat Times*, June 4, 1965; "CORE to Urge House to Block Seating of Five Mississippians," *New York Times*, December 29, 1964; Jerry DeMuth, "'Tired of Being Sick and Tired,'" *The Nation*, June 1, 1964; Peggy Elam, "Monument to Fannie Lou Hamer Awaits Funds," *Clarion-Ledger*, March 9, 1980; "Fannie Lou 'Tell it Like it Is,'" *Harvard Crimson*, November 23, 1968;

Fannie Lou Hamer, "'Sick and Tired of Being Sick and Tired,'" *Katallagete!: The Journal of the Committee of Southern Churchmen*, Fall 1968; Fannie Lou Hamer, "Fannie Lou Hamer Speaks Out," *Essence* 1, 6, October 1971; M.S. Handler, "CORE Hears Cries of 'Black Power,'" *New York Times*, July 2, 1966; Megan Landauer and Jonathon Wolman, "Fannie Lou Hamer '. . . forcing a new political reality," *The Daily Cardinal*, October 8, 1971; Arnold H. Lubasch, "Malcolm Favors a Mau Mau in US," *New York Times*, December 21, 1964; Joseph A. Loftus, "5 Mississippians Seated by House: But Liberals Muster 148 Votes Against Them," *New York Times*, January 5, 1965; Staughton Lynd, "A Radical Speaks in Defense of SNCC," *New York Times*, September 10, 1967; Marian McBride, "Fannie Lou Hamer: Nobody Knows the Trouble She's Seen," *Washington Post*, July 14, 1968; Franklyn Peterson, "Sunflowers Don't Grow in Sunflower County," *Sepia*, 19, 1970; Robert Pfefferkorn, "From one who pursued equality, a plea for love," *Wisconsin State Journal*, January 30, 1976; Bill Sierichs, "'Sin-Sickness' Probed at Crime Meet," *Jackson Daily News*, March 24, 1976; Jonathon Wolman, "Mississippi Elections: By Hook or Crook," *Daily Cardinal,* November 5, 1971; Jonathon Wolman, "Mississippi Elections: Facing an Old Political Reality," *Daily Cardinal*, November 11, 1971; and Roger Yockey, "King Co. 'Adopts' Sunflower County," *The Progress,* March 7, 1969.

Popular essays written more recently provided insight about defining historical moments in Hamer's activism, even as they informed my reconstruction of her life and legacy. I consulted, Carolyn Kleiner Butler, "Down in Mississippi," *Smithsonian Magazine*, February 2005; John T. Edge, "The Hidden Radicalism of Southern Food," *New York Times Magazine*, May 6, 2017; Hasan Kwame Jeffries, "We Need King's Radical Vision. We Don't Need Convenient Heroes," *Southern Poverty Law Center: Weekend Read*, April 6, 2018; Haynes Johnson, "1968 Democratic National Convention: The Bosses Strike Back," *Smithsonian Magazine*, August 2008; and Melissa Harris-Lacewell, "Obama and the Sisters," *The Nation*, September 2008.

Moreover, I wrote *Fannie Lou Hamer: America's Freedom Fighting Woman* from an antiracist and a feminist perspective. The following works informed my approach: *The Black Woman: An Anthology*, edited by Toni Cade Bambara and Eleanor W. Traylor (New York: Washington Square Press, 2005); bell hooks' Institute at Berea College: Teach, Remember, Explore, Celebrate (www.bellhooksinstitute.com); Brittney Cooper, *Eloquent Rage: A Black Feminist Discovers Her Superpower* (New York: St. Martin's Press, 2018); Robin DiAngelo, *White Fragility: Why It's So Hard for White People to Talk About Racism* (Boston: Beacon Press, 2018); W. E. B. DuBois, *The Souls of Black Folk: Essays and Sketches* (Chicago: A. G. McClurg, 1903); Darlene Clark Hine, "Rape and the Inner Lives of Black Women in the Middle West: Preliminary

Thoughts on the Culture of Dissemblance," *Signs*, 14, Summer 1989; Ibram X. Kendi, *How to Be an Antiracist* (New York: One World, 2019); *Black Women in White America: A Documentary History*, edited by Gerda Lerner (New York: Vintage, 1972); Danielle L. McGuire, *At the Dark End of the Street: Black Women, Rape, and Resistance—A New History of the Civil Rights Movement* (New York: Vintage, 2011); Henry H. Mitchell, *Black Preaching: The Recovery of a Powerful Art* (Nashville: Abingdon Press, 1990); Bernice Johnson Reagon, "My Black Mothers and Sisters or On Beginning a Cultural Biography," *Feminist Studies*, 8, 1, Spring 1982; Bernice Johnson Reagon, "Women as Culture Carriers in the Civil Rights Movement: Fannie Lou Hamer." In *Women in the Civil Rights Movement: Trailblazers and Torchbearers*, 1941–1965, edited by Vicki Crawford, Jaqueline Rouse, and Barbara Woods (New York: Carlson, 1990); Belinda Robnett, *How Long? How Long?: African American Women in the Struggle for Civil Rights* (New York: Oxford University Press, 2000); Jacqueline Jones Royster, "When the First Voice You Hear Is Not Your Own," *College Composition and Communication*, 47, 1, February 1996; Rebecca Traister, *Good and Mad: The Revolutionary Power of Women's Anger* (New York: Simon & Schuster, 2018); and Deborah Gray White, *Too Heavy a Load: Black Women in Defense of Themselves, 1894–1994.* (New York: W.W. Norton & Company, 1999).

Index

About the Author

Maegan Parker Brooks.
Photo credit, Frank Miller.

Maegan Parker Brooks, PhD, teaches in the Civic Communication and Media Department and the American Ethic Studies Program at Willamette University in Salem, Oregon. Brooks also directs *Find Your Voice: The Online Resource for Fannie Lou Hamer Studies* (findyourvoice.willamette.edu), a website which hosts a K-12 curriculum project she developed in partnership with civil rights scholars and public school teachers in the Mississippi Delta. All resources on the site are provided free of charge, including Brooks's children's book, *Planting Seeds: The Life and Legacy of Fannie Lou Hamer* (illustrated by Shelby McConville). Brooks has previously published two books about Fannie Lou Hamer. The first was an anthology of Hamer's speeches, which she co-edited with Davis W. Houck, entitled *The Speeches of Fannie Lou Hamer: To Tell It Like It Is*. The second was a rhetorical biography, *A Voice that Could Stir an Army: Fannie Lou Hamer and the Rhetoric of the Black Freedom Movement*, which was named an Outstanding Academic Title of 2015 by the American Library Association. Brooks served on the board of the Fannie Lou Hamer Statue and Education Fund; she also served as a lead researcher for the documentary film *Fannie Lou Hamer's America* and as a consultant for the Fannie Lou Hamer BrainPOP animation.